How to Raise a Sane and Healthy Cat

The enigmatic, endearing cat has been beguiling and bewildering his human admirers for thousands of years. Today, cats fit into our lives more appropriately than ever before. It remains for us to provide the best care, environment and quality of life possible for these very special animal friends. The beautiful model here is Sean Hammond's Marshmellow.

Victoria Kensington

How to Raise a Sane and Healthy Cat

Sean Hammond

AND

Carolyn Usrey

Foreword by Mary Alice Cox, DVM
Illustrations by Joanne Shank-Pollitt
Photographs by Victoria Kensington

HOWELL
BOOK HOUSE

MACMILLAN • USA

Howell Book House
Macmillan General Reference
A Simon & Schuster Macmillan Company
1633 Broadway
New York, NY 10019-6785

Library of Congress Cataloging-in-Publication Data

Hammond, Sean.
    How to raise a sane and healthy cat/Sean Hammond and Carolyn
Usrey.
        p.   cm.
    ISBN 0-87605-797-0
    1. Cats.   2. Cats—Health.   I. Usrey, Carolyn.   I. Title.
SF447.H28   1994
636.8'083—dc20   93–45334
                                                          CIP

Macmillan books are available at special discounts for bulk purchases for sales promotions, premiums, fund-raising, or educational use. For details, contact:

Special Sales Director
Macmillan Publishing Company
1633 Broadway
New York, NY 10019-6785

10 9 8 7 6 5

Printed in the United States of America

Contents

For Sean's girls,
Streaky, Shadow, Denny and Marshmellow,
who have taught him so much
about being a cat

For Christina and David

Acknowledgments

A VERY SPECIAL thank you to Dr. Mary Alice Cox, DVM, who has vetted both our animals and this book with true professionalism and an extraordinary degree of care. The excellence of this work is due in large part to her invaluable service.

Thank you to the many friends, Nancy Brinegar, Christina Usrey, Patti Wood and Roberta Diehl who have given us both their feedback and encouragement. Added appreciation goes to William Kern, Elizabeth TeSelle and Dr. Nancy Hinkle for their expertise and contributions. Thanks to Margaret Viviani who typed much of the original manuscript, and to Cynthia Washburn for her early art work. Thanks also to Chris Harper, whose cooking kept us on task.

Unwilling to employ the inanimate object "it" to refer to the cat, we have chosen to use the male pronouns, to honor Carolyn's cat, Chauncey, who died in 1987.

Foreword

IN THE PAST few years, the cat has climbed in popularity to become the most popular pet in the United States. There are scores of new cat owners, as well as millions of people who have enjoyed the company of cats. For all cat owners, this book will be a valuable source of information on a variety of topics, from tips on selecting a cat to thoughtful advice on dealing with the death of a treasured pet. The question and answer format allows the reader to take an active part, and the topics cover many subjects that will encourage people to become better cat owners. The real beneficiaries of this book will be all the cats whose families are seeking information that will help them improve the quality of their cats' lives.

Mary Alice Cox, DVM

1

Description of the Cat

T HE DESIGN of the cat, his colors, coat patterns, anatomy—gross and otherwise—and how it is all put together give rise to some serious and some not so serious questions. This chapter also has what might even be considered an unofficial guide to cat genealogy; the breed descriptions may enable you to determine your foundling's lineage.

WHAT IS THE RECENT HISTORY OF THE HOUSE CAT?

Humankind and "modern" cats developed at about the same time, and by the end of the last Ice Age, were in forms recognizable as related to the people and cats living today. Possibly cats stole scraps at Stone Age fires, but they were not domesticated until about three or four thousand years ago.

Today's wild cats of Egypt and Europe are both close enough genetically to mate with the house cat. However, only the offspring from Egyptian wild cats can be tamed. Because of this, it is believed our house cats descend from this North African desert cat.

These ancestral cats were lean but well muscled with a moderate body shape. With their short, dense coats, they were well insulated from both heat and cold. Their easy-to-groom fur was either dark self-colored (one solid color) or dark tabby (to help camouflage the hunting cat). Like all feline species, these cats were formidable hunters. They were domesticated early on, to keep rodents and other small pests out of stored grain. The modern Abyssinian looks much like this cat of ancient Egypt.

Once domesticated, the cat was on the move. Beginning about nine hundred years ago, Phoenician trading ships spread cats to Europe, China and India. Longhaired cats developed in Persia. The Romans brought cats to England, and the first recorded planned breeding occurred in 999 A.D. in Japan at the Imperial Palace.

Sailors have always been fond of cats because they helped keep ships' rat populations in check. "Ratting" paid his fare and the cat traveled around the world many times—perhaps this is why the word for cat sounds similar in many languages.

The hardworking cat didn't always enjoy human favor. During the Middle Ages, he was linked to Satanic worship and witches. Even Pope Innocent VIII added to the cat's PR problem by denouncing him and "his people." Anyone objecting to the mass killing of cats, anyone giving a cat a home or even just giving a stray a meal, could be burned at the stake. There were executions—most of the victims were women denounced as witches. *Felis catus* was hounded almost to extinction, and to this day the totally black cat isn't very common.

After England and Europe were decimated by the Black Death, spread by the fleas on rodents, the cat was again appreciated for his ratting skills and his demonic association evaporated.

Even after fifty million years, the modern cat still has the shoulder of an arboreal animal and this gives him grace, surefootedness and the ability to squeeze into tight spaces.

HOW CAN I TELL IF A CAT IS MALE OR FEMALE?

To determine the sex of a cat, lift the tail and look at the cat's rump.

Female

Her anus and anal glands lie under the base of her tail and just below and very close to her anus is the vaginal opening.

Male

His anus and anal glands, like the female's, are under the base of his tail. The penis sheath is just below the anus. Testes are located between the anus and the penis. (They are large and very noticeable on an intact adult, small in the kitten and absent in the neuter.)

WHAT ARE THE ANAL GLANDS?

The anal glands, used in scent marking, are located on either side of the anus. (See diagram.) The cat may express these glands when startled, when

A cat's sex can be determined by observing outer genitalia. This animal is a female.

The anal glands are located on either side of the cat's anal opening in the four and eight o'clock positions.

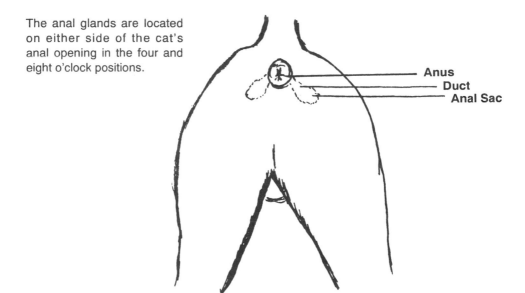

Anus
Duct
Anal Sac

having a bowel movement or when groomed or stimulated in the anal area. The grayish-green material expelled has a strong odor. Fortunately cats are fastidious and will clean up the mess on their fur—so you don't have to.

HOW DOES A CAT'S BREED AFFECT HIS BODY AND HEAD SHAPE?

Depending on the breed, or breed combinations, cats might exhibit one of three body shapes.

- *Cobby—Persian Type.* Broad, flat face with short legs and the body of a "line-backer."
- *Foreign—Siamese Type.* Thin, long face with long legs and a long, thin body.
- *Moderate—Domestic Shorthair Type.* Round face with legs in proportion to body with medium tail.

CAN A CAT'S EAR SHAPE HELP IDENTIFY HIS BREED?

Ear type can often be a better breed identifier than body shape because ears are unaffected by body fat. Essentially there are four principal ear types.

- *Persian Type.* Small, erect, rounded and set low on the cat's head.
- *Siamese Type.* Large, erect, tall and set high on head.
- *Domestic Shorthair.* Medium-sized and erect.
- *Folded Ears*
  — American Curl is medium-sized and folded backward.
  — Scottish Fold is medium-sized and folded forward.

DO SOME CAT BREEDS HAVE LONGER TAILS?

Yes, tails, like ears, are tailor-made. Siamese, with tails at least as long as their body, traditionally have the longest tails. On the other hand, most Manx are born with little or no tail. Most breeds, however, have unflamboyant tails, measuring a little less than their body length.

WHAT KINDS OF EYE-COLOR VARIATIONS DO CATS HAVE?

Eyes can vary dramatically in color, shade and intensity. While green (emerald green to yellow green) is the color most often associated with cats' eyes, yellow is also extremely common. Yellows range from deep orange copper to pale gold. The occasional cat will even have one green eye and one yellow eye.

Although the green/yellow pairing is the most common, other odd-eyed combinations involving one blue eye can be a genetic signal that the cat carries the partly masked gene for albinism. These cats are often deaf in the ear on the same side as their blue eye. Most albinos, pure-white cats with two blue eyes, are completely deaf.

There is another genetic variant for blue eyes. These cats have ancestral origins in Asia. Siamese cats (the original breed) and Himalayans (Siamese and Persian cross) should have brilliant, sapphire-blue eyes.

HOW DOES A CAT'S COAT (FUR) REFLECT HIS BREED?

Every cat's coat can be described in terms of its **length, texture** and **color/ pattern**. Genetic combinations in a particular cat's coat can show just how complicated heredity can be in cats.

Coat Length

- *Long Hair* (e.g., Persian). Fur is approximately two to four inches long, and longer still on the cat's ruff (neck area) and on his tail.
- *Short Hair* (e.g., American Shorthair). Fur is one inch or less, and generally the same length over the entire body.
- *"Furless"* (e.g., Sphinx). This cat looks hairless because his fur is only one-sixteenth of an inch long. His very fine, short, single undercoat without guard hairs feels like suede. Regulation of body temperature can be a real problem for these scantily clad cats. And they can't hide all those wrinkles.

Coat Type

- *Guard Hairs* (coarse, longer outer hairs). Most guard hairs protect from temperature extremes and sunburn. However, some modern mutations—Korat, Sphinx, Rex and American Wirehair—don't have guard hairs.
- *Undercoat* (fine, shorter hairs). All cats have an undercoat. Very plush-coated cats, such as the Korat and Russian Blue, have double undercoats and no guard hairs at all. Some cats, like the American Wirehair or Rex types, have curly undercoats. Their body-hugging fur is kinked or curly and also lacks guard hairs.

Coat Colors and Patterns

There are at least fifty colors/shades recognized by the cat fancy. Ten of the most common are described below.

- *Self-colored*. The cat is all one color, with no shading or stray hairs of any other color.

- *Bicolor*. Bicolored cats are white with another solid color or tabby patches in any proportion. (A cat with one small spot on the stomach would not be a bicolor but rather a flawed self-colored.)
- *Himalayan*. These cats have a light-colored body with darker extremities. Examples of this pattern include the Himalayan, Siamese, Balinese, Ragdoll and Snowshoe breeds.
- *Tabby*. Tabby is believed to be the original pattern of the cat. All tabbies have an "M" on their foreheads, stripes on the legs and rings around the tail. Many have a mark that resembles a "thumbprint" on their ears and stomachs.
    There are three main variations of the tabby theme:
    — *Classic*. Classic tabbies have bull's-eye patterns on their sides and a butterfly-shaped marking over the shoulder blades.
    — *Mackerel*. A mackerel will have vertical stripes on his sides and a stripe centered down the length of the back.
    — *Spotted Tabby or Torby*. These cats have a pattern similar to the other tabbies' but the lines are broken instead of solid.
- *Agouti*. On agouti cats, each hair has bands of color or ticking, with the darker colors closer to the tip. This trait appears only in the Abyssinian or Singapura. Colors are limited to shades of orange, brown and gray.
- *Shaded, Cameo or Tipped*. Each hair is shaded light at the skin to dark at the tip. The shading is subtle, so the hair does not look banded; the cat looks dark till the fur is brushed backward or moved to show the lighter color.
- *Tortoiseshell*. Tortoiseshells combine black, red (orange) and cream in large or small, tweed or solid-color patches. Their paws will alternate light and dark (e.g., right front and left rear are light and the other two legs are dark). Some have a harlequin face (a face divided in the middle with light color on one side and dark on the other). Most tortoiseshells are females.
- *Dilute Tortoiseshell*. These generally female cats are the same as the tortoiseshell above except that their colors are muted to blue, pink and off-white.
- *Calico*. A calico cat is a combination of black, red (orange) and white in large solid-color patches. The large areas of white are mostly on the stomach, legs and face. Technically, calicos are tortoiseshells with the white spotting gene and therefore most of these cats are females.
- *Mi-ke*. This is a Japanese Bobtail Calico pattern that restricts the black and red patches to the top of the head, the tail and a saddle on the back. However, most of the cat's fur is white.

WHAT ARE THE GENETICS OF COAT COLORS AND PATTERNS?

While geneticists believe that the original cats were brown tabbies, through mutations and selective breeding there are now more than fifty colors and patterns. The original colors and patterns are dominant (more likely to appear) over more recent ones. In general, there are some fairly clear patterns in cat genetics: *dominant* vs. *recessive*. Dominant traits show up when paired with a recessive trait from the other parent.

DOMINANT (STRONG TRAIT)	RECESSIVE (WEAK TRAIT)
Darker colors	Lighter colors
Tabby	Most other patterns
Short hair	Long hair
Erect ears	Folded ears
Himalayan (Siamese)	Most other patterns
White-spotting gene	Other colors and patterns

A white-spotting gene can occur with any color or pattern. In fact, any fur color with white (bicolor) is an example of the white-spotting gene. The gene can mask a cat's color pattern by creating lockets or white feet. For example, a tortoiseshell with a white-spotting gene becomes a calico.

Sex-Linked and Sex-Influenced Traits

Sex-linked traits are carried on either the female or the male sex chromosome. Sex-influenced traits aren't carried on the sex chromosomes but their strength or weakness depends on the sex of the carrier. A good example of a sex-influenced trait in humans is "baldness"—a sister and brother may have the same genes, but usually only the brother will be bald. Both types of traits, sex-linked and sex-influenced, tend to appear primarily in one sex.

- *Red (orange or ginger) coat color* is a sex-influenced trait. Seventy to seventy-five percent of red tabbies are male.
- *Tortoiseshell and calico (tortoiseshell with a white-spotting gene)* are sex-linked to the female.

Himalayan or Siamese Genes

The Himalayan or Siamese gene darkens eight or nine points on the cat (ears, face, all four legs, tail—and in the traditional Siamese, the genitalia). This gene is temperature-activated; the warmer the temperature, the lighter the color. Kittens are born white and begin to show their points by three weeks as they spend less time near their mother's warmth. The darker color begins at the cooler tips of the ears, toes, etc., and moves slowly inward.

Temperature sensitivity is more noticeable in outdoor cats, whose points darken considerably in the winter. And while house cats won't show an obvious seasonal change in point color, they will, like all who carry the Himalayan gene, continue to darken throughout life as the circulation in their extremities decreases with age. This gene makes use of nature's solar energy, keeping the animal warm in his extremities—the darker fur absorbs more heat from the sun.

WHAT IS "NORMAL" ANATOMY FOR A CAT?

The internal organs of a cat are similar to those of a human. Yet cats do have wonderfully different bone and muscle structure. Look at the charts on internal body structures. If you count very carefully, you will find that the cat has 230 bones in his skeleton. For comparison, humans have only 206. Most of the difference can be accounted for by the tail.

There are other interesting contrasts too. Pick up your cat and feel the first bend at the paw. This isn't his wrist; that's a little farther up. This bend is his heel; his foot has been greatly elongated to let him run silently on heavy, padded toes.

WHY DO CATS LIKE HEAT?

Normal feline body temperature is higher than ours (101 to 102 degrees) and the smaller body mass requires more energy to keep warm. Finally, cats are hedonists—they love body comforts and simply enjoy the heat.

DO CATS SWEAT AND PANT?

Cats sweat, pant and lick their fur and noses to help keep cool. The evaporating saliva rises into the air, taking the excess heat with it.

A cat may pant to cool his body, or when stressed. Cats generally do not exercise enough to pant from exertion—so a panting cat may need medical attention. See chapter 21 for heat sickness diagnosis and treatment.

All cats have sweat glands in their paws. While the paws aren't the most effective air conditioner, cats do need to sweat to release salts and impurities, as do humans.

Unfortunately, panting, licking and sweating from the paws are not enough to keep your cat cool under extreme circumstances. Don't leave any pet in a closed car or in any other area with poor ventilation. Heat can kill in a matter of minutes.

HOW MUCH FUR DOES A CAT HAVE?

It's hard to believe someone has taken the time to estimate the hair on a cat's stomach. The average cat has approximately 130,000 hairs on his stomach, and stomach hair is thinner than the rest of his coat. So get out your tape measure, grab a cat and round up—way up!

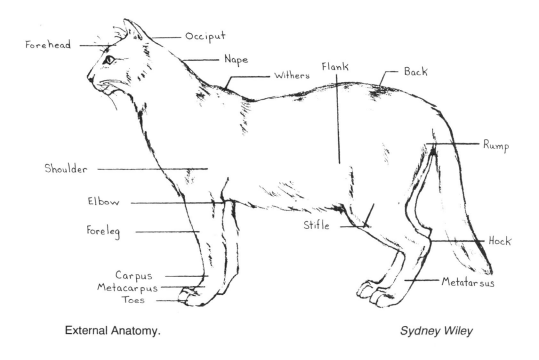

Forehead

Occiput

Nape

Withers

Flank

Back

Shoulder

Elbow

Foreleg

Stifle

Rump

Hock

Carpus
Metacarpus
Toes

Metatarsus

External Anatomy.

Sydney Wiley

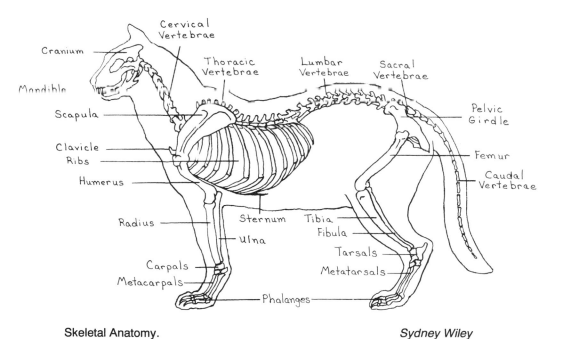

Cervical
Vertebrae

Cranium

Thoracic
Vertebrae

Lumbar
Vertebrae

Sacral
Vertebrae

Mandible

Scapula

Pelvic
Girdle

Clavicle
Ribs

Femur

Humerus

Caudal
Vertebrae

Radius

Sternum

Tibia

Fibula

Ulna

Tarsals

Carpals

Metatarsals

Metacarpals

Phalanges

Skeletal Anatomy.

Sydney Wiley

Reprinted with permission from *Cat Owner's Home Veterinary Handbook* ©1983
by Howell Book House.

9

The rough surface of the cat's tongue is an ingenious natural adaptation that affects eating, drinking and grooming.

A cat's amazing ability to land on its feet after falling from a height may have had a part in the establishment of the "nine lives" superstition. While a cat can right itself in stages as shown by these drawings, it can be injured in a too-short or too-long fall — just like all other animals.

WHY IS THE CAT'S TONGUE ROUGH?

The Velcro-like hooks (*filiform papillae*) were designed to lick the meat off bones, to drink and to keep his fur clean and tidy for better insulation.

HOW WELL CAN MY CAT SEE?

Cats can see well in dim light but not in total darkness. Their eyes are proportionally eight times larger than our eyes, and set in their skull so only the pupil and iris show. This restricts the movement of the eyes, so the cat has to move his whole head to look around. Cats are also extremely farsighted, so they can't see anything that is four inches or less from their face. In his research at Florida State University, Dr. Mark Burkley has found the following:

- Cats see moving objects better than stationary ones.
- While they can see some color, they see only the pale shades similar to early two-color Technicolor films.
- Cats see the same visual images we do and can recognize human faces.

The cat's eye is designed to increase his night and day vision. The tapetum, a membrane layer in the retina, reflects light to increase low-level vision, and the pupil changes size and shape to increase and decrease the amount of light reaching the eye.

The pupil's ability to form a narrow slit is an extremely effective way to cut glare and keep images sharp even in very bright light. Conversely, the capacity of a cat's pupil to open far wider than a human's gives the cat night vision up to ten times better than ours. This advantage in vision can be compared to what we can see on a clear night with a full moon as opposed to an overcast new moon (no moon) night.

WHY DO MY CAT'S EYES "GLOW IN THE DARK"?

The glow is a reflection of whatever light is available off the tapetum on the back of the eyeball. The eye uses this mirrorlike membrane to concentrate the light for improved night sight. Most cat's eyes glow green or yellow to match their eye color. But a blue-eyed cat's eyes will glow ruby red.

WHAT IS THAT SKIN COVERING MY CAT'S EYES?

It's the third eyelid, or nictitating membrane. This membrane helps lubricate the eye and becomes visible when it partially covers the eyes of a sleepy, contented cat. Also, it can cover all or part of the eyes of an ill cat.

WHAT ARE WHISKERS?

Whiskers are a type of modified hair used to increase the cat's awareness of the environment. Cats have these modified hairs as whiskers, eyebrows, chin hairs and hairs at the back of their front ankles. These hairs help the cat sense air currents as small as the air disturbed by the movement of a mouse.

Because a cat is unable to clearly see anything within four inches of his face, he needs these hairs to feel objects near his head and front feet. And as a nighttime hunter, he needs more than eyesight to position prey for the kill.

HOW WELL CAN MY CAT HEAR?

Cats can hear much better than we can—and even better than dogs. Not only can a cat hear both higher and lower frequencies than humans, but his hearing is more acute (cats can hear softer sounds). Unlike many of us who can be tone-deaf, cats can discriminate between half tones on a musical scale, and with their mobile, cone-shaped ears they can locate the origin of a sound within one inch.

WHY DOES MY CAT HAVE EXTRA SKIN ON HIS BELLY?

All felines have loose skin over their abdomens. This bag of sag provides room for the cat to gorge. In the wild, a cat may go a long time between kills and feasts—and gorging becomes insurance against lean times. Gorging is also the way a mother cat brings meat back to her young. She vomits the partially digested meat for her weaned kittens to eat.

HOW CAN A CAT TWIST LIKE THAT?

The cat's spine is very flexible because it's held together by muscles, not ligaments or tendons like our spines.

DO CATS ALWAYS LAND ON THEIR FEET?

Not always. If the distance is too short, the cat doesn't have time to turn over and relax. Given enough time, a cat usually lands on his feet because he instinctively raises his head, which drops the hips and helps him twist into a "standing" position. He then relaxes into a "parachute" shape to reduce speed and ease the force of landing.

If the distance is too long, the cat lands too hard. While cats have been known to survive falls of 120 feet, survival depends on air currents, the surface the cat lands on and his starting position—i.e., whether it's vertical or horizontal. Most of these fallen felines are either badly injured or killed.

The most common injuries for lucky survivors are broken legs and jaws. In recent years, these accidents have escalated to such a high level that Vets have given them a name—HRS (high-rise syndrome).

See chapter 3 for suggestions on how to "catproof" your home and balcony.

WHY DOES A CAT RAISE HIS RUMP WHEN SCRATCHED?

The cat's rump is very sensitive because there are lots of nerve endings in the anal-genital area. Scratching the cat at the base of the tail is stimulating and he "leans into it" by raising his rump. For a few cats, it is so stimulating that they may bite or swat. It is nothing personal; he is just so excited he *must* do something.

DO CATS NEED TAILS?

While the Japanese Bobtail and Manx cats do well without a tail, cats do use them for communication and to help guide and balance themselves when they jump. Tails are also used like a rudder to help the cat right himself in a fall. See chapter 7, "Normal Behavior."

DO ALL CATS CARRY THEIR TAILS UP?

While all thirty-eight feline species, large and small, can lift their tails to signal a feeling of well-being or to spray, only the domestic cat walks with his tail raised.

HOW MANY TOES DOES A CAT HAVE?

On their front paws, most cats have five toes, four to walk on and one on the side called the dewclaw. And on their rear paws, they usually have four toes. There are, however, exceptions to this toe total—polydactylous cats have extra toes, usually six or more toes on each front paw and four or more toes on each rear paw. This inherited trait began with a mutation first recorded in the New England area, and as far as we know, confers no physical advantage on these unusual toe toters.

DO CATS EXPERIENCE DIFFERENT KINDS OF SLEEP?

Indoor cats normally sleep fifteen to eighteen hours per day in stretches ranging from a few minutes to several hours. Of their daily sleep time, about twelve to fourteen hours are catnaps (very light sleep) during which the cat sleeps in various poses and is still aware of his surroundings. These light naps conserve energy and help your cat pass the time.

Outdoor cats normally sleep less—twelve to fifteen hours per day. They must be awake longer to hunt and to defend both themselves and their territory.

When cats sleep deeply, their head drops, their muscles are loose and may twitch and their eyes flicker back and forth behind closed eyelids. Deep sleep lasts at least four hours and it's a time to curl up, dream, relax and repair.

WHY DOES MY CAT SLEEP UNDER THE BLANKETS OR CURLED IN A TIGHT BALL?

The evolution of the cat has not caught up with the can opener, so he still raises his body temperature while in deep sleep to counteract bacteria from the hunted meal. Curling up, lying under blankets and finding warm places all help raise the heat.

WHY DOES MY CAT SLEEP IN SUNNY PATCHES SO MUCH?

Cats like warmth just as we do, but they also have a nutritional reason for sun worship. Cats secrete cholecalciferol onto their skin and sunlight converts it to vitamin D. Then, when the cat grooms, he gets his daily ration of vitamin D. **Note:** Don't let your cat sit in sunlight and then cool off in front of the air-conditioning vent—he can develop both ear and skin problems. Your best option is to keep him away from the vents—both day and night.

2

The Well-Equipped Cat

***

$\mathbf{T}$HERE IS MORE than the initial purchase price in determining the cost of a cat, or any pet. Over the life of the animal, the purchase price is the least of it. This chapter will give you an idea of both the time and the money investment you'll have in his care. Also included are ways to lower the ecological impact of pet ownership.

WHAT SHOULD I EXPECT TO PAY FOR YEARLY UPKEEP?

The estimated first-year cost for food, equipment and routine medical care is approximately $300 to $700, with equipment and flea treatment accounting for most of the price-range difference. After the first year, consumable supplies and regular Vet expenses will run about $150 per year for a healthy cat. Moreover, you may have an increased and/or nonrefundable deposit and/or monthly rent.

None of these amounts include the cost of medical emergencies and illness, which can add hundreds to thousands of dollars. Before you buy equipment, browse through chapter 20—you may be able to make it yourself and save lots of money.

HOW MUCH DOES A CAT COST IN TIME?

All of the times given are estimates for one cat. The times don't always double for two cats, but everything will take somewhat longer. In any case, adding a cat to your home can increase your work time by about an hour a day. The following table will give you a ballpark estimate of the time requirements for optimum care.

Activity	Per Day	Per Week
Brushing fur:		
Longhaired	10 min.	1½ hr.
Shorthaired	—	5 min.
Brushing teeth	—	5 min.
Clipping claws	—	5 min.
Flea control:		
Flea comb	10 min.	1½ hr.
Sprays	—	10–15 min.
Care of equipment:		
Washing bowls	2 min.	15 min.
Cleaning litter box (scoopable litter 2 times/day)	5 min.	½ hr.
Feeding 2 meals per day and refill water bowl	5 min.	½ hr.
Aerobic play for health and fun	10–15 min.	1–2 hr.
Extra cleaning (flying fur, etc.)	5 min.	½ hr.
APPROXIMATE TOTALS: Shorthaired	1 hr.	7 hr.
Longhaired	1¼ hr.	8¾ hr.

CAN I USE HUMAN PRODUCTS ON MY CAT?

Because cats have different nutritional needs and greater sensitivity to toxins and are constantly grooming their fur, products are generally not interchangeable between humans and cats. Read labels carefully. The following list contains general item categories and indicates whether the particular items are interchangeable.

Equipment and Supplies

- Human shampoos or dish soaps can cause fur loss. Use only cat shampoos.
- Human (soft-bristled infant) toothbrushes can be used.
- Human hairbrushes and combs may be used on a cat, but cat brushes and combs will do a better job. Plastic grooming tools can produce static electricity and make his fur stand on end.
- Human nail clippers can be used to trim claws, if they are brand-new and very sharp. Otherwise they tend to split the nail. For a nice clean (and quick) cut, use scissor-type cat nail clippers.

Food

See chapter 4 for a list of good and bad snacks. Cats can enjoy many people foods, **but** keep the following in mind:

- Rich foods (such as creamy sauces and fatty foods) can cause digestive upsets.
- Some foods are toxic; some can even kill.
- People food is not nutritionally sound for cats, so your cat would be more prone to illnesses and may have a shorter life span if fed mostly people food.
- Keep people-food snacks to 10 percent or less of your cat's total diet.

Medications

- Do **not** give human medicines. Example: aspirin and all aspirin substitutes, such as acetaminophen and ibuprofen, are poisonous to cats. There are exceptions listed for the first-aid kit; see chapter 13.

CAN I USE MY DOG'S PRODUCTS ON MY CAT?

Since cats have different food needs and greater sensitivity to toxins, and groom more than dogs, few products are interchangeable between dogs and cats. Read labels carefully. Never feed dog food or give dog (only) medications to your cat. Dog food's nutrition levels can lead to a sickly cat or even to blindness and death. And dog flea products and wormers can poison a cat.

On the other hand, some of a dog's equipment (brushes, small bowls and lightweight leashes) can be used.

WHAT TYPE OF COLLAR SHOULD MY CAT HAVE?

Elastic or breakaway collars are the best choice because they prevent injury. Never use ribbon or yarn for a collar. It may look cute, but if it gets caught, your cat can choke to death. All collars need to have up-to-date rabies and animal license tags attached—and to help a lost cat get home, special-order identification tags should also be on the collar. Indoor cats can accidentally get out.
Note: If your cat frays collars by grooming, you can prolong the life of the collar. See chapter 20 for directions.

WHAT TYPE OF BOWL SHOULD I USE
FOR FOOD AND WATER?

Believe it or not, the choice of a bowl can make a difference. Dispenser-type food bowls, which hold a lot of dry food and keep the bowl full, are not recommended, because the food becomes stale, draws pests (such as roaches) and loses nutritional value when exposed to the air. It is also far better for your cat if you feed meals.

Dispenser-type water bowls, which hold a pint or quart of water and keep the bowl full, are also not recommended, because you can't monitor water consumption as easily, and some cats would rather not drink than drink "stale" water. When selecting bowls, consider the following:

- The bowl should be easy to clean; clean it daily.
- Use metal or ceramic bowls. (Plastic bowls can cause acne under the chin because it's harder to remove the greasy food residue, and plastic is more apt to cause allergies.)
- Bowl shape:
  — Shallow, wide bowls for flat-faced cats
  — Deeper bowls for narrow-faced cats

WHAT TYPE OF SCRATCHING POST/PAD SHOULD I GET?

A good scratching post/pad and a little training can ensure that your furniture stays undamaged. The scratching place should be both inviting and safe. You may need to try several different types and styles of posts and pads to find out what *he* thinks is suitable. If the cat doesn't like what you give him to scratch on, he'll make his own selection among your things.

To discourage demolition of your upholstery, select furniture with smooth, tightly woven fabrics or velour, for these materials don't remove claw sheaths and they aren't attractive scratching surfaces to a cat.

See chapter 20 for directions on how to make your own scratching post, or look for the following if you purchase one in a store or through a catalog:

Height

- A vertical post/pad must be tall enough so the cat can stretch the length of his body.
- Horizontal post/pads may be shorter than his body length if there's room near the pad for the cat to stretch out.
- Floor-to-ceiling posts are fun. Cats like high places, and if you make it yourself, the cost will be reasonable.

Construction

- The post must be sturdy—and for vertical posts, well balanced with a large base to prevent tilting. If the post gives when he tries to use it, he'll use your couch instead.
- A horizontal pad needs to be secured too. Put the lid under a piece of furniture, so it won't travel as he scratches.
- The scratching surface should have carpet, cardboard, rough wood, sisal rope or any material that will catch claws and sharpen them.

WHAT ARE MY CHOICES FOR COMBS AND BRUSHES?

Types of Combs and Brushes and Description

Type	Comments	Cost	Use
FLEA COMB: Small comb with tiny teeth spaced about thickness of a piece of paper. Metal teeth better than plastic.	Rids coat of fleas, eggs, flea debris, loose flakes of skin that larva feed on.	$3–$8	Use on any cat; hard to use on a longhaired cat.
SLICKER BRUSH: Brush with fine, close-spaced, curved metal bristles.	Removes loose fur; stimulates the skin.	$5–$10	Use on shorthaired cats **only**.
MAT COMB or MAT RAKE: Teeth are blunted blades.	Cuts the hair to remove mats; does not leave holes in the fur.	$5–$10	Use on longhaired cats or any cat that mats easily.
PIN BRUSH: Round-ended bristles spaced in cushion base.	Good for general grooming.	$5–$10	Use on any cat.
COMBINATION COMB: Wider teeth spacing; match fine teeth to short fur and coarse to long fur.	Good for general grooming.	$5–$10	Use on any cat.

WHAT SHOULD I LOOK FOR IN A COMMERCIAL TOY?

There are lots of good toys on the market and more are appearing all the time.

Look for unpainted toys that are sturdy and well made. Avoid toys with edges and small parts that can come off or be chewed off and swallowed. Most cats will enjoy toys with dried catnip in them.

Since the main occupation of a cat is hunting, look for playthings that simulate the chase.

WHY DO I NEED A CARRIER?

Convenience. Besides making a cozy bed when you add a pillow, or providing a safe place to eat, or being a convenience when traveling, it's faster to stuff one or more cats into a carrier during an emergency than to put on harnesses, or, worse yet, to tie a frightened, clawing cat inside a pillowcase (type of emergency carrier).

Security. Most cats feel more secure in a carrier during an emergency, and no matter how he feels about the situation, he'll be safer and so will you. Many cats panic and attack when under stress.

Restriction of Movement. Carriers help restrict the movement of an ill or injured cat, who may bite or do further damage to himself by moving around. Carriers also restrain other "movements"—they contain the mess if your cat vomits or loses bladder or bowel control while in the car or on the way to the Vet's.

WHAT TYPES OF PET CARRIERS ARE AVAILABLE?

Note: Chapter 20 has directions for carrier pads to keep the cat from sliding around in his crate.

	Cardboard	Airline Crate (under seat)	Hard Plastic Crate	Fancy Wooden Crate	Soft-Sided Carrier*
Cost (approx.)	$5	$12–$15	$10–$30, depends on size	$25 and up, depends on style	$25–$50
Number of cats	1	1	1–3, depends on size	1–3, depends on size	1
Carry on plane	no	yes	no	no	no
Ship as cargo	no	no	yes for most types	no	no
Escape-proof	no	yes	yes	yes	depends on style
Durable	no	yes	yes	yes	yes
Good for daily use	yes	no	yes	yes	yes
Use in car	yes[†]	no	yes[†]	depends on style[†]	depends on style
Available from	Vets, pet shops, catalogs	catalogs, airlines, pet shops	Vets, pet shops, catalogs	catalogs	pet shops, catalogs

20

| Weight of carrier | light | light | medium | heavy | light |

*Soft-sided carriers are duffel-bag-type carriers, usually made of net and vinyl or of cloth. Or they may be travel bags, similar to baby packs; your cat snuggles inside the sack and you wear it on your chest or on your back.

†To seat-belt these carriers in the car, place carrier on seat, thread the seat belt through the carrier's handle and fasten.

Note: Some cats prefer to use a harness when traveling.

WHAT CAN I USE FOR AN EMERGENCY CARRIER?

Emergency carriers aren't for long-term use, because they're much more stressful for your cat than specially designed carriers and they don't protect the cat from impact or other physical hazards. Conversely, the other kinds of physical hazards—urine, feces and shredding—aren't easy to cope with in these makeshift carriers.

Note: A cat who is in pain or frightened may bite or scratch, no matter how loving and gentle he usually is. He is not mad at you, nor is he trying to hurt you.

Carriers for a Cat with Broken Bones or Internal Injuries

See chapter 21 for stretcher ideas and instructions.

Carriers for the Ill Cat or for Household Emergencies

If you have no one to help you transport your cat, use one of the following:

Pillowcases

- Put the cat inside the case; **do not leave his head outside** with the pillowcase tied around his neck. (The cloth is porous material. **Never** put a plastic bag around the pillowcase.)
- Tie the open end fairly tightly with rope, belt, necktie, etc.
- Remember, the cat can still bite and claw—and urinate—through the cloth. You may want to put a plastic garbage bag on the car seat **under** the tied pillowcase.

Cloth Duffel or "Breathable" Luggage

- **Do not** zip up completely. Leave a half-inch opening in the zipper for air.
- **Never** use plastic to line the bag. While (urine, feces, shredding) damage is always a possibility, you can easily suffocate your cat.

21

Towel/Blanket Wrap

If you have a friend to help you get the cat to the Vet's, you might consider towel wrapping. Done right, towel wrapping can protect you from scratches and bites. See chapter 21 for directions.

HOW CAN MY CAT SAFELY ENJOY THE OUTSIDE?

Try These Equipment Choices:

- Use commercial outdoor enclosures for the window or yard. These units can be expensive.
- Use a large wire dog crate. This is a less expensive portable alternative to most commercial outdoor cat enclosures.
- Use a harness (**never a collar**) and leash. **Do not** tie the cat out and leave him, since he has no protection from other animals. You also need to be with him to make sure the leash doesn't become tangled.
- Build your own window or yard enclosure. See chapter 20 for directions.

WHAT TYPES OF PET DOORS ARE THERE?

These doors can be a great convenience. Inside the house, solid door units can keep small children and medium/large dogs out of the kitty-litter area. Doors can lead into a protected outdoor enclosure or a window porch. But when you use the doors to give your cat free access to the great outdoors, remember that other small animals, like skunks, possums and stray cats, can use any of these units (except the magnetic lock ones) to come into your home.

Solid Door Units

- To install these pet doors, a hole is cut into your wood or metal door. The unit is fitted into the hole and secured with screws. To get in and out, the cat pushes through a flap. These doors may or may not have a catch to lock the flap when you want the cat to stay in (depends on the brand).

Sliding Door or Window Units

- Your door or window is left ajar and a clear panel containing the cat door is placed in the space. Again, the cat pushes through the flap, which may or may not have a catch to lock it when you want your cat to stay in.

Screen Door Units

- These units work like the regular door or window units but they are usually made of screening and can't take much wear and tear.

Fancy Doors

- *Magnetic Lock Doors*. Some fairly expensive units have a magnetic door lock which controls who can use the door. The cat wears a special collar with a magnetic ''key'' that allows the door panel to open when pushed.
- *Insulated Doors*: Often installed in a wall or window, these double doors block the cold wind or summer heat better.

GREENING THE CAT—YOUR CAT AND THE ENVIRONMENT

HOW DO I LESSEN MY CAT'S IMPACT ON THE ENVIRONMENT?

Your choice of supplies and how you use them can make a difference for you, your cat and the ecology. With a little extra effort, you can help the environment and save money too. Try any or all of the following ideas:

Recycling

- Don't buy single-use, disposable items; washing and reusing litter boxes, bowls, etc., doesn't add to the landfill and it keeps your cost down.
- Look for food, litter and equipment packaged in or made from recycled materials.
- Recycle metal and plastic containers.
- Use recycled materials for toys. See chapter 11.
- Reuse large food bags or litter bags as recycle containers for newspapers, cardboard, plastics or aluminum.

Pollution Solutions

- Select a flea treatment with the lowest environmental impact. See chapter 10.
- Use pump sprays for flea treatments instead of aerosols.
- Use low-impact cleaners such as vinegar, borax, baking soda and citrus-based soaps. Read labels carefully. See chapter 20 for the recipes for environmentally safe cleaners.

Food

- Read cat food labels; if the food contains fish, check for the Dolphin Safe logo.
- Do not overfeed your cat; a fat cat uses more of everything.
- Feed a top-quality brand-name food. You use less food and less packaging and you'll have a healthier cat.
- Buy the largest food containers and store food correctly. See chapter 4 for storage tips.

23

Recreation

- Feed the wild birds. Set up the feeder against a window; the birds have a food source and your cat has entertainment. Place your compost pile below the feeders to recycle seed hulls and droppings. (If done right, the pile should be odor-free. See chapter 20 for composting directions.)
- Take your harnessed cat out for a walk or just for a bit of sun.

Other

- Neuter before sexual maturity, at four to five months. Your cat will be more loving and won't add to overpopulation.
- Keep your cat inside and let him out only on a leash and harness or in an enclosure, so he can't hunt wild birds. And you'll have far fewer flea problems.
- Do regular home health checks (chapter 12) to catch health problems early and to prevent their spread. See your Vet at least once a year for both vaccinations and routine checkups.
- Adjust your heat or air conditioning when you're away or asleep. Programmable thermostat controls can earn their purchase price back in a short time and many can be installed without professional help. Whether hand-set or programmed, the heat should not be set higher than 80 degrees and the air conditioning should not be lower than 55 degrees.

HOW CAN I LOWER THE ENVIRONMENTAL IMPACT OF HIS LITTER BOX?

Conventional litter use in a one-cat household can add more than one ton of litter waste to a landfill over a six-year period.

Use a flushable litter or choose a composting litter. Composting litter should be used on ornamental plants only.

Toilet-trained cats or cats who use septic-tank-type boxes preclude litter mess, expense and odor.

You can read about litter in chapter 5. Meanwhile, here are some environmental tips for the litter box.

- Don't use litter liners. While litter-box liners make changing the box quicker and less messy, they add to the landfill. Even liners labeled biodegradable will not decompose in landfills for decades and many of these biodegradable plastics must be exposed to sunlight to degrade. Washing the box has less impact on the environment, especially with low-impact cleaners.
- Use a metal slotted spoon instead of a plastic litter scoop; it does the job more thoroughly, lasts far longer and can be recycled.
- Select a litter that is either compostable or flushable and has no additives except for baking soda or activated charcoal. Many cats object to perfumed scents and look for other, less acceptable places to do their business. Keep in mind that you will use a smaller volume of clumping litters compared with traditional clay litters.

WHAT ARE THE BENEFITS OF REGULAR GROOMING?

Besides reducing the general mess and the need to chemically flea-treat both your cat and your home, daily and weekly grooming sessions can deepen your relationship with your pet, help prevent health problems and aid in early detection of illness.

If you combine grooming with safe flea treatment, you can reduce the need for sprays and improve their effectiveness. Additionally, a good brushing will also minimize the need for hair-ball treatments for your cat. See chapter 10 for more information on fleas.

Grooming also saves money in surprising ways. Regular grooming reduces the amount of flying fur and hair buildup in the TV, VCR and computer. A service call to vacuum hair out of an expensive piece of electronics can be more than $50.

If your cat goes to a professional groomer, you should select one who uses organically based supplies and chemicals with the lowest environmental impact.

WHAT CAN I GROW OUTSIDE TO HELP KEEP
FLEAS AWAY?

Since you can bring fleas in after working in the yard, it's important to keep the yard as flea-free as possible. Grow marigolds, painted daisies, pennyroyal and mums; they will repel fleas, look pretty and add their bit of oxygen to the atmosphere.

3

Choosing a Cat

THERE ARE many factors to consider when selecting a first pet or even a second or third, and it's important that you make your commitment to a pet on the basis of informed choices. The sad truth is that the overwhelming majority of animals taken in by animal shelters are there because their owners failed to make responsible decisions about pet ownership.

First of all, pet selection may not even be an option. Check your lease for pet clauses; pets may be prohibited or restricted by number, size or species. Even if pets are allowed, you may have to pay a larger rent, a deposit or even a nonrefundable deposit.

If you already have a pet, does he want to share his space with another animal? What type of pet would be best?

In addition to pet selection guidelines, this chapter will help you get things set up before you bring him home.

WHAT CAN I EXPECT TO PAY FOR A CAT?

The initial purchase price is influenced by whether the cat is a mixed breed or a purebred of pet, breeding or show quality.

Mixed breeds are free or nearly so. If you get a cat or kitten from a shelter, expect to pay a nominal fee. Often this fee covers your first Vet visit and reduces neutering costs. The fee also helps defray the shelter's expenses for the animal's care.

Purebred pricing varies with the quality of the cat and with the reputation of the cattery. These cats can cost from a mere $20 to thousands of dollars. Typically, a purebred will fall into one of the following categories:

- *Pet Quality*. Pet-quality cats do not perfectly fit the breed description. These cats are less expensive than other purebreds but should **not** be used in a breeding program because of faults in appearance or health-related problems. Examples of faults which do not affect health or temperament are coat length, texture, color or markings, face shape and length of body or overall size. The cat will still make a wonderful pet and companion when neutered. Some pet-quality cats may have health problems such as heart defects, kidney problems or other genetic abnormalities. While these cats can also be fine companions, you may have ongoing health issues to deal with. Neutering these pets is imperative to ensure that these genetic problems aren't passed on to further generations.
- *Breed Quality*. These purebred cats are good examples of their breed and are healthy animals too. They can be used in a reputable breeding program, but may or may not win in shows. They can still be good companions as neuters.
- *Show Quality*. Show-quality cats are healthy, outstanding examples of their breed. The most expensive of the purebreds, they can be used in a reputable breeding program and will win in shows. These cats can also be good companions as neuters.

DO I HAVE TO BUY A PUREBRED CAT TO BE ABLE TO ENTER A SHOW?

Cat shows aren't just for the picture-perfect purebreds with five-part names and six-page pedigrees. Any feline, including those neutered and possessing undecided lineage, can perform in the show ring.

Today's cat show has something for everyone. They can be fun, educational and hard work—and if your special cat isn't a show-off, you can still enjoy yourself as a spectator. For more information on cat shows, see chapter 11.

A cat can be championed in any of the following categories:

- intact purebred cats
- purebred kittens
- neutered/spayed purebred cats
- household pets (HHP), which include both mixed breeds and purebreds, who have no papers

Note: HHP must be neutered/spayed if six months or older. Declawed cats cannot be shown in some of the clubs.

WHAT DOES "PAPERED," "REGISTERED" AND "HHP" MEAN?

When you buy a kitten or cat, keep in mind that a registration paper isn't a legal certification—or even an indication—of the cat's health or temperament.

Nor is it a guarantee that the kitten you buy is a quality example of his breed. Kitten mills and many backyard breeders do big business by registering their kittens with little or no regard for their quality. A well-tempered, healthy "alley" cat will be a far better pet than a poor-dispositioned, ailing purebred.

Papered and Registered

These are different terms with **identical** meaning. To be papered/registered, a cat must meet the following two criteria:

- Both parents must be papered and of the same breed.
- Their breeder must certify to the cat club who the parents are.

HHP (Household Pet)

HHP is a show category, a sort of grab bag of cats without papers. Kittens over six months old must be neutered/spayed to be shown and some of the clubs do not allow declawed cats. A cat can lack papers for one of the following reasons:

- A purebred was not registered or his papers are missing.
- The cat has mixed heritage. "Mixed" applies to cats who are unregistrable because
  — one or both parents are unknown,
  — parents are of different breeds or
  — one or both parents, even if known, are unregistered.

HOW DO I REGISTER MY CAT?

If you purchase a purebred, he should come with registry papers.

If you don't have a purebred or if your purebred has no papers, you can still "register" the cat for cat show purposes only. Write to one or more registries you're interested in and ask for the paperwork relating to household pets. Make sure that you get a set of papers for each cat you want to register.

Fill in the paperwork and don't forget to enclose the fees when you mail it back.

WHAT IS THE CAT FANCY?

"The Cat Fancy" is a nebulous term for the wonderfully fanatic world of cat lovers, cat shows and professional breeders. The people, the information, the enthusiasm and love of cats are all part of it. So when a premier cat magazine needed a title, what better name than *Cat Fancy*!

HOW CAN I FIND OUT IF MY CAT WANTS A COMPANION?

Some cats can't tolerate competition with other cats but will enjoy companionship with a dog or some other species. Other cats are as Kipling described—"the cat that walked by himself"—and they want no other life forms in the house but you.

Before you make any final decisions, evaluate your cat's personality, for timid, shy cats may prefer to be alone.

To begin with, you might decide if your cat falls into any of the following "loner" categories:

- Cats with behavior problems may do better alone—at least until their behavior improves.
- Older cats, who have always been "only" cats, most likely will not want to change.
- Cats who react strongly to strays outside their windows may not want to share with another cat but may accept a dog or rabbit.
- Cats who have a strong negative reaction to other cats or animal scents on you or on your clothes will not be happy sharing.
- Cats who lack self-confidence may prefer to be an "only" cat. (See chapter 7 for information on evaluating his level of confidence.)

If your cat is described above or if you're just not sure, you can test your cat's willingness to have a new roommate by trying the following:

- Ask a friend to visit with their pet for several hours. The animals, especially the visiting pet, should be leashed. (For the most reliable test, the visiting pet should be the same species, breed and age you are thinking of adopting.)
- Invite one friend and their pet at a time. Test no more than one such combination per week.
- Observe your cat's reaction. See the Companion Chart below:

Companion Chart: Your Cat's Reaction to a Visiting Pet

Does Want This Species as a Friend.	May or May Not Want This Species as a Friend; Arrange One or Two More Visits.	Does Not Want This Species as a Friend. For Safety, Remove the Visitor Immediately.
Offers to play.	Sits up on a high place and observes *without* hisses, ears back or puffed tail.	Attacks with tail puffed, ears back; biting to draw blood.
Touches noses and/or sniffs.	Leaves the room; shows more indifference than fear or aggression.	Hides with eyes dilated. May pant and refuse to come out, even when the visitor has been gone for some time.
Grooms other animal.	Mild hissing without full aggression or defense display.	Sprays or house-soils after the visitor leaves.
	Ignores the other animal.	Makes household members the target of displaced aggression.

HOW CAN I TEST TO DETERMINE THE CAT'S PERSONALITY?

Dominant, submissive and shy are examples of the personality extremes. Most cats have a mixture of these traits and are an "average" cat. The average cat is the most flexible and easygoing of the personality types. But any personality type can be a happy, well-adjusted pet with training, socialization and the right roommates. See chapter 7 for training and socialization guidelines.

Dominant Cats Will:	Submissive Cats Will:	Shy Cats Will:
be the winner of kitten games.	give up easily in games with other kittens; turn belly-up in surrender.	freeze or run when approached by other kittens or people.
be assertive and outgoing with other kittens and people.	be quiet and slow to warm up to others; hang back with mom cat.	not willingly interact with people or other animals.
be the first to explore places and people.	be one of the last to explore new places and may take days or weeks to warm up to people.	stay in corners, boxes or other easily defendable places.
struggle to turn over when held belly-up in your arms; not want to surrender.	become limp or freeze when turned over belly-up in your arms.	become rigid when turned over belly-up in your arms; "cry," hiss, growl; may bite or scratch when touched.
be fearless and ready to try anything; carry tail up.	be reluctant to try new things.	avoid new things; not carry tail upright.
greet and smell everyone.	hang back.	be fearful of new people; fearful of being touched, approached or picked up.
nudge the other kittens away from food.	give up his own food when challenged.	give up his own food when challenged.
always be on top when kittens pile up to sleep.	tend to be on the bottom of the pile.	tend to be off to the side of the pile.

HOW DO I SELECT A CAT?

There are many things to consider when selecting your first cat or when adding to your family. First, read a good breed book to learn more about the different breeds, so you can pick one that will fit into your home and your lifestyle. Some cat breeds are quieter or more vocal than others; some breeds are more social than others; some breeds require more care—and there are other ways in which cat breeds differ. Before you choose a cat, you should consider the following:

Money and Time. Do you have the time and the financial resources to give the cat the kind of love and care he needs? See chapter 2 for estimates of time and money commitments.

Allergies. Does someone in your home have allergies? You may still be able to have a cat in the house. See chapter 19 for more information.

Space. There are no set spatial requirements for a cat, **but** it needs room for sunny naps, litter boxes and other equipment. Overcrowding can cause health and behavior problems, and territorial cats may begin to spray when over-crowded.

Male or Female. After neutering, males and females are very much alike.

Kitten or Adult. Kittens are definitely more adaptable. The adult's behavior patterns and personality are already developed. Adult cats do have advantages; they are more settled and less active and you'll know exactly what you're getting.

Personality Type. Decide what personality you want. Shy cats may always need to be alone for their well-being: they become distressed easily. Very dominant cats are harder to train and may also need to be alone or with a submissive cat because they try to run the house and everyone in it. Two or more dominant cats may have problems living together because they fight and/or spray to mark their territory. Average cats easily adjust to new situations, people and pets, and are the easiest to train.

Longhaired or Shorthaired. While longhaired cats have an exotic beauty that most shorthairs lack, a shorthair is much easier to care for. Long hair needs daily grooming.

Mixed Breed or Purebred. A mixed breed is a surprise package and as a companion will bring you as much love and satisfaction as any purebred. Purebred personalities are more predictable, although personality and grooming needs vary from breed to breed. The biggest drawback can be cost, which varies widely depending on breed and quality.

One Cat, Two or More. No more than two cats should be in a small apartment. As a rule, if space allows, two or three cats get into less trouble than one lonely cat looking for a good time. Of course, two or more cats will require more time and expense. Whatever the arrangement, quality care should be the primary concern. Do your present pets want more company? You should have no more cats than the resident cat(s) is (are) comfortable with.

Age and Gender Combinations. Two primary rules apply. Kittens younger than five months are most easily accepted by a resident cat, as are older kittens of the opposite sex.

HOW OLD SHOULD A KITTEN BE WHEN ACQUIRED?

Kittens should be at least eight weeks old when separated from their mother. But twelve weeks is even better because the kitten has had time to learn how to be a cat.

WHERE CAN I FIND A CAT/KITTEN?

There are many places to find a new companion. Remember that cats from your local paper, from the pet store or from individuals may come from backyard breeders. These animals can have some built-in problems.

Purebred

- Breed ads in cat magazines
- Breed ads in local papers
- At cat shows
- Asking people where they got their cat
- At humane shelters (if papers are not important)

Mixed Breed or Household Pet (HHP)

- At humane shelters
- In the local classified section of your paper
- Asking neighbors, relatives, co-workers

WHAT ARE THE ADVANTAGES/DISADVANTAGES OF THE DIFFERENT PLACES ONE CAN ACQUIRE A CAT?

Professional Breeder

The best place to purchase a purebred cat of any quality, for companion or for show, is the professional breeder. They:

- Know about the breed, understand genetics and have a firm breeding program aimed at certain breed improvements.
- Are active in showing cats and breed many champions and grand champions.
- Are members of breed clubs and professional organizations.
- Have high-quality pets who are healthy and have a sound temperament.
- Produce healthy cats/kittens who are cleared for testable communicable diseases and whose vaccinations are up to date.
- Have well-socialized, friendly cats that are raised in the home.
- Have a waiting list for kittens because the queen is not bred every time she is in heat; she is allowed to rest and recover between litters.

- Require signed spay/neuter agreements for pet-quality animals.
- Require that you return a kitten that "doesn't work out."
- Interview and investigate prospective adoptive families and do not sell kittens to everyone who asks. They are concerned that their kittens go to good homes.

Kitten Mills

In kitten mills (commercial breeders of animals), queens of dubious quality (even if papered) are bred every time they are in heat with toms of equally dubious quality. The animal is most often considered an object, a unit to be manufactured and sold. The standard of care for these animals is usually low-quality—little space and poor nutrition and health care.

Backyard Breeders

In general terms, backyard breeders are small-time operations (smaller than kitten mills) with no breeding program to improve the breed. Consequently, their kittens are usually below the standards of the professional breeders. They tend not to show their cats; in fact, their "purebred" animals may or may not be registrable or a quality representative of their breed. And unfortunately for both the cats and the buyer, these pets may have built-in genetic or acquired health problems.

Backyard breeders include the next-door neighbors who wanted Fluffy to have just one litter to show the children the "miracle of life." The family may care about their pet, but they don't know the genetics or breeding problems of their breed. Nor do they understand the problems of overpopulation and the health concerns of cats in general. These breeders won't insist on neuter/spay agreements for pet-quality kittens. Less concerned with the type of home the kitten will go to, they are also unlikely to accept a returned kitten. Many times these breeders are just making the pet earn back his purchase price or making a little money on the side.

Pet Stores

The quality of pet-store animals can vary greatly because the kittens can come from professional breeders, kitten mills or backyard breeders. Although some stores buy top-quality, healthy kittens from professional breeders, it's hard to prove where most pet-store stock is acquired.

Too often money is the primary concern. Kittens are bought from mills or backyard breeders, stores are understaffed and the animals left in small cages for weeks. Some stores give health guarantees to "replace" a pet if the pet becomes ill or dies within a specified period, but these generally don't cover the temperament problems that can come from kitten mills and backyard breeders.

Animal Shelters

The animal shelter or humane association is a good place to find a mixed-breed cat, or with some patience a purebred or purebred-appearing cat. Consider the following reasons for animal shelter adoption:

- These shelters rescue and care for animals otherwise abandoned or given up.
- If you are willing to keep looking, many purebred cats can be found, but the cat will not have papers.
- The animal will usually be in good physical health.
- You may or may not know the animal's experiences or breeding but surprises can be fun.

WHAT DO THE CLASSIFIED ADS REALLY MEAN?

Backyard breeders and kitten mills are the common placers of classified advertisements for purebreds. If the ads list several breeds or more than one litter at a time, or mislabel the breed (i.e., do not know the proper name of the breed), you aren't dealing with a professional breeder.

Read the ads carefully, and read between the lines. "Cute, feisty kittens—free" may translate as young kittens who are not well socialized, may well be wild and have behavior problems. "Need home for special cat, not good with children" may mean that the cat has already scratched or bitten a child—with or without provocation.

Ask questions. Why are they looking for a new home? What experience has the cat had with other pets and people in the home? What health care have they had? May you meet the parent cats?

By the way, if you find yourself in a position to advertise a cat or kitten because you can no longer give it a good home, put a price, even a small one, on the animal. Too often the middlemen for animal laboratories pick up their cats through "free" ads.

HOW DO I KNOW IF THE CAT OR KITTEN IS HEALTHY?

Selecting a healthy cat will save you money, time and possibly heartbreak. Kittens should be at least eight weeks old (twelve weeks is better). Here are some guidelines to help you make a wise choice:

- Check the breeder's reputation:
  — Ask about their reputation at the local humane association, shelter or Veterinarian.
  — How many cats/kittens does this person have? A kitten mill will have many queens and many litters for sale at one time.
  — How often does this person have kittens for sale? Each queen should be bred only once a year at the most.

- Check the breeder's physical environment. It should be clean and free of odors.
  — How much space does the queen have? The kittens should be raised "underfoot."
  — Check the nesting area. Is it large enough for the queen and kittens to sleep and play, and for the queen to begin litter-box training?
- Ask the breeder questions about shots, health care, worming, general care, flea control, and ask if the kittens are FeLV (feline leukemia) negative. Insist on written documentation noting dates and the Vet's signature for all tests, test results **and** vaccinations. (Vaccinations given by breeders can't be officially verified; you and the breeder will be better off if a formal veterinary record is established.)
- Check all kittens in the litter, parent(s) and other animals present. Kittens should be bright, springy, altert and active. Note the following:

  General Appearance. Alert, active, lively, good muscle tone.

  Mobility. Agile and graceful, surefooted, able to jump on/off objects.

  Body. No lumps, masses, sores; no foul odors.

  Coat and Skin. Glossy and well-groomed fur with no bare patches, no mats, no fleas; smooth and supple skin.

  Chest. Quiet breaths, no rattles except purring.

  Eyes. Clear and bright, reflect light at night, no drainage; nictitating membrane (third eyelid) retracted.

  Nose. No drainage, supple, may be dry or moist—and into everything.

  Mouth. Gums should be pink (not blue or grayish)—unless they are naturally pigmented; teeth firm in gums and white with no black spots (cavities) and no tartar; no foul mouth odor.

  Ears. Clean and dry with healthy skin; no foul odors or drainage.

  Anus. Clean; no foul smell.

  Urine and Feces. Urine is clear yellow; feces are dark brown, moist and well formed; animal does not strain to eliminate. Check the litter box; it should have no diarrhea and no "sick" smell.

WHAT DO I DO AFTER I DECIDE ON A CAT?

To avoid problems and to reduce the homecoming stress for both you and your new pet, prepare for the cat's arrival by catproofing the house; see information below. And it's always better if you've purchased needed supplies beforehand; see chapter 2.

For purchased cats, ask about acquiring the pedigree and get a written agreement on the kitten's health, the return policies and any breeding or neutering requirements. The health agreement (which should come with the kitten) should include dates and Veterinarian signatures for all tests, test results and vaccination records. Some breeders give their own shots; unfortunately, these unofficial records are not always reliable.

Take any new pet to the Vet for a health checkup and for his first shots (if needed) within twenty-four hours. Even better—make an appointment to take the animal to the Vet on the way home. There are "return of merchandise" laws, so any animal purchased at a pet store needs to have an immediate health check. Also, if you are bringing a new cat into a multiple-cat household, you may want to have your present cat(s) retested for FeLV (feline leukemia) to prevent infection of the newcomer.

If possible, keep the newcomer in isolation for two to three weeks. This means that you maintain separate facilities and that you wash up after visits. This period is long enough for most diseases to show up, before you expose your existing pets to the new cat.

WHAT SHOULD I CONSIDER BEFORE I GIVE A CAT OR KITTEN AS A GIFT?

Is the child, or even the adult, ready for the responsibility and the time and money commitments a pet requires? You want your gift to be a pleasure and joy for the next twenty years, not a mistake that ends up at the animal shelter or, worse yet, dumped on the roadside.

After concerns regarding commitment and responsibility have been dealt with, discuss the following with all of the involved people.

- Do they want a cat or would they prefer a different kind of animal?
- Do they want a kitten or a cat?
- Do they want a specific purebred? Is breed a concern?
- What personality type do they want to live with?
- When? Timing is important. Avoid holidays; quiet times are best.

BRINGING THE CAT HOME

This section includes information on how to catproof your home and the best way to introduce a new animal to the household members, including your other pets. Remember to check your lease for pet clauses **before** you bring him home.

WHAT SUPPLIES DO I NEED WHEN I GET THE CAT/KITTEN?

A whole new environment can be stressful for the cat; he'll do better if there are no sudden changes in food, water and litter. Make arrangements for the following **before** you bring your cat home:

Carrier or Harness. Take it with you to get the pet.

Food. Make any changes gradually over a week or ten days. It may be best to keep to the same diet.

Water. If the new pet is used to a different water supply, bring home some of that water. Gradually change the water to your home supply by adding a little of your water every day.

Sanitary Arrangements. Learn what arrangements the cat presently uses. Buy that brand of litter or ask for enough litter for a day. See chapter 5 to evaluate that litter or to get more information in case you need to change the setup.

HOW CAN I CATPROOF MY HOME TO MAKE IT SAFER?

Setting up a safe environment isn't enough; you must make safety precautions lifelong habits. The following will help your cat avoid both behavior and health problems.

INSIDE THE HOUSE

Sinks and Cabinets

- Check under and behind the sinks and cabinets for holes and seal them closed.
- Install latches on cabinets. Keep tobacco, cleaning supplies of any type, poisons, other chemicals *and candy* out of reach.
- Keep all medicines, cosmetics, personal-care items and other similar items in a cabinet or drawer.
- Keep cupboards closed unless you want furry food and dishes.

Large Storage Areas and Trash Containers

- Do not allow the cat access to storage areas such as the attic and basement. Keep the doors latched.
- Check when closing doors that your pet is not locked in closets or cut off from the litter box. Train the cat to leave the area when you tell him, "Out."
- Use covered trash cans in the kitchen or put the trash can under the sink and lock the doors with child locks or a locking hook and eye. Garbage can be very interesting to a cat but it can also be deadly.

Balconies

- Keep cats off open balconies, or have the areas enclosed for safe access. Keep the doors latched.

Windows and Doors

- Check that window screens are secure and unbroken. Do not open windows without screens. Replace half screens; cats can remove them.

- Go in and out carefully—so that your cat doesn't get out. See chapter 8 for training ideas.
- Tie up mini-blind and drapery cords. A cat can get caught in the cords and strangle.

Appliances and Furniture

- Do not leave appliance doors open; check before using all appliances.
- Watch kittens when opening the oven; they are lured by the smells and don't understand the danger.
- Secure or unplug dangling electrical cords. A playful cat can be hit by a falling iron or hair dryer.
- Train him to stay off the gas stove or store the clean pans on the top so he doesn't have any space; he can singe his whiskers or fur on the pilot light.
- Check the knobs on the stove; while the newer models have safety features so the cat can't turn on the burners, older stoves do not.
- Be careful using built-in footrests on chairs. See that there are no animals resting in the space underneath. The same caution applies to sofa beds and other such movable furniture. And know where the cat is when you're in your rocking chair too.
- Periodically check the underside of beds, couches and chairs. When these items have tears or holes in the bottom, it can be a siren call to a cat. Once in, it's difficult to get him back out without causing further damage.

Table and Dresser Tops

- Anything he can reach with a paw is a toy. Either keep these surfaces cleared of objects or train him to leave things alone.
- Keep small objects (hair ribbons and yarn, buttons, coins, rings) out of reach.
- Remove temptations from counters or tables and train him to stay off counters. Remember that the plastic that temptation came in is also inviting—and dangerous!

Hazards Associated with Other Pets

- Use one of these ideas to keep a cat from using the dog's pet door:
  — Close it off and let Fido in and out yourself.
  — Install a magnetic pet door that opens only when the pet wears a matching collar. Put the collar on your dog only.
- Use a hood on your aquarium whether it contains fish or other animals. This prevents escapes and cat visits. An under-gravel filter or bio wheel will keep filter material from curious paws.

Product Safety Precautions

- In general, any product labeled as a hazard for children is also a hazard for pets.
- Select safe cleaning products both for the safety of your cat and for the environment. See further information in chapter 6.

- Remove or make inaccessible all poisonous plants and any plant with serrated leaves. Read on in this chapter for a chart on poisonous plants and tips for making plants inaccessible.
- Do not use poisons to control pests where the cat could get to the poison or to the poisoned insects.
- Any object small enough to fit into his mouth can be swallowed. Unfortunately, many of these objects cannot pass through the cat's system without damage. Bowel blockage is common and can be remedied only by surgery.
- Avoid toys that have small parts that can be removed, and regularly inspect toys. Discard any toys that are badly worn or damaged.
- String, yarn, thread, rubber bands are all very dangerous. The cat plays with the object and eats it; these items can wrap around his teeth and tongue, or tangle in the bowels. Not only can they cut into tissues, they can block air passages and cut off circulation. **Never attempt to remove any of these tangles from a cat's mouth or anus. Get the cat to your Vet immediately.**
- Cats can ingest lead metal directly from their environment or indirectly by grooming it off their fur. Lead is in old paint chips, in drinking water from old pipes and in improperly glazed pottery used for water or food bowls.

IN THE GARAGE

- Close off all access to the garage to keep wild animals out. They can be a danger to you and your cat if they slip into the garage.
- Clean up any spills or drips from the car. Clay litter is great for absorbing these toxic messes. Pets will lick up sweet-tasting antifreeze, and it takes less than a teaspoon to kill a cat.

OUTSIDE THE HOUSE

- Close off all access to crawl spaces for the safety of your cat and to keep wild animals out.
- Read labels for chemicals used in your yard.
- Keep strays out of your yard.
- If you park outside, bang on the car hood before starting the car. Outdoor cats will crawl onto the motor to get warm.
- Do not let your cat out when you are mowing the lawn or after spraying.

CAN I KEEP BOTH HOUSE PLANTS AND CATS?

Yes. Plants help clear the air in our homes, so they can be good for you and your cat. Spider plants or airplane plants are great indoor antipollution green machines and are both easy to grow.

Some plants, however, are toxic, and others with serrated leaves can cut a cat's mouth or lacerate his stomach lining—leading to blood-laced vomiting. See the chart below, in which items marked with an "X" are toxic to cats.

Note: If you have any questions about a particular plant, ask your Vet, or call the poison hot line; see chapter 21. For ideas on how to protect your plants from chewing or soil digging, see chapter 8.

Plant	Bark	Leaf and/or Stem	Seed	Bulb	Flower	Berry	Root
almond			X				
amaryllis (surprise lily)				X			
apple			X				
apricot			X				
arrowhead vine		X					
asparagus fern		X					
azalea (in quantity)		X					
Baltic ivy		X				X	
bittersweet						X	
Boston ivy		X				X	
boxwood	X	X					
burrs such as cocklebur and burdock	Will cause mats that must be cut out.						
buttercup	X	X					
cactus and other spiny plants	The spines mat fur and may penetrate skin.						
caladium		X					
calla or arum lily		X					
castor bean			X				
cherry—black, bitter, sweet or choke	X	X					
chrysanthemum (mums)		X					
creeping fig		X					
crocus		X		X	X		X
crown of thorns	Sap is an irritant to eyes and skin.						
daffodil or jonquil				X			

Plant	Bark	Leaf and/or Stem	Seed	Bulb	Flower	Berry	Root
dieffenbachia (dumb cane, mother-in-law plant)		X					
elephant ears		X					
English holly		X				X	
English ivy		X				X	
foxglove	X	X					
grass awns, such as foxtail, wild barley, ripgut grass	The awn is the part of the seed which can push itself into the skin and move through the body. In this case it must be surgically removed. On a superficial level, it can cause mats.						
hemlock	X	X	X			X	X
hyacinth		X		X	X		X
hydrangea	X	X	X		X	X	X
iris or flag			X				
Jerusalem cherry						X	
larkspur (delphinium)		X	X				
lily of the valley	X	X					
marigold		X	X		X		X
mistletoe		X				X	
	The oil can cause allergies.						
morning glory			X				
mountain laurel	X	X	X		X	X	X
mushrooms (wild)	Toxic parts include the cap or stem and root.						
nicotiana		X					
oleander	X	X					
periwinkle			X				
philodendron		X					
poinsettia	Sap is an irritant to the eyes and the skin.						
poison ivy, oak and sumac	These will not harm the cat, but the cat can pass oils (and poison ivy, oak, sumac) on to you.						
rhododendron	X	X	X	X	X	X	
rhubarb		X					
schefflera		X					

Plant	Bark	Leaf and/or Stem	Seed	Bulb	Flower	Berry	Root
snow on the mountain	Sap is an irritant to the eyes and skin.						
spider plant (airplane plant)	Concentrates toxins from the house into the leaves.						
thorn apple			X				
trumpet vine			X				
tulip				X			
walnut						green hull	
weeping fig (ficus)		X					
wisteria	X	X	X		X	X	X
yew	X	X	X				

Two Suggestions to Safeguard Your Cat—and Your Plants

- To protect your cat, hang suspected plants high in the windows where the cat can't reach them, or you can train the cat not to bother your plants.
- Grow a shade-loving yard grass for the cat in a wide flat container on a sunny sill; it can be small for snacks or large enough to sleep in too.

HOW DO I INTRODUCE A NEW CAT TO MY HOUSEHOLD?

It's important to start off right to avoid problems.

If You Have No Other Pets

If you're getting a new cat or kitten to replace a lost cat or one that has recently died, vacuum well and wipe or mist white vinegar on safe surfaces **before** you bring the new cat home. The vinegar neutralizes the lingering scent of the old pet and makes your environment less threatening to the newcomer. New cats, even neutered ones, may spray inside the house to claim the territory as their own. The same applies if you move your ''old'' cat into a new home. If the previous owners had a cat, get out the vinegar!

- Set up all the equipment you need.
- Take a carrier with you to pick up the cat.
- Open the carrier in the room with the litter box. Leave the cat closed in the room and allow him to explore.

- Later, when he is calm and comfortable with you and the space:
  — Let the cat explore more of the house.
  — Show him where the food and water bowls and the scratching post are.
- Keep things low-key for a few days to let him get used to his new home.

If You Have Other Pets

Follow the same steps above **except**:

- Do not give the new cat attention (other than feedings)—no matter how cute! Don't pet or even talk to the newcomer until the other animals have accepted him.
- Give your other pets extra attention **when they are well behaved**, and ignore inappropriate behavior.
- Refer to the new cat as your other animals' pet or brother/sister. (No, they can't understand the words but they will understand your body English. Also, hearing their names paired in a positive way will help them bond.)
- Daily, wipe each animal with the same cloth. This creates a colony smell composed of all the individual body scents.

4

Food and Nutrition

THIS CHAPTER tells what type of diet a cat needs, gives instructions on how to read food labels and provides other nutritional tidbits, including recipes and lists of good and bad snacks. Remember, your cat is what he eats. Be smart, let him eat smart; you'll have a healthier pet and fewer Vet bills.

DO CATS HAVE SPECIAL NUTRITIONAL NEEDS?

Cats are true carnivores (meat eaters) and they need a diet of 30 percent protein. They also need food high in saturated fats for vitamin D and hormone production.

The extra protein is needed for a cat's specific amino acid, vitamin and mineral requirements. And cats are efficient carnivores. While they can metabolize some plants with such nutrients as vitamin A, they can absorb vitamin A only from meat.

WHY DO CATS EAT GRASS AND SOMETIMES MY FERNS?

Grass is a natural source of dietary fiber that also gives relief from many gastrointestinal upsets. Eating a little seems to be for the taste. Eating a lot is a way to induce vomiting, to help relieve hair balls or some other stomach distress.

WHAT SHOULD I FEED MY CAT OR KITTEN?

Feed your cat any national name brand of commercial cat food which is labeled "field-tested" and "100% nutritionally complete" for the age of your friend. If your cat isn't particular, you can feed a variety of flavors.

The costlier Veterinarian-recommended, high-quality foods can in the long run actually cost less than grocery store brands because your cat will need less food, defecate less and remain healthier.

Read the labels and make sure the food is nutritionally right for your cat. (See the question below.) It's unwise to buy food labeled "for all ages." Cats of different ages have different nutritional needs. Kittens under a year old grow at an accelerated rate and need concentrated food, labeled "kitten food." If a cat is at least one year old, he needs less concentrated food; on a rich diet he'll become fat and be more prone to health problems. Elderly cats or cats with chronic health problems may need prescription diets.

Try to keep snacks and treats (people food, commercial cat treats, etc.) to 10 percent or less of the total food intake.

WHAT SHOULD I LOOK FOR ON THE FOOD LABELS?

New research shows that foods containing at least 30 percent *animal* protein and a low level of magnesium play a major role in the prevention of feline lower urinary tract disease (FLUTD), a new name for FUS. Unfortunately, even if the food meets these standards, federal guidelines prohibit a statement concerning the prevention of FLUTD unless the food is specifically formulated for that purpose.

The ingredients on a food label are listed in the order of amount, from the most to the least used ingredient. The analysis of the food is given in percentages of **minimum** daily needs to prevent diseases related to vitamin and mineral deficiencies—not necessarily to provide optimum levels of nutrition. The first ingredient(s) listed should be *animal-based protein*. Note that meat by-products mean organ meats, such as heart and liver, that are highly nutritious for cats. Avoid foods that list ingredients such as salt, chemical preservatives, food dyes and sugar.

Any product labeled "for intermittent feeding only" or "not to be fed as a sole diet" is **not** a cat food to be given daily but rather a supplement or snack.

WHAT ELSE SHOULD I LOOK FOR WHEN SELECTING PET FOODS?

As you select packages of food, use common sense, and buy only bags and cans in good shape. Avoid outdated or damaged packages. If the food smells "off," do not use it and report it to the company. Most brands will have an address or phone number to deal with customer complaints.

Buy the largest sizes and learn how to properly store the food. Read on for storage instructions.

WHAT PEOPLE FOODS CAN I FEED MY CAT OR KITTEN?

Commercial cat foods are specially formulated for a cat's nutritional needs. These needs are so specific that even a diet of people-food fish, like tuna, can cause vitamin deficiencies leading to convulsion, paralysis and death. Additionally, a diet of table scraps is not a healthy or balanced alternative for a cat.

Occasional "good" snacks can be a healthy way to work variety into your cat's diet without upsetting his nutritional balance. Remember, snacks should be kept to preferably 10 percent, and definitely not more than 15 percent, of total food intake.

If your cat is elderly or has medical problems, check with your Vet before giving him any treats.

Good Snacks

- Raw or cooked vegetables, plain, no sauces
- Fresh fruit
- Cheese and yogurt
- Meat drippings
- **Cooked** meat or **cooked** eggs
- **Cooked** poultry. (make certain all bones are removed)
- **Cooked** soup bones
- Liquid from water-packed meats and fish

ARE THERE ANY PEOPLE FOODS THAT CAN HURT MY CAT?

Yes. And the consequences can range from mild sickness to death. The most common feeding mistakes are **raw** meat, poultry, fish or eggs and **bones**. The raw (uncooked) products contain bacteria and your cat can become ill with food poisoning. Bones, except as noted in the previous question, may splinter and the sharp ends can puncture the cat's digestive system. Yes, strays and feral cats eat bones, but their life span is also much shorter due to their diet and lifestyle. Below is a general list of the "don'ts." If you have any concerns about a particular food that is not included, contact your Vet. It's better to be safe than make your cat sorry.

Really Bad Snacks

- *Uncooked* meat, fish, poultry or eggs
- Bones (especially chicken and other small bones)
- Alcoholic beverages in any form
- Rich sauces
- Onions, raw potatoes, coconut and coconut oil
- Corncobs (may cause blockage)
- Chocolate in any form
- Candy, desserts or any other sweet foods
- Sodium benzoin (preservative used in soft drinks and in apple drinks)

CAN I GIVE MY CAT A VEGGIE DIET?

No. The cat is a carnivore, not an omnivore (plant and meat eater) or a herbivore (plant eater). In reality, cats won't be tempted very much by a vegetarian diet. Also, plant protein cannot supply some required amino acids, including taurine. And a cat without taurine will become blind.

SHOULD I FEED HIM A SPECIAL DIET TO PREVENT PROBLEMS?

No. The best nourishment for the average healthy adult cat is a name-brand, high-quality maintenance diet. Besides, you can't accurately predict which cats will develop which medical problems.

HOW MUCH FOOD SHOULD I GIVE MY CAT DAILY?

The amount of food your cat really needs depends on:

- The variety and brand of the food
- His age and body size
- His activity level
- His health
- The season (more food may be needed in winter to keep the body temperature up)

With higher-quality foods, less is needed and less should be fed. The per-meal amounts described assume you're feeding a top-quality diet.

Kittens. Give 2 tablespoons of kitten food per meal. Another tablespoon per meal can be added if the kitten demands more. Evaluate the animal's weight every two weeks and adjust the food accordingly.

Adults. A kitten eats like an adult when the Vet changes its diet to adult food—usually at nine to twelve months. For every ten pounds of body weight, feed ¼ cup of dry food per meal **or** 2 slightly rounded tablespoons of wet food per meal. After ten days, evaluate the cat's weight and adjust the amount of food. To keep from having a tubby—or too thin—tabby, be sure to evaluate your cat's weight at least four times a year.

Pregnant or Nursing Females. Queens need another ¼ cup of food per day. Either feed an additional ¼ cup meal or give her ⅜ cup of food twice daily. Although the weight of a nursing queen will be easy to evaluate, an expectant mom cat—who grows more round as the pregnancy progresses—will be harder to assess.

HOW OFTEN SHOULD I FEED MY KITTEN OR CAT?

Feeding Table

Age	Number of Meals per Day
Four weeks	(Introduce kitten food) 3 to 4 meals
Six weeks to three months	(Mother will wean) 6 meals
Three to four months	5 meals
Four to seven months	4 meals
Seven months to nine months	3 meals*
Nine months to one year	2 meals*
Two to ten years	2 meals
Ten years and over	3 to 4 meals[†]

*Change to adult food when your Vet advises.

[†]Change to senior food when your Vet advises.

WHY SHOULD I FEED MY CAT MEALS INSTEAD OF LEAVING FOOD OUT ALL THE TIME?

In the wild, a cat would make a kill and then could go twelve to thirty-six hours or even longer on it. So the cat's body is biochemically set up to handle meals, not all-day snacking. It's actually good for an adult cat to be hungry for a few hours (no matter what he says).

A healthy adult cat (one to ten years of age) usually does better with two meals a day. For others, two meals per day may not be enough; kittens, senior cats, ill or recuperating cats may need to be fed smaller, even more frequent meals. Consult your Vet about feeding schedules for cats with special needs.

Cats can become overweight with free-feeding (food left out all the time). If your cat is already obese, it's impossible to put him on a diet with the food out. Some cats will become anorectic (seriously underweight) because the constant smell of food short-circuits the hunger reflexes.

There are other disadvantages too. If you free-feed in a multi-cat household, you can't tell how much each cat is eating. One cat may be eating far less than usual or not eating at all. The loss of appetite can be a symptom of a serious medical problem; you may not know there is a problem until it's too late.

Feeding meals also helps build a positive relationship between the cat and his person. Bonds are strengthened because your cat depends on you for food, as he once depended on mom cat.

Finally, remember that food left out all the time loses nutritional value and encourages bugs and rodents.

HOW DO I CHANGE FROM FREE-FEEDING TO MEALS?

Follow the directions below. The secret to success is tough love. Don't fall prey to a plaintive, begging meow. Cats are smart, and catch on after two to three meals. If you have more than one cat, set out bowls placed at least twelve inches apart for each cat. A permanent feeding place for each cat is best.

Directions

In the morning:

STEP 1   Feed half of the cat's total food.
STEP 2   Leave the food for ten to fifteen minutes only.
STEP 3   Then pick up **all** leftovers. Toss or store (see question on food storage below).
STEP 4   **Do not feed the cat at all during the day.** When the cat complains, play with or pet the cat, or you can leave the house, but do not give in!

At bedtime:

STEP 5   Feed the cat the other half of his daily ration.
STEP 6   Leave the food for ten to fifteen minutes only.
STEP 7   Remove **all** leftovers.

HOW DO I DEAL WITH CATS ON DIFFERENT MEAL SCHEDULES?

The very young, old or convalescent need to eat more frequently than a healthy adult. Feed the cat who needs more meals on schedule. The other cat can be given a small snack of raw vegetables or a few pieces saved from a previous meal. If he tries to steal food, isolate the cat who needs the meal and then feed him.

HOW CAN I TELL IF MY CAT IS AT HIS IDEAL WEIGHT?

Test him just before a meal. Stand your cat up and gently feel his ribs and stomach.

Appearance	Probable Weight
Ribs slightly noticeable to touch; stomach is flat.	Ideal weight.
Ribs barely noticeable by touch; stomach is rounded.	Overweight; see your Vet.
Ribs and backbone very noticeable to touch; ribs and backbone may be visible; stomach concave.	Underweight; see your Vet.

WHY SHOULD I WORRY IF HE IS OVER- OR UNDERWEIGHT?

The overweight cat is more likely to develop diabetes and fatty liver disease. He is also less agile and may have a hard time grooming himself. The added weight also puts more stress on his heart and joints. And fat cats are more expensive to maintain.

The underweight cat is not receiving sufficient nutrients. He will be more likely to become ill—and cranky.

HOW CAN I HELP MY CAT LOSE WEIGHT?

Even cats have not been neglected in the marketing craze for low-calorie foods in the battle of the bulge. Several premium brands now offer reduced-calorie cat foods. The idea is to serve the same amount of diet food that your cat normally consumes. Or you can simply reduce the amount of regular food you give him and stop feeding high-calorie snacks. Water and vegetables can be added to fill the cat up.

Consult with your Vet about an exercise routine. In general, ten to fifteen minutes of aerobic play is enough to tone those muscles and burn that fat.

WHY WON'T MY CAT EAT HIS FOOD?

If he is normally a good eater and suddenly stops eating, see your Vet and follow her directions for care. Cats normally don't eat well when they are ill, so you'll need a clean bill of health before you take any action.

Once you know the reason is not medical, consider the following:

- What are his normal behaviors?
- Does he play food games, rejecting the first thing you offer or refusing leftovers from a can?
- Does he have problems with hair balls?
- Is the food offered coming directly from the refrigerator?
- Is food left down all the time?
- What type of food are you offering him? Some cats have different ideas of what makes a gourmet meal and will not eat certain flavors.

HOW CAN I ENCOURAGE MY CAT TO EAT?

If the doctor has given your finicky feline a clean bill of health, try the following suggestions.

- If you have been free-feeding, change to meals. Your cat can build up hunger between meals, and you'll be better able to monitor his intake.
- Some cats won't eat cold canned food. The food can be warmed by one of two methods:
  — Put a meal-sized portion in the microwave (use a microwave-safe container) for fifteen to thirty seconds. Stir the food and check the temperature before serving, since hot spots created by microwaving can burn your cat's mouth.
  — Put a meal-sized portion in a container and let it rest in a bowl of hot water. (Do not wet the food.)
- If the cat ignores his available fresh food and just wants what is in the next unopened can, try a little tough love; most cats will adjust in a day or two. Here's what to do.
  — Offer the cat a meal.
  — Wait ten minutes.
  — No matter how little he has eaten, if anything, put away any leftovers.
  — Do not feed the cat anything till the next mealtime.
  — No matter how much he whines or pleads, **no cheating**.
  — Offer him his meal again.

Note: Do not let your cat go for more than three days without eating unless your Vet approves.

HOW SHOULD I STORE CAT FOOD?

Try leaving an open can of fish-based cat food out for a while in a warm kitchen, and you and your nose will appreciate the value of adequate cat food storage. Whether canned or dry, left-out cat food also draws pests and loses its nutritional value.

51

Canned Food Storage

- Serve only enough for one meal at a time.
- Remove the rest of the food from the can and put it into a sealable plastic or glass container.
- Refrigerate.
- Store unopened cans in a cool, dry place.

Note: If you shake the can before you open it, the contents will slide out more easily.

Dry Food Storage

- Serve only enough for one meal at a time. (Do not leave food out at all times.)
- Pour the remainder into a catproof, airtight container.
- Store in a cool, dry place, inaccessible to pests or pets. If he is able to open cupboards and help himself to extras, see chapter 8 for help.

WHY WATER?

You may not see your cat drink much water, but he does need it. Most of his bodily functions and chemistry must have water to work efficiently. A cat or kitten on a dry food diet will probably drink more water than a cat on canned food, but the total water intake will be about the same. Clean the bowl and give him fresh water daily.

If your pet seems thirstier than usual, it might be a sign of a serious health problem. See your Veterinarian immediately.

IF I OFFER MILK, DOES HE NEED WATER TOO?

Even cats that can drink milk also need fresh water daily. Nutritionally, milk isn't considered a liquid; it's more of a food. Additionally, some cats are lactose-intolerant. Missing the enzymes needed to digest it, these cats get diarrhea and gas if they drink milk.

ARE THERE RECIPES FOR CAT SNACKS?

Yes. The following recipes are good snacks and make a great gift for your pets or for friends with pets. Both dogs and cats like these treats, which will keep in a plastic bag at room temperature for many months. With four different flavors, there is one to suit every palate.

RECIPES FOR ANIMAL SNACKS

Add **one** of the following protein flavors to the basic recipe below:

1 can of chicken broth

or

1 can of condensed cheddar cheese soup

or

1 6-ounce can of oil- **or** water-packed tuna fish, including the can's liquid, and ½ cup of water, processed in a food processor/blender for fifteen to twenty seconds. If you use the oil-packed tuna, reduce the amount of butter by 2 tablespoons. If you use water-packed tuna, reduce the amount of water by 2 tablespoons.

or

1 10-ounce can of beef consommé

Basic Recipe

4½ cups whole-wheat flour
1 stick butter or margarine
½ cup wheat germ
2 cloves garlic
2 tablespoons molasses
¼ cup unbleached or white flour

Mix one of the protein flavors above and all other ingredients **except** the unbleached flour. Knead lightly on a floured surface, using the unbleached flour to keep the mixture from sticking. Roll out the dough to a thickness of ⅛ to ¼ inch. Cut with a floured cookie cutter and place on ungreased sheet. (We use bone-shaped cutters.) Bake, on top rack, at 350 degrees for twenty minutes. Turn each biscuit over and return to the oven for another fifteen minutes. Turn the oven off and leave the biscuits in the oven to dry out. The oven's low humidity is ideal, for unless the biscuits are thoroughly dry, they'll mold. When the biscuits are very dry and cool, store them in an airtight container.

WHY DOES MY CAT REFUSE TO TRY NEW FOODS?

Although cats are curious, they are creatures of conservative habit when it comes to food and other comforts. Kittens that are exposed to different situations and a variety of foods are much more adaptable as adult cats and more willing to try new foods when they grow older.

HOW CAN I GET MY CAT TO EAT A NEW FOOD?

Whether a cat needs a change of diet because of health or for some other reason, it can be a challenge to get him to accept new food. You can camouflage the change by making it so gradual that your cat won't notice the switch. (If you are changing the diet because of serious illness, you may not have the luxury of a gradual change. Consult your Vet about the best way to make the transition, and if necessary, resort to force-feeding.)

Under normal circumstances, to change a cat's food habits, substitute the new food (⅛ to ¼ of the total) for part of his usual food. Keep the ratio the same for three or four days. Gradually (twice a week) increase, again by another ⅛ to ¼ , the amount of new food in his bowl. In no time at all, your cat will be happily dining on his new food.

WHY DOES MY CAT SOMETIMES VOMIT RIGHT AFTER EATING?

Cats vomit easily. In the wild, they'll often regurgitate hair, skin and bones. Indoor cats vomit too, for a variety of reasons. They may have hair balls, blockage from eating nonfood items or some other type of blockage. Some cats throw up when they eat too fast or because the food was cold. If your cat vomits occasionally, don't worry about it. It's not unknown for cats to regurgitate food immediately after eating and then reingest it.

Vomiting can, however, be a symptom of illness. If your cat vomits regularly, or if he vomits blood or foreign objects, see your Vet immediately.

HE EATS TOO FAST. WHAT CAN I DO?

When cats eat too fast, they are prone to vomiting after meals and may bother their housemates by stealing their food. One of the following ideas should help slow his eating:

- Divide the food into smaller, more frequent meals.
- Scatter the food over a large platter or tray or put it into several bowls or saucers in different locations.
- For canned food, add water so he has to lap it up.
- For both canned and dry food, leave a spoon in his bowl or add **large** marbles or **large** marble-sized stones to his food so he has to root out the food.

5

Sanitation Arrangements

T HIS CHAPTER tells how to care for the litter box and describes litter types and alternatives to litter. See chapter 8 if you're having a problem with house soiling.

WHAT TYPES OF LITTER ARE THERE?

You have many litter choices today and new products are coming out each year. The table below lists the most common litter types. Flushable litter is conspicuously absent from the table—to find a flushable litter, you need to look for individual products. Any litter that is flushable will be specifically labeled on its container. Keep in mind that these litters are disposable only in a municipal sewer system—not in a septic field. And you should **never** flush litters, even into city sewers, if they are not labeled for toilet disposal.

Litter Types

Litter Type	Cost	Odor Control	Mess	Health Aspects
Plain sand	Cheap	None	Tracks	Dusty*
Plain clay (generics)	Cheap	None	Tracks	Dusty*

Litter Type	Cost	Odor Control	Mess	Health Aspects
Fancy unscented clay (brand names)	Moderate	Varies with the brand.	Tracks	Most have reduced dust.
Fancy scented clay (brand names)	Moderate	Covers odor; some cats object to fragrance.	Tracks	Most have reduced dust.
Cedar shavings (compostable)	Expensive	Covers odor; some cats object to cedar smell.	Less tracking	See note below chart.*
Shredded newspaper (compostable)	Cheap	None	Wide strips do not track much.	Most ink.
Clumping†	Moderate	Excellent odor control	Tracks	Cleaner than other fillers
Biodegradable commercial litters of corncob, recycled paper and other natural sources (compostable)	Expensive and hard to find outside specialty catalogs	Good	Less tracking than clay	Less dusty than clay

*Some authorities are questioning the health effects of using clay or cedar litters. The dust from the cheaper clay litters is hard on both cat and human respiratory systems.
†Cats tend to like these fine-grained litters better than traditional clay because the texture is much easier on soft paws.

WHAT TYPES OF LITTER BOXES ARE THERE?

There are many styles of litter boxes but only two major requirements. First, check the construction. The box should have sturdy walls which direct the drainage into the box. Second, the box must be big enough for an adult cat to stand up and turn around in. Here are some of your litter-box options:

Disposable Boxes

These small cardboard boxes come complete with clay litter and are meant to be used only for a few days. Use it and throw the whole thing out. While they are an expensive alternative, these disposable boxes are great for trips or for a contagious cat.

Open Boxes

An open box can be as simple as an old dishpan or it can be a commercial plastic litter box. The only drawback is that scratched litter and spray can go over the sides, especially if the box isn't very deep.

Covered Boxes

Covered boxes can be uncomplicated affairs with a plain removable lid, or fancy with an air filter on the top, or fancier still with both filters and fans. Any kind of covered box will help control flying litter and direct urine back into the box if the cat sprays. And if for some reason your covered box leaks when your cat sprays, you can fix the problem yourself. See chapter 20.

Special Boxes

There are several choices for "litterless" litter boxes. Read on.

WHAT CAN I USE FOR A TRAVEL LITTER BOX OR TEMPORARY BOX?

Any plastic-lined cardboard box big enough for the cat to turn around in and four inches deep will do for most cats. If you're dealing with a sprayer, however, you'll need a box at least three inches higher than his rump. Make sure one side of this extra-deep box is cut down for an entrance. To line the box, use a **thick** plastic garbage bag, large enough to fold down over the sides of the box.

If you're traveling, take a twist tie along with you or use a drawstring bag to line the box. This way the bag can be closed around the litter while your cat's in his crate, and with the bag tied, you'll have less spilling—and less smelling. You can buy disposable litter boxes through catalogs.

Use the cat's regular litter type to avoid rejection of the box; new litter combined with the stress of traveling can have messy consequences. And if you are at all unsure of your cat's acceptance of the temporary box, use clean litter from his box at home. This litter, although dry and without feces, already carries his scent and, unlike new litter, will strongly attract him to the box.

WHERE SHOULD I PUT THE LITTER BOX?

Put the litter box in a quiet, out-of-the-way place, away from your cat's food and water bowls. Many people keep the box in the bathroom, since tracking is more easily controlled and you can conveniently dump daily feces and flushable litter into the toilet.

If you have small children, you may prefer to keep the litter—and the odor—in a garage or basement. Install a small pet door to give your cat access to his litter and to keep small children and other pets away from the box.

Note: If you put the box in your garage, catproof the area and be aware that your cat can get out when the garage door is up—or, worse yet, get run over as you back the car out. In particular, make sure your radiator is not leaking antifreeze; a tiny amount licked off a soiled paw can kill your cat! Use a special less-toxic antifreeze.

WHAT TYPE OF LITTER TOOLS AND ACCESSORIES SHOULD I USE?

Whatever the type of litter, to help it last longer, reduce odor and keep it in usable shape, you are going to need a scoop. The clumping litters are great because scooping daily removes clumps of urine along with the feces, leaving the litter in almost-new condition.

While they initially cost more than special plastic litter scoops, metal tools will last much longer and are ultimately a better buy. An inexpensive solution is a slotted cooking spoon or skimmer. Either makes a wonderful scoop and they won't break easily like plastic scoops.

If you don't have flushable litter in a box next to the toilet, a large-mouth jar with a lid makes cleanup neater. Kept beside the litter box, the jar can hold the solid waste from your daily cleanings. Put about a quarter inch of baking soda in the bottom of the jar and keep the lid on between ''deposits'' to reduce odors.

You can also use litter liners to cover the inside of the box and hold the litter for easy disposal. Unfortunately, most cats can tear the plastic and put holes in most liners. And while they make your job faster and easier, liners do add to our landfills. It's better to simply wash out the box.

HOW CAN I CONVINCE MY CAT TO ACCEPT A CHANGE IN THE TYPE OF LITTER OR A NEW LOCATION FOR THE LITTER BOX?

Sudden changes upset some cats, and to tell you they are unhappy with the new arrangements, they'll leave little damp messages. Some extra precautions on your part can prevent this problem.

To Change the Type of Litter

Gradually substitute larger amounts of the new litter over time. Make sure you allow time to see if your cat accepts and regularly uses the new combinations. Begin the substitution with ⅛ to ¼ of the total amount of the litter. Slowly increase by these amounts until all the litter is changed over.

To Change the Location of the Box

If your setup allows, gradually (over a period of one or two weeks) move the box one foot or two feet at a time closer to the new location. Of course, trailing the litter box through your dining room may not be an attractive option. In this case, confine him with the litter box for a few days; when he shows acceptance of the new arrangement, let him out. For a week or two, you might continue to feed him in the room with the litter.

HOW DO I DISPOSE OF LITTER?

Most litters, including clay clumping litters, have to be put into the trash. Compostable and flushable litters are the only litter classifications that don't add to our already overburdened landfills. Compostable litters are used on ornamental plants only (never use them on vegetables or around fruit trees). For a list of compostable litter types, see the litter information table given above. chapter 20 will help you compost and still keep you on speaking terms with neighbors.

Other specially labeled litters can be flushed down a toilet on a city sewer system but **not into a septic tank or septic field**. Don't assume that your fine-particle clumping litter is flushable. Read labels.

Irrespective of how the litter is disposed of, pregnant women and immune-suppressed people should not clean out the litter box. Cat feces can carry toxoplasmas (see chapter 13). If there is no other person to do the job, these vulnerable individuals should wear a mask and rubber gloves. After finishing any litter chore, **everyone** should wash their hands and face with an antibacterial soap.

HOW CAN I STOP THE LITTER FROM SCATTERING?

Some litter types are more easily kicked and tracked away from the litter box. See the litter table given above. Using a covered litter box will help if you have an energetic scratcher. If you raise the box on a platform about six inches off the floor, your cat, as he prepares to jump down, will spread his back paws and push off, shaking more litter off his feet and back into the box. A safe and simple way to catch the litter just outside the box, before it is tracked around the house, is to put a deep-pile washable rug or a textured plastic runner next to the box.

HOW DO I CONTROL ODORS FROM THE LITTER BOX?

If you can smell dirty litter, imagine how your cat feels—his sense of smell is much more sensitive than yours. If he turns his nose up at the box, you'll be amazed at his creative selection of new places to do his "business."

To avoid problems, try the following:

- Use 1 to 1½ inches of clay litter **or** 2 to 3 inches of clumping litter and the other litter alternatives.
- Use ¼ to ⅓ cup of baking soda mixed into any type of litter.
- Clean out feces and wet litter once a day (twice a day is even more effective).
- Use one box for every one or two cats.
- Fill a small open container (small cup, saucer or baby food jar) with cheap imitation vanilla with whole spices (cinnamon stick, clove or anise) to absorb odors. Leave the container near the litter box or a nearby floor vent to fight odors. As this mixture evaporates, add water, and every three months recharge the vanilla. Once or twice a year dump the whole thing and start a new batch.

  NonScents markets a volcanic mineral which helps absorb odors. We've had particularly good results with their net bag of "rock" pieces.
- Put a few whole cloves or other fragrant whole spices in your vacuum cleaner bag to release a pleasant scent in the air as you clean.

I DON'T WANT THE MESS AND HASSLE OF A LITTER BOX. ARE THERE ANY OTHER CHOICES?

Yes, there are other litter-box options. One of the best of these new ideas is the Royal Flush. It consists of a box rather like a traditional one, but with the addition of a mechanism that flushes the mess down the drain. You connect water from a washer hookup and pipe to a floor drain. After the cat uses it and leaves, a timer is activated and the waste is flushed after a three-minute delay. The prototype we bought worked great and quickly paid for itself in litter savings. No mess, no fuss and no smell!

Toilet training is another option, and like any litter choice, potty use has its drawbacks. While the cost of litter and its odor are eliminated, you might need to devote an entire toilet to your cat, especially during the training period. And, of course, you'll need to flush for him and clean the toilet bowl one to two times a week.

HOW DO I TOILET-TRAIN A CAT?

While physically handicapped, older or timid cats may not adjust to sharing the toilet with you, many cats will be willing to make these changes. Keep in mind that cats take their litter habits personally. A giant new step in sanitary arrangements can turn a fastidious feline into an indiscriminate house soiler overnight.

There are several commercial products to help you toilet-train Kitty. Or you can set up a system by yourself. Either way, the training time may take from eight to twelve weeks. As a rule, the more gradual the change, the more acceptable to the cat.

STEP 1 Move the litter near the toilet.
- If the litter box is not near the stool, move it there. See information above on how to change the location of the box. Once it's in place, wait one week.

- If the litter box is covered, remove the lid and wait one week.
- To control litter being kicked around, make an aluminum-foil shield as follows:
  — Measure the total length of all four box sides.
  — Measure a length of aluminum foil to match.
  — Fold the foil over the long way.
  — Tape this shield to the top edge of the box.

STEP 2   Gradually raise the level of the box until it's even with the toilet seat.
- Raise the litter box no more than three inches per week. Be certain that the box doesn't slide or that the base underneath won't move.
  — Suggested materials to stack under the box: bricks, blocks, tied bundles of magazines or newspaper.
  — To secure the litter box to the base, use bungee cords, cords, packing tape, duct tape.
- When the litter box is even with the stool seat, leave everything as is for one week.

STEP 3   Fasten the litter box on the stool seat.
- Move the litter box off the stack and onto the stool seat and fasten the box with short bungee cords; leave it as is for one week. For you to use the stool, remove and replace the box. Get rid of the stack; you don't need it anymore.

STEP 4   Rest a plastic bowl with litter on the toilet bowl rim under the toilet seat.
- Remove the box and place a plastic bowl with litter in the stool. The bowl should:
  — fit securely under the seat, resting on the rim of the stool.
  — be a soft plastic so you can cut it with a knife.
- Your cat will step **into** the bowl to use the litter.
- For you to use the stool, remove and replace the bowl.

STEP 5   Reduce the amount of litter.
- Slowly reduce the amount of litter in the bowl over two weeks.
- As the amount of litter is reduced, you will have to clean the bowl more often. Some cats will insist that you clean it every time it's used. Keep it clean so he will want to continue using it instead of your bathroom rug.

STEP 6   Cut a hole in the bowl and enlarge it until the bowl isn't needed anymore.
- When the litter is gone, cut a hole in the center of the bowl about the size of a quarter. Continue to clean the bowl.
- After one week, slowly begin to enlarge the hole. As the hole grows larger, the cat will be forced up onto the seat of the stool.
- After two weeks, the cat should be using the stool with no bowl.

Remember: You will need to flush for the cat. The stool will need to be cleaned far more often, but you don't have to mess with litter! If your cat has problems at any step, go back to the last step where he was successful and stay there for one week. Then start again but make a smaller amount of change over a longer time (i.e., wait ten days between steps instead of one week or enlarge the hole a smaller amount at a time).

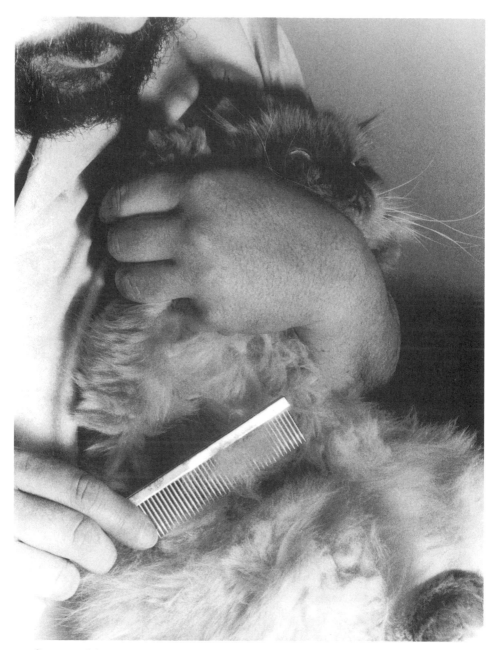

Cats need frequent, regular grooming using the correct brush and comb. Long-haired breeds should be groomed even more often than shorthairs. Grooming helps avoid internal blockages of ingested hair and enhances the beauty of every cat.

6

Cleaning—House and Cat

CATS DO CREATE a certain amount of mess. Your clothes and couch will be a little furrier, hair balls will appear on the carpet, nose prints will dot the windows and the dust bunnies will be large and prolific. While this chapter will help you cope with the mess, there will always be more. If you hate cleaning up fur, groom your cat; you'll have less mess and you'll all be happier.

CLEANING THE HOUSE

Because diluting stains is one of the secrets to cleaning up after pets, a hand-held cordless wet/dry vac is great for spot cleaning. It is more effective than paper towels, and ecologically sound.

HOW DO I CLEAN UP VOMIT?

To clean up vomit, first use a paper towel to pick up and then dilute the remaining stain with plain water. Sop up the water with more paper towels (or a wet/dry vac) and finish with any good household cleaner.

HOW DO I CLEAN UP URINE AND SPRAY?

Specific products on the market claim to clean and deodorize cat urine and spray. You can certainly try some of them, but you'll probably get mixed results at a hefty price. Plain white distilled vinegar is both cheap and effective. No, it doesn't have a perfumed deodorizer, but post-treatment vanilla is far better than potpourri or other cover-up scents because it actually absorbs odors. See the cleanup chart in this chapter.

If the item soiled can be machine-washed, use the pre-wash cycle with about a half gallon of white vinegar added to the wash water. Then wash on the regular cycle with detergent, a quarter gallon of vinegar and Borax (follow package directions). Depending on the manufacturer's instructions, air-dry or machine-dry.

Below, the first directions given are for cleaning urine on a flat surface. However, if you find a soiled floor area near a wall or near any vertical surface, you should assume the cat has sprayed the wall. Follow the directions for cleaning spray and treat the surface area as well.

If your cat shows undue interest in the scene of the crime, after cleaning leave some citrus peel in the area. If the cat can smell the urine, he will probably urinate there again.

To Clean Urine on a Floor (Flat Surface)

STEP 1   Use wet/dry vac or paper towels to wipe up. Get the area as dry as possible.

STEP 2   Use plain water to dilute and then vac up the water or blot with paper towels.

STEP 3   Rinse with distilled white vinegar. Use vinegar liberally if the cat urinated on a carpet, couch or other fabric. Make sure the vinegar soaks into the object as deep as the urine. For old stains, let the vinegar soak in for fifteen or twenty minutes; let the vinegar air-dry; go directly to step 5.

STEP 4   Wet-vac or towel-dry the area.

STEP 5   When the area is dry, cover generously with baking soda and **leave for several days**. For areas where there has been repeated soiling, leave the baking soda down for a month and cover with heavy plastic sheeting. The plastic should extend one foot beyond the stain in all directions. Change the baking soda at least twice a month and mist very lightly with water weekly; the baking soda works better when slightly damp.

STEP 6   Clean up the baking soda. Use a brush and dustpan to clean it up because baking soda isn't good for your vacuum cleaner. Then rearrange the furniture so the spot is inaccessible.

STEP 7   Put a small dish or open baby food jar with vanilla or leave an unlit vanilla-scented candle near the area. Be careful if you use liquid vanilla; it will permanently stain if spilled.

To Clean Up Cat Spray (on Vertical Surfaces)

Obviously, treating a vertical surface is a little trickier and some wall coverings may be damaged by the vinegar and baking soda. Washable surfaces do respond best to treatment. Before you begin, **spot-test the wall covering** in a location out of view. Don't forget to treat the floor beneath the sprayed wall.

STEP 1   Wipe the wall with a damp paper towel.

STEP 2   Soak the area thoroughly with white vinegar. It can be applied with a spray bottle or on a "vinegar rag" taped or tacked over the stain.

STEP 3   Rinse the wall with water. Make sure the vinegar is rinsed well to prevent a chemical reaction with the baking soda in the next step.

STEP 4   Dust baking soda on the damp wall.

STEP 5   Tack an oversized piece of thick plastic over the cleaned area until the odor vanishes. This will deny your cat the pleasure of remarking the spot. Also, if he sprays the plastic, the backsplash might be more than he bargained for.

If an outside cat has sprayed the side of the house, first use vinegar as described above to remove the odor. Then place ammonia-soaked rags or your own cat's feces around the edge of your property. To further intimidate intruders, shake a rattle can (closed can with rocks or marbles inside) when you see a cat in your yard. Read chapter 8 for more information.

HOW DO I CLEAN UP FECES?

Use a paper towel to pick up the feces. Then mix water and white vinegar in equal proportions. Use this mixture to clean up any residue.

Chart on Cleanup

Product	Relative Cost	Advantages	Disadvantages
Distilled white vinegar	Inexpensive	Easy to use; does not stain; easy to store; nonpolluting; chemically neutralizes.	May not be as strong as other cleaners; temporary astringent smell.
Deodorants or deodorizing agents	Expensive	Pleasant scent covers odor for people.	Does not remove source of odor; aerosol sprays are not good for the environment.
Enzymes	Concentrates or dry are inexpensive; ready-to-use are expensive.	Destroys source of odor.	May stain or lighten fabrics; once mixed cannot be stored.

Product	Relative Cost	Advantages	Disadvantages
Soap and water	Inexpensive	Cheap and readily available	Works only on nonporous surfaces; may leave residual odor.
Ammonia	Inexpensive	None	Intensifies the odor of urine.
Citrus-based cleaners	Moderately priced	Cleans up mess and stops odor; smell is offensive to most cats.	Not available in all areas
Commercial all-purpose cleaners	Relatively expensive	Cleans up the mess; stops odor for people only.	Some may be toxic if not thoroughly rinsed away; does not remove odor for cat.

HOW DO I PROTECT MY HARDWOOD FLOORS?

Old floors can be refinished and sealed; new floors can be sealed when laid. For easy cleanup, seal wood with a minimum of two coats (three coats are better) of a polyurethane finish.

HOW CAN I CLEAN CAT HAIR OFF MY CLOTHES AND FURNITURE?

For emergency, no-frills cleanup, try available household items.

- Use masking tape. Tear off six- to eight-inch strips and press the sticky side on the fabric. Repeat till clean.
- Use a clean, damp sponge to wipe off hair.
- Use cat's soft brush or an old hairbrush or toothbrush to brush the fur off.

Products specifically designed to clean up fur can be cheaper in the long run. These items can be bought through catalogs or in pet supply stores. Here are some of your options.

- Fur squeegee. Used like a window squeegee to scrape off hair.
- Pet-hair grabber. Permanent sticky surface. Wash with water to clean and reactivate.
- Rolls of sticky paper. Peeled to a new sheet and thrown away. This product is initially less expensive but will eventually cost more than the reusable squeegee or grabber.

HOW DO I REDUCE THE AMOUNT OF FUR FLYING?

Groom your cat daily with dampened brushes or use a grooming glove to remove dead surface fur.

Note: Grooming gloves are not meant for in-depth grooming but they're great for surface hair. See catalogs or pet supply stores for gloves.

HOW DO I CLEAN THE CAT'S EQUIPMENT?

If the cat's equipment is not cleaned regularly and appropriately, it can become a source of odor or disease and trigger avoidance of the litter box. Make sure that you rinse off cleaners carefully; most cleaners can be toxic or offensive to cats. Follow manufacturer's directions if possible.

Litter Box and Scoop

- Once a week, empty all the litter and clean the box with a mixture of water and one to two drops of household bleach. Rinse **very** thoroughly and dry. Refill. Do **not** use ammonia for cleaning any litter-related equipment; it intensifies the urine odor.

Water Bowls

- Once a week, wash the bowl with dish soap and thoroughly rinse.

Food Bowls

- Dry-food dishes: wash with soap and rinse, weekly.
- Wet-food dishes: wash with soap and rinse, daily.

Grooming Tools (should be done weekly or monthly depending on number of cats)

- Clean out hair after each use. A self-cleaning brush is the easiest and most convenient. Or use a plastic fork to slip between the teeth and lift the fur.
- Wash with a cat shampoo and an old toothbrush and rinse **very** well.

Toys (clean as needed)

- Hard-surfaced toys can be cleaned with cat shampoo or baking soda and an old toothbrush. Rinse **very** well.
- Soft toys can be wiped with a damp cloth or toothbrush, or vacuumed.
- Replace paper toys.

Bedding

- Bedding can usually be machine-washed and machine-dried.

Collar, Harness and Tags

- Leather equipment should be cleaned as needed with saddle soap.
- Nylon equipment and tags should be washed as needed with cat shampoo and an old toothbrush. If the metal from the tags or tag hooks leaves smudges on his fur, cover them with a light coating of clear fingernail polish.

Crate

- Hard plastic crates can be wiped with a damp rag. Use cat shampoo or baking soda and an old toothbrush to remove stubborn stains.

CLEANING THE CAT

WHY DOES A CAT GROOM?

Cats hunt by stealth and an odorless cat is a better hunter. Also, when cats live together in a colony, grooming allows the milder individual scents to blend into a colony scent.

Grooming, besides being a comforting reminder of their mother's TLC, cleans the cat's coat. And a clean, neat coat is a better insulator against heat and cold.

MY CAT LICKS HIMSELF. WHY DO I NEED TO GROOM?

Your cat grooms (cleans) himself by licking and nibbling his fur, and while most cats do a pretty good job, they can always use some help. Your involvement on a regular basis deepens your relationship with your cat—and helps avoid hair balls. Longhaired cats, in particular, need extra help with tangles and matting. Regular grooming lets you detect health problems earlier.

WHY DOES MY CAT CHEW AND PULL ON HIS BACK CLAWS?

The cat is cleaning and sharpening his back claws.

The grooming tool shown here consists of closely-spaced, short teeth and is especially suited to removing excess hair from short-hairs during shedding.

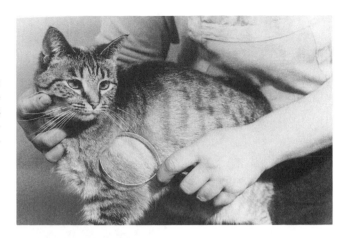

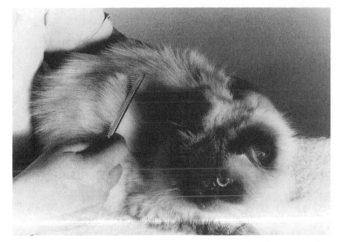

The correct comb for a cat will depend on its coat type, but every comb should have a smooth surface with blunt-tipped teeth to avoid scratching the skin.

The mat comb is an excellent tool for breaking up snarls and tangles with a minimum amount of stress to the cat.

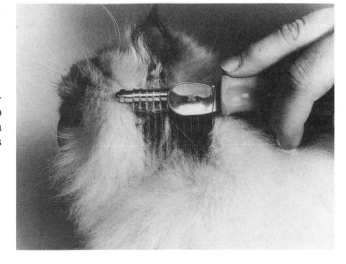

WHEN SHOULD I START GROOMING MY CAT?

Begin grooming your cat when he is four weeks old or as soon as you get him. The earlier he is exposed to the routine, the better.

HOW OFTEN DO I GROOM WHICH "PARTS"?

Daily

- *Longhaired Fur*. Light combing daily and thorough combing once a week. These cats are prone to matting if not regularly combed; mats can be painful, tear skin and create raw areas which support fleas and infection.

Weekly

- *Shorthaired Fur*. Comb weekly; during spring and fall shedding, comb two to three times per week.
- *Ears*. Check weekly; clean as needed.
- *Teeth*. Once or twice a week is enough for most cats; more often for old cats or cats who develop plaque readily.
- *Back Claws*. Clip weekly; they need to be kept very short. A kitten's claws will need clipping more often than an older cat's claws.
- *Hair-Ball Preventative*. Commercial preparation.
  — For longhairs, give weekly; two to three times a week during spring and fall.
  — For shorthairs, give every other week; weekly during spring and fall.

Biweekly

- *Front Claws*. Clip once every two weeks.

As Needed

- *Eyes*. Clean as needed.
- *Bathe Cat*. Give baths as needed.

HOW DO I GROOM (BRUSH/COMB) A CAT'S FUR?

While equipment varies, the process is much the same for all cats. Don't be embarrassed and bypass any part of the cat's body. The most likely places for the cat to have problems with his coat are armpits, stomach and groin. Remember to always comb out a cat **before** any type of bath. Grooming time gives a great opportunity to check the condition of his fur. Look for fleas; check for lumps, sore areas and any other abnormalities.

Equipment

- *Furless Cats.* Use a grooming glove, soft brush or chamois cloth to firmly "wipe" him down.
- *Curly-Coat* or *Short-Coated Cats.* Use a slicker brush, pin brush, general or fine grooming comb or flea comb.
- *Medium-* and *Long-Coated Cats.* Use a general grooming comb or pin brush, and if needed, a dematting comb.

General Process

Remove his collar. Working with the grain of his fur, start at his shoulders and work back to the end of his tail. Turn him over and groom his stomach, armpits and groin. Turn him over again and attend to his face and legs.

Gently but firmly, comb his fur so that it's all lying flat and unsnarled. If you find a mat, do not pull on it—that hurts. Use a dematting comb or your fingers to tease it out. Clean the fur off the comb or brush as needed. When you finish, remember to replace his collar.

WHAT IS HAIR-BALL MEDICINE AND WHEN IS THE BEST TIME TO GIVE IT?

Hair-ball medicine lubricates hair balls or adds fiber to help the cat pass the fur ingested when grooming. If the fur doesn't pass through the cat's intestines, he may vomit up the hair ball or the hair can form a blockage that needs to be surgically removed.

To give a petroleum-based preventative, measure (on your finger) the amount recommended on the package. It's great if he'll lick it off your finger, but if he doesn't like the flavor, you can wipe it off on the roof of his mouth or rub it on his front leg and paw. Don't worry, he'll groom it off. Fiber products are easily mixed in with the cat's food, and most cats don't mind the addition.

WHAT IS A SLICKER BRUSH AND HOW DO I USE IT?

This brush is designed for cats with short, slick coats. It will penetrate the fur to the skin, so it's wonderful for removing dead fur. Don't use this brush, however, on longhaired or dense-coated cats, because the angled, close-set teeth can "grab" the fur. Needless to say, this is uncomfortable for the cat.

Work with the grain of the fur. The easiest approach is to point the handle toward the cat's rump so the teeth go with the fur; don't drag the brush backward against the hair. Brush from the top of his head toward the tail, but don't use the slicker brush on his face. A toothbrush works beautifully here and is soft enough and small enough to maneuver safely around eyes, mouth and nose.

Use the slicker brush gently but firmly—and keep in mind that those little thin teeth can be irritating to your cat's skin if you press down.

If your cat hasn't been groomed in a while, fur will quickly build up on the brush. You can clean the brush as needed by using a fork to lift fur out of the teeth.

The slicker brush is such a great hair catcher; try it on your short-napped Oriental rugs or carpets. It will pick up the stubborn cat (and dog) hair your vacuum leaves behind. But if you use the brush on your rugs, make sure you wash it with cat shampoo and dry it thoroughly before you use it on your cat.

WHY DOES HE HAVE DANDRUFF AND WHAT CAN I DO ABOUT IT?

There are several reasons for dandruff.

- If the dandruff occurs only in the winter, it may be caused by the very dry air. Add a humidifier for him, the furniture and you.
- If the dandruff occurs year-round, it may be from one of these reasons:
  — He grooms poorly because he wasn't taught how to do it by his mother, or he's too fat to do it correctly.
  — His diet needs to be improved; low-quality food can cause dandruff.
  — His food is always available. He free-feeds and grazes all day. Since his body is always digesting, it doesn't have time for other housekeeping duties.

It's easy to test for the cause of dandruff by elimination. Help with his grooming for two weeks, and then reevaluate. If he improves, poor grooming was the culprit. Continue to help him groom and put him on a diet if needed. To test for a dietary link, change him to meals for two weeks and evaluate, or switch to a better-quality diet for the same period.

HOW DO I CLEAN MY CAT'S EARS?

Clean ears are important for a cat's overall health.

While only your Vet can clean the ear canal and diagnose/treat ear problems, you can clean his *outer* ears with a damp cloth. Wipe the inside of the outer ears but don't drip water into the canal itself. **Never** use a cotton swab (or any item smaller than your elbow) in the ear canal.

If your pet produces a large amount of ear wax, but doesn't have mites, your Vet can give you an ear-cleaning solution.

To use the ear-cleaning solution:

STEP 1   Position the cat on his side on your lap. Towel-wrap him if needed; see chapter 13 for directions.

STEP 2   While holding the outer ear, squirt five to ten drops into the ear. Do not let go of the outer ear.

STEP 3   Gently squeeze the outer ear to move the fluid around.
STEP 4   Position a tissue or paper towel over the ear and let go of the outer ear. The cat will shake his head to remove the liquid.
STEP 5   Repeat with the outer ear.
STEP 6   Wipe any excess off with a clean towel.

WHY DO I NEED TO BRUSH MY CAT'S TEETH?

Your cat needs his teeth brushed for the same reasons you need to brush your own teeth—to retard the buildup of tartar, prevent cavities and maintain healthy gums. Gum disease, gingivitis, can lead to tooth loss and life-threatening systemic infections.

As with any grooming routine, tooth brushing is best started when your cat is a kitten. Cats fed only soft foods, old cats and ill cats may have more dental problems and will need more frequent brushing.

HOW CAN I TELL IF MY CAT HAS TARTAR?

Open his mouth and look for dull, off-white or yellow patches near the gum line. He'll probably have bad breath and red swollen gums. If he does have tartar, see your Vet to have the cat's teeth cleaned. Tartar left untreated can lead to cavities and gingivitis (infected gums).

HOW DO I BRUSH MY CAT'S TEETH?

Use **only** commercial cat toothpaste or a clean, water-dampened toothbrush. With cat toothpaste, use the amount called for in the directions. Hold the cat as if you were giving a pill; see chapter 13. Gently but firmly rub the toothpaste on the cat's teeth with your finger or a gauze square or a pet/infant toothbrush.

HOW DO I CLIP MY CAT'S CLAWS?

Start clipping claws when the kitten is four weeks old or when you get the cat. The earlier you start, the easier the job later on.

It's best if you put the cat on his back on your lap. Hold the clippers in one hand and with the other grasp the cat's paw and gently squeeze the toe to expose the claw. Here are some helpful guidelines:

- Back claws—cut most of the white part off.
- Front claws—trim only enough white so you don't feel any claws when you brush upward on a relaxed paw.

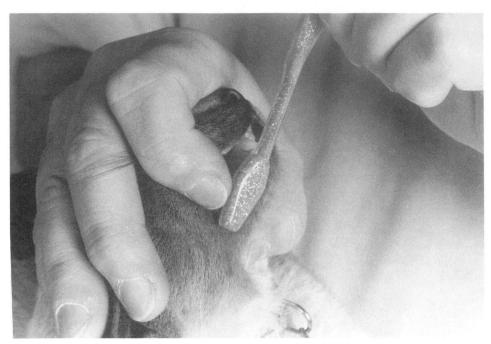

There are several preparations made especially to clean your cat's teeth. The job is made much easier though if you accustom your pet to this attention as a young kitten.

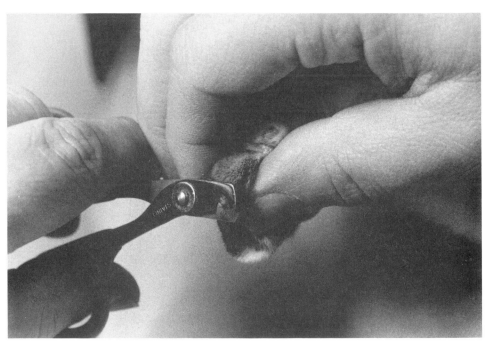

To trim your cat's claws, press gently on each toe and remove only the pointed tip that is exposed. Avoid cutting too close otherwise profuse bleeding could result.

- Trim the claws from the side; don't cut from the top of the claw to the bottom.
- If the claw is rough after cutting, run your nail file over the end to smooth.
- Make sure you cut all the claws, including the dewclaw (higher, side claw).
- If you clip the claw too close and the claw bleeds, try the following:
  — Use your finger to put pressure on the cut end until the bleeding stops.
  — Run his claw across a softened bar of soap.
  — Dip his claw in styptic powder.

HOW DO I CLEAN MY CAT'S EYES?

Position the cat on your lap, and towel-wrap him if necessary; see chapter 13. Using a clean cloth or a piece of dry gauze, gently wipe the fur around the cat's eye. Wipe from the nose to the outside of the eye. Do **not** wipe the cornea or attempt to keep the eye open as you clean the fur.

Any discharge that does not look like tears could be a symptom of a health problem. Consult your Vet before medicating your cat's eyes.

WHEN SHOULD I BATHE MY CAT?

A bath isn't a cat's idea of a good time and should be reserved only for the following:

- Special occasions.
- When the cat is too ill to groom.
- When the cat gets a toxic or poisonous substance on his fur.
- When the cat becomes excessively dirty.
- When the cat has a skin problem that may be helped by a medicated bath.

HOW DO I BATHE MY CAT?

There are three choices for baths: dry, damp and wet—three different baths for different occasions. A dry bath is suitable for a mildly soiled cat or stud tail (oily fur at the base of the tail). The damp bath is good for helping the ill cat or for cleaning off surface dirt. The wet bath is for shows, for flea control or for a cat who is really filthy or has a toxic substance on his fur.

For any bath, follow these guidelines:

- Gather all materials needed in advance.
- The bathroom, if escape-proof, is the best room to use.
- Thoroughly comb his fur and remove all mats **before** the bath. Trim his claws!
- Be gentle but firm; don't yell at or chastise your cat, you will only frighten him more.
- Discourage panic or any other undesirable behavior.

- Keep the cat's tail toward you; teeth and front claws should be pointed away from you.
- If you anticipate getting scratched during the bathing process, use a cat sack, a finely woven net sack which allows shampoo and water to get through to the fur, and yet prevents the cat from taking a swipe at you.

Dry Bath

In a dry bath, fine, dry cornmeal is dusted into the cat's fur to soak up excess oil and other dirt. For easy cleanup, cover the workplace with several layers of newspaper. Then remove one layer at a time as needed to control the mess. Carefully fold the paper to contain the cornmeal and discard it.

STEP 1   Dust dirty areas of your cat's coat with the cornmeal.
STEP 2   Leave the meal on for five minutes.
STEP 3   Comb out the cornmeal with a medium comb or pin brush.
STEP 4   Repeat as needed until the fur is clean.
STEP 5   Dust the fur with cornstarch.
STEP 6   Comb out the cornstarch with a fine comb.

Damp Bath

STEP 1   With the cat on your lap or a convenient surface, use a clean damp cloth to wipe with the grain of his fur. Give special attention to his face and genitals.
STEP 2   Dry-towel him with a clean dry towel.

Wet Bath

Use **only** cat shampoo and be very careful **not** to get shampoo and water in his eyes, mouth or ears. A spray attachment to the sink faucet makes this job go faster and easier. (If your cat strongly objects to the water, use a cat sack.)

To keep yourself dry and clean, you'll need a waterproof apron. A large trash sack with slits cut on the seams for your head and arms gives great protection. And if you put a strip of clear tape at each end of the slits, it will last for many baths.

STEP 1   Put a towel or bath mat in the bottom of the kitchen sink or tub to give the cat better footing and to lessen fear. If you will be giving baths often, consider cutting a suction-cup type of bath mat to size for your kitchen sink.
STEP 2   Put a large cotton ball in each of the cat's ears, to keep them dry.
STEP 3   Wet the cat's fur from the neck to the end of his tail. Apply cat shampoo and work up a lather.
STEP 4   Rinse his fur **very** well and gently squeeze it to remove water. Continue until the water runs clear. If you see any residue, rinse again until all the soap is gone.

STEP 5   Squeeze the fur as dry as possible, then blot it gently with a towel. The cat will want to shake. Simply hold a large towel over him to catch the spray. For a longhaired cat use a wide-toothed comb or brush to comb his fur as it dries. Combing will keep his fur from tangling. Since his skin will be extra tender after a bath, be very gentle.

STEP 6   Keep him warm until he's fully dry. For both longhaired and shorthaired cats, use a hair dryer, on low to speed drying. Another method is to put a gooseneck lamp with a 100-watt bulb about ten to twelve inches above his head while he's curled up in a box or in his bed.

HOW CAN I REMOVE TAR, PAINT, GREASE AND OTHER CONTAMINANTS FROM MY CAT'S FUR AND FOOT PADS?

Grease, oil-based paint, tar and other nonpolar chemical substances need to be dissolved in another oil. Try using a small amount of cooking oil to loosen these nasties, and then follow up with a dry bath or a wet bath. (A dry bath can do a better job removing the oil.) Don't be tempted to use paint removers or household cleaners—they can be just as toxic as what you're trying to remove.

Call your Vet if your cat has a toxin on his fur and has been grooming.

7

Normal Behavior

A WELL-SOCIALIZED, well-mannered cat will be happier and more content with himself—and a greater joy to your life. A well-adjusted cat will also save you time, energy and money. If you understand a cat's behavior, training and socializing your cat will be much easier. In effect, this chapter teaches you to both understand and speak "cat."

Even if your potential lease has a no-pet clause, a well-trained cat may be exempted if you ask your landlord first.

This chapter describes normal behaviors, and while the hunting, killing and eating of prey are normal cat behaviors, they can cause problems. Hunting is more fully covered in chapter 8.

DO CATS "THINK"?

Cats do think but not as people do—not in sentences and concepts. They do communicate with other cats, consciously leaving messages like "I was here" or "This is my territory" when they use clawing and scent markers.

You've probably already found out how manipulative cats can be. In experiments with Skinner boxes, cats were just a little slower than chimps in opening the box for treats—by the way, dogs came in a poor third.

Cats have an excellent associative memory too. Dr. Benjamin L. Hart, in the September/October 1975 issue of *Feline Practice*, wrote that in behavioral tests only primates and cats are able to learn tasks at a faster rate by watching another do it first. Cats are quick to pair an event with a particular action or smell, so they can easily remember the behavior that triggers a booby trap. Once burned, a cat will not jump on a hot stove again, or a cold one either.

CAN CATS LEARN?

Cats are born with some knowledge (instinct or "hard-wired" knowledge) and yet, like us, they must learn other things.

Intraspecies (cat to cat) communications such as puffed tails and hisses are hard-wired. Sometimes learning fine-tunes an instinctive behavior. For example, stalking or chasing a moving object is hard-wired, but how to stalk effectively and kill cleanly is learned.

Cats learn by associative memory and demonstration. Mom cat shows the kitten how to use the litter. She teaches the kittens what prey is and how to kill it, if subjects are available. A cat born and raised in a house with small rodents or birds will not recognize them as prey.

Interspecies communication, such as staring at his empty food dish to get you to feed him, is also learned by association and demonstration. Your cat learns where you store the food and stares to remind you he is hungry. Activities like using a paw to take food out of a small jar are learned behaviors too.

CAN CATS BE TRAINED?

Yes! Cats can be taught everyday household manners and special tricks because they are smart. But a cat won't do or not do an action just because you say so. Your cat sees you as an equal

A cat won't grasp what you are trying to teach through punishment. If you hit him, he'll learn to fear you but won't learn not to repeat the "crime." When correction or discipline is called for, use ideas discussed in chapter 8.

A cat learns better with motivation. He'll remember lessons when there's something interesting in it for him, such as praise or a treat.

To teach household manners, you first must remove temptations. Don't leave the chicken out to thaw on the counter; move the priceless antique out of the path to the window with the best sunbeams; hang the plants up high in the window, out of his way, and cover the aquarium.

Another must in training a cat is to give him alternatives to inappropriate behaviors **before** there is a problem. Select toys and a scratching post that he'll want to use instead of your furnishings. You may also want to adopt two cats together as playmates. Boredom can lead to behavior problems. If you interact with your cat, he'll be more social and more content to "follow the rules." If inappropriate behaviors have already become a habit, let the environment help; see chapter 8 for ideas.

CAN MY CAT LEARN TO DO TRICKS?

To teach your cat special tricks, you'll need a deep, trusting relationship. Decide what you what him to do on command, such as wave his paw, hold a pose or sit up. To start, pick something he does on his own. Carry treats with you at all times and watch him.

When you see him do a trick type of action, say a one- or two-word command and reward him. Then it is just a matter of time and practice. He'll soon learn to associate the command with the action—and the action with the treat. You can also use the treat to entice him to do something like spinning around to "follow" the piece of food. Continue to reward him until he responds to each short command. But keep the training sessions short—cats don't like to spend too much time each day on any one project, except naps.

If you're serious about turning your cat into a trickster, you should consult *The Educated Cat* by George Ney, which is devoted to trick training for cats.

DO CATS DREAM?

Yes. According to brain-wave studies, cats, like most mammals, do dream. But they are not telling what they dream about. Watch your cat as he sleeps. When his paws and tail twitch or his eyes rapidly move from side to side under the lids, he's dreaming.

WHY DO CATS SNIFF AT URINE STAINS?

You might say that cats have a nose for news. As disgusting as it seems to us, urine and feces carry information like a neighborhood newspaper.

Experts think the information includes:

- Individual scent identity of a cat
- Age
- General nutrition and state of health
- Mood—frightened, angry, content
- Gender
- Breeding cycle—if applicable
- Territory ownership (the more the spot is marked, the more time the cat has spent there)
- Size of the cat (the height of the spray is slightly higher than the cat's hips)

WHY DOES MY CAT DROOL WHEN I PET HIM?

Unless there is a medical problem, your cat drools because he is *so* relaxed.

WHY DO CATS LIKE THEIR NECK AND CHIN SCRATCHED SO MUCH?

It feels so good! The chin and neck areas are difficult for the cat to groom. A cat enjoys being clean, and when you scratch or brush his neck and chin, you not only clean the fur but get his scent on you (same as in head bumping)—then you smell "correct" to your cat.

WHY DO CATS BURY THEIR FECES?

Because cats hunt by stealth, they need to keep themselves and their territory clean and odor-free so it's harder for prey to detect them.

Conversely, cats will leave exposed feces, and urine, at the edges of their territory to mark it—as a "paws off, this is my space" warning to other cats. These territories can be as large as three to five acres. In the wild several females will have adjacent territories and a male will have a larger territory overlapping theirs.

DO ALL CATS CHASE MICE?

All cats are attracted by movement. But some cats are more interested in mousing than others. True mousing is a learned ability; a cat will chase but may not catch and kill the mouse—depending on his skill and experience.

The mother cat teaches her kittens how to mouse—if she knows how and if mice are available.

CAN I TEACH MY CAT TO CHASE MICE?

Nope. Your cat is already a mouser or not. Kittens learn catch-and-kill techniques very early, and almost always from their mother. This is why few cats dumped along country roads survive. Most are likely to starve before perfecting their technique.

IS A CAT BEING CRUEL WHEN HE PLAYS WITH A MOUSE?

Within his worldview, no, the cat is not trying to torture the mouse. As cruel as it seems, the cat's slow torment of his captured prey is normal behavior. Cats may have several reasons for their actions:

- If the cat is young, he may be practicing how to hunt.

- If a mother is teaching kittens how to hunt, she needs to demonstrate repeatedly and the kittens need to practice.
- To release stress or excitement; as humans play games, the cat may play with the mouse to relax and have some fun.

Note: Be careful if you decide to "rescue" the victim. The cat or the prey may bite you. Besides the pain and the chance of bacterial infection, any warm-blooded animal can carry rabies.

IS MOUSING A BAD IDEA?

Cats are exposed to added dangers when mousing out of doors. These dangers include the following:

- Parasites such as fleas and worms
- Diseases contracted both from prey and from other cats
- Injuries which can easily become infected
- Secondary poisoning (e.g., the cat catches a slow-moving poisoned mouse and ingests the poison already in the mouse's body)
- The usual dangers of running loose (see chapter 9)

If for whatever the reason, your cat must mouse, minimize the risk to him by following these guidelines:

- Do not put out bait or traps.
- Feed the cat a healthy diet. A healthy, well-muscled cat can hunt better and will be better able to resist the dangers of mousing.
- Keep vaccinations current and regularly check for injuries and infection.

Remember, an outdoor mouser may also hunt other animals, like songbirds, chipmunks and rabbits. The hunting drawbacks described above still apply—and if bunny bashing is repugnant to you, you might want to keep your potential mouser inside.

HOW DOES A CAT KILL A MOUSE?

Regardless of the preliminary chase and the amount of play with the prey, the coup de grace is always the same. The cat jumps on the mouse to stun him. Then he bites the mouse's neck and shakes his own head to break the victim's neck. You may notice this head-shaking behavior when he eats or when he plays with his catnip mouse.

IS MY CAT CONTENT AND SELF-CONFIDENT?

The table below describes the body language of both a content, self-confident cat and a cat who lacks self-confidence. Cats, like people, generally show a range of behaviors and moods. Look at the lists and at how your cat usually behaves. You'll see that his habitual behavior more closely matches one list or the other.

At a given moment, the amount of self-confidence he displays indicates how he feels about that particular situation. Not surprisingly, his behavior in this instance is called situational behavior.

Habitually contented cats are better pets because they're usually able to adjust to changes and to other companion animals with greater ease.

While the cat's habitual behavior or basic personality can't be changed, there are some things you can do to help a cat become more at ease and confident in his own home. For more information, see chapter 8.

Content and Self-Confident	Not Content and Self-Confident
Sleeps on windowsills, the bed, the middle of the floor, any comfy or sunny spot.	Sleeps in enclosed out-of-the way places or under the covers on the bed.
Sleeps with his people at night; sleeps on his people during the day.	Sleeps alone in easily defendable places.
Holds his tail upright or out when walking.	Holds his tail low or between his legs when walking.
Tail is still or tip is gently flipping when in repose.	Tail is pressed to the body or under the body when in repose.
Ears are upright and relaxed, occasionally twitching to locate sounds.	Ears are laid back against the head.
Whiskers are fanned to the side of his face or forward. Cat uses them as sensors.	Whiskers are pulled back tight against his face.
Eyes are open or partially closed.	Eyes are wide open with pupils dilated. The cat is watchful.
He plays, stretches and moves with easy grace.	He does not play easily or seem relaxed. His movements are stiff.
He cuddles and seeks attention from people and other pets.	He is shy and a loner, preferring to keep to himself.
He purrs and kneads when he's with people or other animals. Meows when he greets.	He exhibits constant or extended or "crying" meows.
Note: Siamese and related cats will be noisier.	

WHAT IS MY CAT TRYING TO TELL ME?

Yes, cats do communicate. They use sight, sound, scent and body language to express a great many messages, including how they feel, territorial claims or the readiness to mate. The cat can also give mixed messages about a situation. For example, he may be fearful and yet willing to aggressively defend himself. So listen and look at his whole body for the full message. A cat can also change his mood very quickly.

House cats have a wider variety of communications than their wild cousins. One of the changes we have made is to keep the cat more infantile throughout his life. So he'll continue to use kitten messages and add the adult messages to that.

There has been enough research and observation so that experts have a pretty good idea what the following messages mean. As with any other language, if you want to be proficient you must study. Watch and listen to your cat. Note his actions and reactions in different situations.

Note: A cat displaying angry or fearful responses is dangerous and should be left alone. Both emotions can lead to a lightning-quick attack.

Head Messages

The Voice

While the Siamese is renowned for his "talking," all cats can make a wide variety of sounds, including consonants, vowels and diphthongs. Try making quiet greeting sounds to him; see if you have a "talker" who will parrot the sounds back to you.

- Purring can indicate contentment or distress depending on the circumstances. Many cats have two purrs. Listen to your cat in different situations. His purr may vary by pitch, intensity and/or volume.
- Meowing, the most common call, changes meaning with circumstances, and varies in pitch, volume and tone. What he wants can often be deduced from the situation. If he is staring at the refrigerator or at his empty dish, he wants food. If he is standing at a closed door, he wants you to open it.
  — The more strident the call, the more demanding he's being. He wants what he wants, *now*.
  — The soft meow is a greeting.
  — A higher-pitched, pleading call is what a kitten uses to call to mom cat or human replacement parents.
  — Staccato, repetitive meowing is interrogative.
  — Purring while meowing says, "I'm pleased with the world. How's it with you?"
- Closed-mouthed "nurr" (less than a growl) means "Stop picking on me. Go away, please."
- Growling is a threat or the message of "No!" or "Stop!"

- Hissing is a serious warning; he is likely to bite or scratch next.
- Murmuring, a soft calling, is a plea for attention.
- Screeching or caterwauling is used when his emotions are raised to a fever pitch. This can be part of very active play, or is emitted while hunting, or is a preliminary to a fight.
- A scream or screech indicates pain, or warning that you will hurt his tail if you finish that step.

The Mouth

- Mouth closed or talking with lips relaxed indicates a happy cat.
- Mouth open, lips tensed or lifted to a sneer indicates he is thinking about subduing something with a bite.
- The flehmen response—a very still cat slightly opens his mouth, a glazed look in his nearly closed eyes, and may lift his lips somewhat in a grimace—means he's directing a scent into the Jacobson's organ in the roof of the mouth behind the gum ridge. He's intently investigating a particularly interesting smell because he likes it. This is most commonly a response to sexual scents.
- Grooming just a lick or two shows embarrassment or uncertainty when feeling threatened. To quote from *The Abandoned* by Paul Gallico: "When in doubt, wash."
- A long yawn, displaying most of his teeth and his tongue, means a relaxed cat. The tense cat will not yawn.

The Nose

- Sniffing (and sometimes licking) another cat's anal-genital region is an indication of social ranking. The cat who presents is acting in an infantile manner and the other cat's sniffing and licking is reminiscent of mom cat's care of her kittens.
- Touching noses between cats is another intimate greeting.

The Whiskers

- Fanned forward indicates interest.
- Held to the side means relaxed.
- Pulled back against the neck, out of the way, shows fear or the readiness to fight.

The Eyes

- Pupils suddenly dilated indicates fear or a startled state. As the pupils enlarge, the cat has a wider field of view, increasing his ability to find where the threat is.
- Pupils suddenly closed to mere slits mean he is ready to take on Godzilla, if needed, to make the world safe for catnaps again.
  Note: Light will make pupils change from large and round (dim light) to vertical slits (bright light). The pupil action noted above happens regardless of the amount of light present.
- Prolonged eye contact or staring is a challenge. The first to look away (including you) is the more submissive.

The mouth and other structures of the cat's face can be very expressive, sending a wide variety of messages to other cats and human observers.

Among cats, touching noses is a sincere gesture of friendship.

- When his eyes are half closed, he is relaxed and settling in for a nap.
- Submission is indicated by the cat's averting his eyes.

The Ears

- Ears pointed forward or moving to catch a sound show interest in what is happening.
- As he draws his ears back toward his neck, he indicates increasing displeasure with the world. He wants his ears out of danger if a fight starts.
- He may twitch his ears irritably when unsure or upset.

The Head

- Rubbing his head (and rump) on other cats, people or objects is an example of scent marking. His lips, chin and the area with less fur in front of the ears all have pheromone glands. He's leaving his personal mark on things: "This is mine" or "I live here." This is a more intimate statement than spraying. He is not asking for anything, just making a statement. Rubbing a figure eight around your legs is an emphatic and demanding variant on the flank and head rubbing. He is reminding you that you are his assistant and he wants something—often food.
- A relaxed, self-confident cat holds his head high, whiskers fanned out to the side and ears up and relaxed.
- A submissive cat, with head held low and forward, will approach another to be groomed on the top of the head; the lowered-head position shows submission.
- Head bumping occurs when a cat touches his forehead to the forehead of another cat or to any reachable part of his human. Head bumping is a very intimate greeting that is not shared with just anyone.

Paw Messages

- Flipping a front paw is a mild curse. It comes from flipping the paw to remove something.
- Shaking a back paw while walking away is a harder curse. It comes from shaking litter off the paws.
- Paw raised or a bop on the offender's forehead is a threat or the message "No!" or "Stop!"
- Claws extended and swatting is "War."

Body Messages

- The belly-up position means surrender in a confrontation. But it can also mean "I trust you unreservedly," for he is displaying the most vulnerable part of his body.
- A cat demonstrates his submissive relationship to another cat by crouching low. He presents a nonchallenging facial expression and the smallest target possible.

Rump Messages

- A cat sprays while backing up to a vertical surface. The trembling tail is held straight up and he may tread with his back paws as he releases a small amount

Head bumping is considered an intimate gesture reserved only for the people and animals of which a cat is most fond.

The cat shown here displays body language that transmits its ease and supreme self-confidence.

By rolling over and exposing its underside, a cat signals its complete trust. This is an extremely vulnerable position and a tremendous compliment to any human.

A tail held high, slightly curved at the tip is yet another sign of a very self-assured feline.

The cat on the left shows by his erect tail and confident manner that he is happy with his world. The cat on the right has noticed something that has taken his interest and he will move closer to investigate.

The movement of the tail tells the observer that this cat is trying to decide on an action in the face of a stimulus.

Can there be any doubt that this cat is both unhappy and frightened?

of urine. Both males and females, intact or neutered, can spray, but it is far more common in intact cats.

- There are more pheromone glands on the rump. See "The Head" in this section.

Tail Messages

- In general, a cat walking and carrying his tail high and not bushed is a happy cat.
- A relaxed, self-confident cat stands at ease with tail held high—often with a curl at the end.
- The tail is gently curved and raised slightly when a cat becomes interested in something. As his interest peaks, he begins to wave it. If he is puzzled by what is happening, the curved tail will rise and the tip will turn to the side.
- Tail waving has several meanings depending on the tail's speed and the part of the tail that is moving.
  — The relaxed cat may gently wave just the tip of the tail.
  — The cat intent on stalking a real mouse or a catnip dummy will wave his whole tail, starting slowly and increasing speed until his whole rear end is moving. He's building up momentum in order to pounce.
  — The undecided cat may twitch his tail, much as people drum their fingers while thinking. When he stops, he has decided.
  — The angry or fearful cat will whip his tail from side to side and may also puff his tail. How fast and how much of his tail is moving indicates the level of his displeasure. If his tail is low and thumping on the floor, he is more likely fearful than angry. He may change the elevation of his tail as his mood changes.
- The female in heat will carry her tail off to the side, so it is out of the way for mating.
- Tail puffing, in which the fur stands on end, indicates several things. If just the hair near his rump lifts, he's uncertain. When he puffs his whole tail, he is really upset or startled. Or instead of puffing his tail he may raise it in an upside down "U" shape behind him. When startled, he may also express his anal glands.
- A truly frightened cat will put his tail between his legs.

Full-Body Messages

- One cat always grooming another indicates social ranking. The cat who grooms is dominant.
- The cat who is always on the top of the heap in a pile of sleeping cats is dominant.
- Mounting behavior is not always sexual. Dominant cats will grab a submissive cat's neck and momentarily mount. Males and females can be in either position.
- Running to greet with tail erect is how kittens return to mom cat or a beloved human.
- Sitting close together, touching noses, sleeping curled together and mutual grooming are signs of friendship.
- The full "Halloween cat" display is one of defense. With arched back and fur standing on end, he positions himself sideways to the threat, and tries to look as big as possible: "You do not want to mess with me!"

When two cats sit closely together it is taken as a sign of friendship, a session of mutual grooming or other intimate contact.

Typical examples of threatening or defensive postures — the "Hallowe'en cat".

Typical spraying posture.

The typical attitude of a fearful or apprehensive cat.

- A female cat rolling around like a "fish out of water" in front of an intact male is indulging in sexual foreplay. The same display in front of people is a sign of affection.
- Hiding or a frozen posture indicates the cat is frightened or insecure.
- When you are holding a frightened or insecure cat, he may grasp you with his paws.

HOW DO CATS PURR?

Recent research, by Dr. David Rice at Tulane University, has finally solved the mystery. The cat vibrates the muscles surrounding the larynx (voice box). Because the muscles, not the larynx, make the purr, the cat can purr while breathing or even while meowing.

WHY DO CATS PURR?

Most adult cats have two different purrs: contented and distressed. The purrs will vary individually in intensity and volume. (Listen to your cat during different situations to tell which is which.)

One theory is that a cat purrs because he associates the sound with his mother's purr and her nurturing during his infancy.

WHY DO CATS KNEAD?

Kittens knead their mother's breast to stimulate the flow of milk. Adult cats knead as a holdover from kittenhood. Consequently, most cats knead when contented and relaxed. Some cats, however, knead under stress.

WHY DOES MY CAT RUB ON OBJECTS AND PEOPLE?

The cat is marking (placing odors) using pheromone glands. These subtle odors tell other cats that this place or person is taken. These odors reinforce his sense of place—even to the point of helping a cat find his way home if he has strayed.

WHY DOES MY CAT SNIFF ME WHEN I RETURN HOME?

Your cat can tell from sniffing you and your clothes what other animals you have touched and where you were. For example, the workplace is an everyday smell whereas the steak house will smell different. Restaurant smells can bring about that "And where is my share of the dinner?" investigatory sniff.

WHY DO CATS SHED HAIR WHEN DISTRESSED?

Cats "let their hair fly" as a defense so an attacker will get a mouthful of fur and not flesh. Prey often do the same thing; birds will molt feathers in fear.

WHAT IS CAT SPRAY AND WHY DO CATS SPRAY?

Cat spray is urine, just like the urine released in the litter box. The difference is *why* and *where* the cat urinates. And yes, female cats do spray. Cats that are neutered before sexual maturity (by five months for a female and eight months for a male) are less likely to spray.

The spraying stance is noticeably different from squatting to urinate. A spraying cat backs up to any upright surface and sprays urine on it. His tail is erect, vibrating, and his back paws may tread. Some cats will go through all the actions of spraying without releasing urine. Pheromones may or may not be released in the absence of urine—experts are not sure.

The primary reason for spraying is to leave a message and the location of the urine makes the message more noticeable.

Indoor spraying out of the box can be caused by stress. Also, indoor cats may spray near a window; they see another cat and mark their own territory, even if it is inside. Outside spraying marks territory, particularly borders.

EARLY TRAINING—SOCIALIZATION

Early training or socialization is extremely important for the cat's development. The kitten is more easily trained and learns more quickly. This is the time to instill the good manners you want in an adult cat.

HOW DO I PICK UP AND HANDLE A CAT?

Always be gentle. Move slowly and quietly, supporting the cat from underneath; cats are calmer with something under their feet and are less apt to strike out when they feel secure. In effect, if the cat's leg is dangling, he's being held incorrectly. Hold him against your chest or over your shoulder. Some cats, however, like to be held cradled belly-up in your arms.

Never pick up cats or kittens by the scruff of the neck. Yes, mom cats can pick up a kitten and carry him by the neck, because young kittens have a reflex to relax when mom cat does it. This instinctive ability weakens as kittens mature,

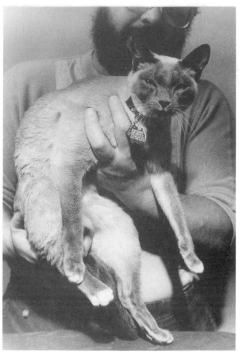

When picking up or handling a cat, it is important to make sure the animal is well supported and comfortable. These photos demonstrate the proper way to lift and handle your cat and still keep its trust.

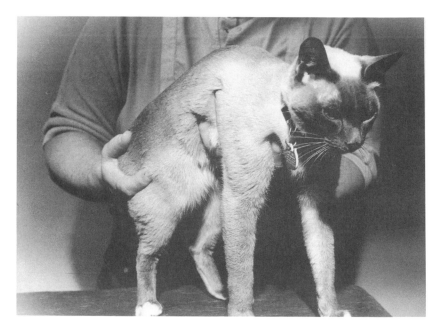

and our hands aren't suited to triggering the reflex, even in the youngest kittens. Also, **never** pick up a cat or kitten by the tail or legs; it will not only frighten him, it may injure him. His response may injure you!

HOW DO I MAKE FRIENDS WITH MY NEW CAT?

When you are both relaxed, set the cat on your lap or next to you. Stroke, the cat, gently but firmly, all over. Accustom him to handling so you can regularly groom him and check for injuries.

Don't leave food always available. Mealtimes help bond a cat to his food source (you). Stay with him while he eats, but don't bother him, just be present.

Talk gently to your new pet and set aside at least ten to twenty minutes a day for active play. Cuddling and stroking a cat also helps you unwind.

If there is a problem getting him to accept you, the cat may have been abused in the past or he may just be severely timid. Try the following to build trust:

- Confine the cat to a bathroom. Put his food and water bowls on one side of the room and put the litter box on the opposite wall. Also, move bedding and toys into the bathroom with him.
- Don't leave his food down; visit for his meals, sit with him while he eats, but don't bother him.
- Visit the cat. Sit on the floor and read a book. **Ignore** him. Wait for the cat to make the first overtures. As he gains confidence, increase your interaction. Let him sniff you and accept you as nonthreatening.

    Regardless of the cat's personality, don't proceed at a faster pace than the cat is comfortable with, and when you speak to him, speak quietly. Move your hand (fingers curled in to protect the tips from bites) to the cat's level, and then closer to his nose so he can sniff you. You can present either the back side of the hand or the palm. Once the cat is comfortable, reach out and scratch him under the chin or behind the ears.

    Never drop your hand unannounced onto the cat. While your goal is to show affection, he will see a move that is both powerful and threatening.

WILL THE CAT HURT MY NEW BABY?

No! While a cat may be attracted to the baby's body warmth and the smell of milk, the likelihood that the baby will squirm, kick, hit or pull fur far outweighs any presumed advantages to the cat.

Calmly let the cat investigate, smell and get accustomed to the baby's furnishings in the nursery **before** you bring the baby home. If the cat has not yet been neutered, get it done two to three months beforehand. A neutered cat will be less stressed by the change a baby brings to a household.

When you bring the baby home, let your cat meet him/her. Without showing any apprehension, let the cat sniff the baby. Your cat will need lots of praise for just being a cat, and special praise for any positive action relating to the baby.

Also, give your cat some special time and attention while the baby sleeps. This is a good time to groom and play. A cat who is pleasantly tired from play is at peace with the world.

If you, as a parent, have any concerns about the baby's safety, deny the cat access to the nursery when your newborn is sleeping. Either put up a screen door to the baby's room or close the door and use an audio monitor to listen in on your child. Closing off the room is a must if your cat begins to mark nursery items.

When the baby's bed is in a room that can't be closed off or if you need to protect a stroller bed, cover the bed with netting. You can find it at any store that sells baby things. Fasten it snugly so it won't sag when the cat checks it out.

As your baby grows, it's more likely that you'll need to protect your cat from the baby. Read on for help with building a loving relationship between your child and the cat.

HOW DO I REWARD MY CAT?

If you're pleased with his behavior, try the following: Make eye contact and stroke your cat. Using his name, speak soothingly, or if you want to be more catlike in your praise, blink slowly when you make eye contact. And if you like speaking to your cat, you can tell him you love him in another way. Make eye contact, look away for a few seconds and then look back at the cat with your eyes half closed.

HOW DO I TEACH MY CHILD TO BE KIND TO ANIMALS?

Children will look to you for cues on how to treat the cat. Set the right example by **your** words, tone of voice and actions. Do not overburden the child with pet care responsibilities beyond his/her age and abilities. When a child views a pet as a burden, a close, loving relationship is less likely.

8

Behavior Problems

MOST "behavior problems" are the cat's natural reaction to his environment. Usually misbehavior is the symptom of a problem, not the cat's being malicious or vindictive. For example, cats will urinate out of the box for different reasons—a dirty box, pairing the pain of a urinary infection with the box or because another cat in the home has attacked him coming out of the box.

Other problems arise from stress, improper socialization and learned behavior. Understanding the source of the problem is essential, because no matter how hard you try to correct your cat, you won't get results until you adjust your retraining techniques to the cause of the behavior.

And while it may be a little late to remind you, prevention is still the best cure.

HOW DO I CORRECT MY CAT'S BEHAVIOR?

Misbehaving is the symptom of a problem, not the cat's deliberate attempt at revenge.

Physical punishment isn't appropriate and won't be successful, because the cat does **not** understand the concept. A cat hit for punishment learns to fear hands, because to him the hands attacked for no reason.

To discipline effectively, remember three key rules: **Never** hit a cat. **Never** call the cat to come for discipline. **Never** use the cat's daily name when disciplining.

Correction or discipline teaches the cat the rules he must live with. And

A light tap on the nose with one finger is an effective means of communicating displeasure. Physical discipline should rarely go further than this.

If you encounter a sudden behavior problem with a previously well-behaved cat look to the cat's health and surroundings for root causes.

it's important that he understands that you're the dominant animal. When you discipline, look at your cat with your eyes wide open and challenging. Use an authoritative, deep voice when saying "No" or when correcting a behavior.

There are measures your cat will understand. For behavior problems while interacting with a cat, try the following:

For Minor Infractions

- Hiss. Use an open-mouthed, back-of-the-throat, loud, hard *h-ch-ch* sound, not a *s-s-s* sound.
- Toss a set of keys or a soft-drink can with stones in it **near**, not at, the cat. Simultaneously say "No" in a deep, stern voice. Soon the cat will respond to the word "No" alone.
- Cover his eyes for three to five seconds.

For Major Infractions

- Using one fingertip, **tap** (do not hit) the cat on the nose/forehead area. This tap is the equivalent of the light tap, claws in, that mom cat gives to a rambunctious kitten.

If the cat continues the same behavior, try the following:

- Hold his scruff (the skin at the back of the cat's neck) with one hand and cover his eyes with the other.
- Lift **only** the cat's front paws (not back paws) off the floor and quickly, but **gently**, shake the cat from side to side **(twice only)**. Do not shake the cat too hard; you don't want to damage his spine. The idea is to simulate what the mother cat would do as a last resort.

ARE THERE SPECIFIC CORRECTIVE MEASURES WHICH WORK FOR INDIVIDUAL PROBLEMS?

Yes. To be truly effective the correction has to address the particular cause of the behavior. Unfortunately, the cause may not always be evident, or there may be more than one reason for the misbehavior. So study what is happening, what happened just before the event, and try to discover the underlying cause. Then refer to the charts below. Each addresses a behavior problem with more than one possible cause. Scan through the rest of the chapter too—some problems, such as house soiling and aggression, are detailed in individual questions.

Some of the corrective measures below involve spraying original flavor Listerine on a forbidden area. Most cats disapprove of the smell, but we won't be able to smell it after a few minutes—the cat will.

Behavior Problem: Jumping on Counters or Tables

Possible Cause	Correction
Temptation of food or dirty dishes	Keep area clean; wipe counters with vinegar. Set booby traps.
Pathway to good nap place	Provide new pathway. Set booby traps.
An attention getter	Ignore the behavior totally but set booby traps.

Behavior Problem: Jumping on the Stove

Possible Cause	Correction
Warmth and height	Set booby traps; store pans on top of stove so there is no room for the cat.
Food/dirty pans	Keep area clean. Wipe with vinegar.

Behavior Problem: Eating Plants/Chewing on Electric Cords

Possible Cause	Correction
Boredom or cravings	Spray plants or cords with Bitter Apple, original flavor Listerine or vinegar. Or spray leaves with water and dip edges in powdered ginger. Combine and repeat for stubborn cats.
	Wrap electric cords with double-sided sticky tape or duct tape with sticky side out.
	Play with cat. Give fresh catnip two or three times a week. Grow grass indoors for cat.
Illness, pain	Visit Vet. Spray plants. Set aside playtime.
Stress or a sudden change in lifestyle	Spray plants. Reduce stress. Give catnip. Playtime.

Behavior Problem: House Soiling

For more information, see the next question.

Possible Cause	Correction
Health problems	See Vet regarding FUS and other illnesses.
Litter-box problems:	Clean litter daily. Keep box in a quiet,

Dirty litter	easily reached place. Use same brand of litter. Put one to two inches of water in the tub if he urinates in the tub.
Change in location	
Change in litter type	
Inaccessible litter	
Stress	Reduce stressors. Increase playtime and attention.
Territorial disputes:	Add more litter boxes. Find a new home for one or more cats. Clean the outside of the house. Spritz your clothes with distilled white vinegar to eliminate other cat's scent.
Too many pets in house	
Mismatched animal personalities	
Outside cats marking on your house	
Smell of other cat on your clothes	
	Seek professional help specific to the individual situation.

Behavior Problem: Biting People

Possible Cause	Correction
Cat is encouraged to roughhouse and play with human hands, etc.	Stop all roughhousing.
	Apply discipline technique described earlier.
	Play games with toys to expend energy and protect hands. Get professional help if needed.
Improper socialization	Use nonthreatening movements; move slowly, speak gently. Get professional help if needed.
Stress	Reduce stressors. Normalize routines. Set aside playtime and quiet time. Get professional help if needed.
Displaced aggression	Get professional help.

Behavior Problem: Clawing

Possible Cause	Correction
FOR CLIMBING CURTAINS: Boredom, attention getting, effort to get a better view	Clip the cat's claws regularly. Get him a companion, new toys. Tie curtains out of the way. Spray Listerine on curtains daily for three to four weeks.
FOR CLAWING FURNITURE: Sharpening claws and territorial marking	Clip the cat's claws regularly. Then cover the place where the cat has been clawing plus several inches to every side with one of the following: clear plastic wrap, aluminum foil, masking tape with sticky sides out or commercial covers. Leave the covering that works

FOR CLAWING OR BITING TOILET PAPER: Boredom, attention getting, sharpening claws, territorial marking	in place for at least a month while you retrain with the scratching post. If covering does not work, set up booby trap with empty soda cans. Clip the cat's claws regularly. Get him a companion, new toys. Attach a toilet paper protector (check ads in cat magazines).

Note: There are directions for reducing stress in chapter 13, how to clip claws in chapter 6, and how to make booby traps later in this chapter.

HOW DO I DEAL WITH HOUSE-SOILING PROBLEMS?

This is one of the most common and exasperating of problems since there are so many reasons for this behavior. Remember, though, cats are **not** vindictive. Your cat isn't getting back at you by trying to destroy your things.

Besides relieving the pressure of a full bladder or colon, cats use urine and feces to communicate with other cats. In essence, by his very behavior, he is explaining why he is leaving urine and feces—our noses are just not sensitive enough to understand the message in its natural, odoriferous form.

Find the Problem

First you'll have to figure out *why* he is house soiling. Here are some of the more common reasons:

- The box is too filthy to share a room with, let alone sit in. Every cat has his own limit with respect to filth. Some cats insist on just-cleaned litter whereas others will use the box as long as there is any litter left among the feces. Most cats, however, fall somewhere in between.
- He is stressed about something in the environment—someone moved into or out of the house, schedules may have changed so he is left alone more—or he may have been harassed or attacked by another animal while in the litter box. Changes like a new carpet, a switch in litter brands—almost any change—can cause stress in a sensitive cat.
- He feels his territory is threatened for any of the following reasons:
  - Too many animals in the house
  - The sight or smell of a foreign cat spraying the outside of the house
  - New animals in the house
  - Moving into a new place where a cat had once lived
  - The smell of other cats on you
- The litter setup is not to his liking. The problem may be one or more of the following:
  - The litter box is in a busy place.
  - The box is too close to his food and water bowls.

— Scented litter, the clay is larger or smaller than usual or other sudden changes in material.
— The litter box is or isn't covered.
— He prefers the feel of the potting soil to his sharp-edged clay litter.
- The box is too small for him to turn around in and get comfortable, or the sides are too short and without a hood (when he sprays, it goes out of the box).
- He is "lazy." You keep the box in the basement and he sleeps and eats upstairs— or it may be that he would have to cross the territory of another cat in the house.
- He missed the early socialization lessons on house manners. He may be a former outdoor cat who has never experienced a litter box.
- He is ill. Cats with lower urinary tract disease or bladder infections are prone to leave small puddles whenever they can get urine out.

Correcting the Problem

Take your cat to your Vet for a urinary health check. If he gets a clean bill of health, rule out as many of the remaining possible causes. Determine what changes need to be made to reduce stress. Next clean all the places which you know, or even think, he may have soiled. If your cat is using the tub or sink instead of his box, leave one to two inches of standing water to dampen his desire to misbehave.

Try adding temporary litter boxes—cardboard boxes with a plastic bag for a liner—to see if more boxes will help. You can put the extra boxes where he has been leaving his messages. When he is using the boxes regularly, you can slowly move them to where you want them and reduce the number. This can also be an opportunity to test different types of litter.

If house soiling is a very long-term problem, or there are factors you cannot change, try confining him to a very small room such as a bathroom or a large wire dog crate. The idea is to confine him so he has no choice but to use his litter box. Do not let him out in the house unless he is on harness and leash and you can watch him (like house-training a small puppy). Do this for one month, then **slowly** let him earn his freedom. Just after he has used the box, usually after a meal, let him be free for an hour or two. Praise him. Gradually allow him to be out longer as he proves he can be trusted.

Note: In a multi-cat household it can be hard to determine who is the culprit. Your Vet can help by giving one cat at a time sodium fluorescein. This is a harmless chemical that will color the cat's urine under fluorescent lights.

IS THERE ANYTHING I CAN USE TO CONTROL SPRAYING?

The best way is to have him or her surgically sterilized before puberty (no later than five months for a female or eight months for a male) so spraying doesn't start. If your cat has already started spraying, you can try one of two diaperlike alternatives described in the February 1993 issue of *Cat Fancy*. Neither of these products (listed below) will stop the spraying, but they may save your home until neutering can be done and during the few weeks after surgery. (It takes four to six weeks for all the hormones to be eliminated from the cat's body.) If your neutered cat is still spraying after eight weeks, see the preceding question.

Product: She's (A paper towel can be folded inside these pants for more absorbency.)
Write to:

UPCO
Dept. CF
P.O. Box 96
St. Joseph, MO 64502

Product: Cataper (diaperlike pants for cats)
Write to:

Millie M. Edwards
Dept. CF
9206 Palm Shores Drive
Spring, TX 77379

SHOULD I LET MY CAT SLEEP ON FLOOR VENTS?

NO. The hot, dry air damages the cat's skin, fur and overall health. Mucous membranes dry out in the mouth and nose and can lead to lowered immunity.

WHY SHOULD I WORRY ABOUT MY CAT CHEWING ON CORDS, PLANTS AND OTHER OBJECTS?

Ingested items, whether leaves or electric cord insulation, may block bowels or cause other internal injury requiring surgery. In addition, plants with serrated leaves can easily cut tender mouth and throat tissue. See chapter 3 for a list of toxic plants. (Most house plants will cause vomiting even if not toxic.) Electric wire laid bare by sharp teeth can cause shocks, burns and even death.

HOW DO I BUILD BOOBY TRAPS?

Harmless booby traps that show your cat that a particular activity is no longer fun are a good way to stop unwanted behaviors. The greatest thing about a booby trap is that you don't have to correct the cat; the booby trap does it for you, and it continues to work even when you are asleep or out of the house.

If you want a booby trap to succeed, **remove all temptations from the**

area. And don't forget to provide alternatives. If you want to prevent him from using an unacceptable "roadway" to the window or other good spot, give him a new route when you booby-trap the old.

With all the methods described below, spray the booby trap with a cheap perfume or original flavor Listerine. Your cat will associate the smell with the booby trap's discomfort. After a period of time and experience with this "booby trap" smell, the cat will be repelled by the smell alone, so eventually the perfume or Listerine will be all you need to dissuade him.

Don't be discouraged if a particular plan fails; you may need to try different methods or combine ideas until you find the one that works for your cat.

To Stop the Cat from Getting on a Shelf or Counter

Balance a strip of cardboard (6″ × the length of the counter) on the edge of the counter. Put empty cans on the back edge so that when the cat jumps up, the whole thing will fall over. Make sure there are no hazardous objects below for the cat to fall on. The object is to startle the cat, not to cause injury.

To Stop the Cat from Walking in Certain Areas

Use one of the following:

- Lay lightly rumpled sheets of aluminum foil over the off-limits area so they make noise when the cat touches it.
- Lay Con-Tact paper, sticky side up, over the area. Change the paper at least weekly, as it will lose adhesiveness.
- Apply strips of double-sided sticky tape over the area. (The type used to lay carpet is the most durable.) Change it as needed to maintain a sticky surface.
- Use the shelf or counter idea given above if appropriate to the area.
- Wipe the area with plain white distilled vinegar two to three times a day.
- Tape fully inflated balloons in such a way that when the cat jumps on the forbidden area, he lands on the balloons and breaks them with his claws.
- Set a small wooden mousetrap, lay it **upside down** on the area, cover with a large (12″ × 12″) piece of lightweight paper. When the cat jumps up there, touching any place on the paper will set off the trap. The bottom of the trap will harmlessly lift the paper and make a loud snap when it shuts.

To Stop a Cat from Scratching and Clawing an Area

The cat must have a scratching post as an alternative to the furniture; see chapter 2. Put the scratching post near where the cat is scratching now. When the cat has used **only** the scratching post for two weeks, gradually move the post to where you want it—a foot at a time. Try the following ideas:

- Tape or tack fully inflated balloons in the area so the cat will break them with his claws.

- Cover the scratched area and several surrounding inches with plastic wrap or aluminum foil.

To Keep Him Out of Potted Plants

- Cut a circle of wire screen two inches bigger than the pot. Cut a small hole in the center of the screen to accommodate the plant stem, and make a slit on both sides of the center hole (but not out to the edge of the circle). The slit will allow you to lower the circle of screen over the plant foliage. Fold the screen edge down over the pot lip and tape or tie string around to hold it in place.
- Place large stones in the pot to cover the soil.

To Discourage Him from Sleeping on the Floor Vents

One of the following should do the job:

- Buy clear plastic vent guards at the hardware store.
- Cut a cardboard "collar" (4″ tall and long enough to bend around all four sides of the vent). Use tape or paper clips to fasten the collar to the vent.
- Bend chicken wire to form a box with five sides (four sides and a top; the bottom will be the vent). Use tape or paper clips to fasten the cage to the vent.

HOW DO I KEEP THE CAT OUT OF THE TRASH/GARBAGE?

Try one of the following ideas:

- Put the trash can under the sink and lock the cabinet with a child protection lock (available in many stores) or a hook-and-eye. You can get hook-and-eye latches that have a spring latch if your cat's the engineering type.
- Use a trash can with a lid. Since cans tend to be lightweight and easily tipped, put a brick or two in the bottom under the trash bag to give it more weight.
  — If the can has a flat lid, put a weight on the lid.
  — If the can has a peaked, swinging lid, keep it away from counters or tables where the cat can sit and pry it open from the top.
- Put the trash can in a fancy wooden holder available in specialty stores.

CAN I STOP THE CAT'S RUNNING AND PLAYING LATE AT NIGHT?

While it is normal for a cat to play at night when he would normally be hunting, you can change his play schedule. Try the following:

- Feed your cat two high-quality meals a day—one-third of his food in the morning fifteen to twenty minutes after you get up and two-thirds at night just before you go to bed.
- Play with him for ten to fifteen minutes one to two hours before his second meal.

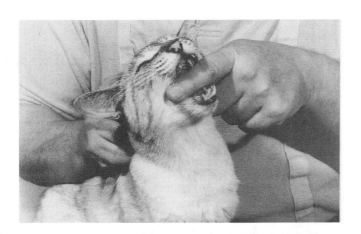

Being the target of a cat attack is a serious matter. You must know how to disengage the attacker as shown in these photos. If the attacker is your own cat, you are well advised to seek the help of a pet therapist for both your sakes.

HOW DO I STOP MY CAT FROM RUNNING OUT EVERY TIME I OPEN THE DOOR?

If the cat learns that the world is a dangerous place when he is not wearing a harness or is in his carrier, he won't want to dash out the door. The idea is, in effect, to booby-trap the outdoors by scaring the cat when he sets an uninvited foot outside. Here's how:

- One person hides outside with a noisemaker—an air horn, whistle or metal pot and spoon. It's important for the outside accomplice to hide where the cat can't see, hear or smell him. So the accomplice has to be very quiet and stay downwind (the breeze goes from the cat toward the person).
- The other person stays inside and "accidentally" leaves the door ajar.
- The second the cat peeks out, the unseen outsider makes a loud noise to chase the cat back into the house.
- Repeat on different days and at different times as needed until the cat is conditioned not to step outside.
- During this time, take the cat to the car in his harness or in the carrier for a treat.

WHAT DO I DO WHEN A CAT ATTACKS ME?

Cat attacks should never be tolerated. To prevent attack, you'll need to address the cause; see the behavior charts herein. If you have an attack cat, make an immediate appointment with a pet therapist for your safety and his sanity.

If you find yourself being attacked, there are some things that you can do.

First

- **Remain calm.**
- Do **not** pull away. This does more damage to your body and excites the cat more, because it's the action of prey and can make the cat more aggressive.
- Grab the scruff of the cat's neck.

To Disengage His Teeth

- Push toward the biting mouth so his jaws open. Then remove your hand (or other part).

To Disengage His Claws

- Release his claws from your hand or other part by moving toward his paw and unhooking his claws. You can ask another person to help; it's easier for someone else to take the cat's paw and move it to release the claws.

When the Teeth or Claws Are Disengaged

- Still holding the cat's scruff, with the other hand hold the cat's rump to turn him and immobilize him **belly-up**.
- Stare at cat until he won't meet your eyes and he relaxes his body. (He is conceding the argument.)
- Talk quietly to the cat ("Now things are better" and such).
- Gently toss the cat so he lands some feet from you **or** put him in another room and close the door for a while.
- Do **not** touch or come near him for at least one hour. This will give both of you a chance to calm down.

WHY GRAB THE CAT'S SCRUFF WHEN HE ATTACKS?

Because grabbing the scruff triggers a reflex for the cat to relax somewhat. Although the reflex is weaker in an adult cat than it is in a kitten, the cat is conditioned to relax more when held by the scruff.

HOW DO I RESTRAIN A CAT?

For full-body restraint, there are several options.

- Towel-wrap; see chapter 13.
- Use a cat sack, a commercial mesh bag to contain the cat. Available through catalogs.
- Use a pillowcase. Place the cat in a heavy pillowcase with only the cat's head out; securely tie the pillowcase around the cat's neck but **not** so tight that he can't breathe. (You can still be scratched through the cloth.)

HOW DO I STOP MY CAT FROM HARASSING MY SMALLER PETS?

The extreme and often least acceptable solution is to isolate one pet in a separate, closed-off room. However, there are ways to live and let live without jeopardizing anyone's quality of life. And don't forget to give the cat lots of praise for nonhunting behaviors.

Fish. Cover the tank with a heavy tank top made for aquariums. Or you might place the tank in a difficult or impossible spot for the cat to reach.

Caged Rodents (hamsters, gerbils, etc.). Reinforce latches with twist ties. Put a weight on light plastic habitats to prevent the cat from knocking them over.

Birds. Hang the cage high and away from curtains, shelves or any adjacent items a cat can climb. Allow the bird out **only** when the cat is locked out of that room.

HOW SHOULD I HANDLE A CAT DISAGREEMENT OR FIGHT?

Cats do a lot of posturing to avoid a fight. These hissy fights can start over such things as territory, the smell of fear on one cat, food, toys or a trip to the Veterinarian. And a cat can move from fear to fight in a second.

Cats will argue loudly during a disagreement, with only the threat of physical damage. They make a great show with their noise and defensive postures. They hiss, spit, yowl and stand sideways or in a "Halloween stance" with puffed-out tails. These disagreements don't require human interference, because the combatants tend to stay two to three feet apart. The argument usually ends with one cat backing down.

Because it's best to let the cats work out their own territorial or dominance arguments, interfere **only** if both cats indicate they are really ready to fight. Intact cats are more likely to progress to a fight or those that are otherwise severely stressed. They will be noisy and they set their whiskers back tightly against their jaws with their ears pulled tightly against the skull and their tails will be puffed. Their pupils close down to a slit, and they assume a defensive posture. The cats will then quickly close the distance between themselves to do battle. If their postures indicate that a fight is imminent and the cats have not yet made physical contact, throw a large towel or blanket over each combatant.

- To stop a fight, try one of these ideas:
  Outdoors:
  —Throw a large bowl of cool water on the cats.
  Indoors:
  —Throw a large lightweight pillow at the cats.
  —Make a loud noise, or yell "Stop!"

Do not touch the cats until after they have calmed down; wait at least half an hour to interact with the cats, because when fully primed for a fight, a cat may attack you by mistake.

HOW DO I PROTECT WILD BIRDS AND OTHER SMALL ANIMALS FROM MY CAT?

The only way to protect wild birds and other animals is to keep your cat indoors and let him out only on a leash or in an enclosure. Bells are not much help; most cats can learn how to stalk silently.

WHY DOESN'T HE EAT WHAT HE CATCHES?

While all cats instinctively attack moving objects, a kitten learns how to hunt and what to eat from his mother. An adult cat from a nonhunting mother

Cats will fight over territories, food, mates or a variety of other reasons. Most frequently cat fights never progress beyond the threatening posture stage. Open combat, however, is always possible and in those cases, cat owners should know how to break up fights without touching the combatants. That's the best way not to get hurt yourself.

usually does not hunt effectively—and if he does catch a mouse, he doesn't know it's food.

WHAT SHOULD I DO IF MY CAT HAS CORNERED AND/OR HURT AN ANIMAL?

The most laid-back and lazy kitty may be tempted by the movement of a small animal. While it can be unsettling to us, it's a normal and natural activity for the cat. But it is also dangerous for him—little mouse bites can lead to big health problems for both of you. If your cat has cornered an animal, do **not** just grab him—he's excited by the hunt and may bite you instead. Here are some things you can do to help:

Inside the House

Call your cat or distract him with a toy. If that fails, use a broom to shoo him into another room and close the door. Live animals can be cornered and caught in a small box or jar and released outside. See below for severely injured animals. Make sure you wash both the pickup equipment and your hands to prevent spreading disease. Now release your cat, but don't touch him till he calms down.

Outside the House

If the prey is alive and just cornered, dump a pan of water on the cat. He should run away and allow the prey to escape—for now.

For Severely Injured Prey

If the prey is severely injured, ease the cat away with a broom or with water (if outside). Most of us aren't capable of judging whether an injured animal is mortally wounded, and yet none of us want to see an animal—even a mouse—suffer needlessly. Call your local Animal Control or a humane service organization. (In urban areas, most Animal Control facilities are open twenty-four hours a day.) Don't feel like you're passing the buck when you call; these organizations can do what we can't—they can evaluate, rehabilitate and, if necessary, euthanize humanely.

They may require you to bring the animal to them for evaluation. If you find yourself needing to transport the injured animal, use a broom or a heavily gloved hand to ease it into a box. An animal that can still move around will need a covered box, so make sure the box or its covering has airholes. If the box is small enough, you can enclose it inside a tied pillowcase.

If you need help and animal services are unavailable, call your Vet for advice—or you may want to take the animal in for evaluation or euthanasia.

WHY WILL TOMS KILL KITTENS?

Intact males will kill litters so the queens will come into heat earlier (because the breast feeding has stopped). In the evolutionary scheme of things, this means that the tom's new bloodline will start earlier.

WHAT IF THIS CHAPTER DID NOT SOLVE MY PROBLEM?

While we have tried to address many common problems, cats are inventive. They can always think of more ways to get into trouble. If all else fails, check your yellow pages for a pet therapist or try calling one of the four well-established, credible hot lines listed below.

1. The Dr. Louis J. Camuti Feline Consultation and Diagnostic Service of the Cornell University Feline Health Center
   Telephone: 1-800-548-8937
   This line is open weekdays (except holidays) from 9 a.m. to noon and 2 p.m. to 4 p.m. (EST). There is a $25 credit call charge per call.
2. San Francisco Society for the Prevention of Cruelty to Animals
   Telephone: 1-415-554-3075
   This line is open through voice mail twenty-four hours a day. A volunteer will write to you with respect to your problem within a day and call you within two days. The service is free.
3. Tree House Animal Foundation, Inc.
   Telephone: 1-312-784-5488
   This line is open every day from 9 a.m. to 5 p.m. (CST). There is no fee for the service, but you will have to pay long-distance charges.
4. University of Pennsylvania School of Veterinary Medicine
   Telephone: 1-215-898-3347
   This line is open twenty-four hours a day via answering machine. Your call is promptly returned by veterinary students. While there is no service charge, you'll be responsible for long-distance charges.

9

Lifestyles of the Sane and Healthy

T O BREED or not to breed, that is the question. Or rather that is only one of the questions you'll need answered to ensure that both you and your cat have lifestyles of the sane and healthy.

In addition to information on neutering, two other major lifestyle choices, declawing and indoor vs. outdoor, are discussed in this chapter. Making choices that are right for both you and your cat can avoid many problems and heartaches later.

TO BREED OR NOT TO BREED

I DON'T WANT MY CAT TO MISS ANYTHING. WHY SHOULD HE BE NEUTERED BEFORE SEXUAL MATURITY?

Neutered cats, male or female, are healthier cats with glossier coats and generally better manners. Younger kittens (after eight weeks) generally have no more problems with this surgery than those neutered at more conventional ages (five months for females and eight months for males). Early neutering has gained more national acceptance recently. The Humane Society of the United States now strongly recommends neutering both cats and dogs *before* puberty.

If you need a financial incentive for neutering your cat: licenses, which are required in many cities, are usually much less expensive for neutered animals.

- Unneutered **male** cats
  - Are more likely to get reproductive system cancer and other diseases.
  - Are more likely to roam.
  - Are more often involved in fights.
  - Are less people-directed.
  - Have less tolerance for multi-cat households.
  - Have strong body odor.
  - Have a very strong-smelling litter box.
  - Are prone to spray anywhere.
- Unneutered **female** cats
  - Have more stress from repeated heats, even if not bred, than from spay surgery.
  - Have more medical problems and stress with the birth and care of one litter of kittens than with a spay operation.
  - Can die from birth complications.
  - Can produce two or three litters a year for as long as she lives.

Note: After seven years this can mean 420,000 cats from one female! The increased population and lack of good homes can lead to starvation, disease—and worse.

- Neutering before sexual maturity helps to
  - Keep the cat "kittenish"—playful and friendly.
  - Keep the cat people-directed.
  - Reduce the urge to spray and to roam in both sexes. (Intact males **will** spray and intact females are likely to spray.)
  - Reduce the chance of breast cancer in females.
  - Eliminate reproductive organ cancers.
  - Diminish the smell of a tom's urine.
  - Limit genetic defects.

DOES IT STILL HELP TO NEUTER AFTER SEXUAL MATURITY?

Yes! You'll have a happier, healthier cat. And no matter when your pet is neutered, it won't contribute to the tragedy of overpopulation.

About six weeks after surgery, you'll be glad to note that litter-box odor will be less strong; it takes that long for all the sex hormones, the cause of the strong odors, to exit the body. Also, the urge to spray will diminish as the hormone level drops. Gradually, calm will settle in and your cat begins to relax with you.

WON'T MY CAT BECOME LAZY AND FAT WHEN SPAYED OR NEUTERED?

No, a cat becomes overweight because of overfeeding. Even normal, healthy cats will appear lazy, because they sleep twelve to fourteen hours per day. See chapter 4 for weight and feeding evaluation.

HOW MUCH DOES SPAY/NEUTER SURGERY COST?

While costs will vary widely by region, prices for neuter and spay operations in most areas are kept reasonably low to encourage responsible pet ownership. And most communities have provisions for lower-cost or free surgery. Contact your local animal shelter or humane society and ask if they have a neuter/spay program. If you can't get help locally, Friends of Animals, a national assistance program, sells inexpensive certificates which are redeemable for low-cost surgery at 1,300 Veterinarians across the United States. You pay $38 for a female and $25 for a male. Costs do change, so you might call to confirm current rates. The address is:

Friends of Animals
Dept. CF
P.O. Box 1244
Norwalk, CT 06856
1-800-321-PETS

IF A FEMALE CAT IS "IN HEAT," WHAT DOES IT MEAN?

Being "in heat" or "in season" means that she is an intact female who is receptive to sexual activity. Tom cats (intact male cats) will pick up on the changes in her body odor, a chemical "open for business" signal, that can carry for miles. You'll soon notice these yowling lotharios standing in line to court her and there will be the inevitable fights for her favors. And unfortunately, most of this very noisy activity takes place at night.

A female cat may mate with more than one male. Her screams will signal the end of intercourse. The penis has barbs on it that are curved back toward the male's body and they rake the female's vagina as he withdraws after intercourse. This abrasion stimulates ovulation in the female. So while a female will go into heat on a regular schedule, she won't ovulate until she mates. Unfortunately, this ensures that almost every mating will produce offspring.

Females will generally go into heat two to three times a year—although it's not unheard of for some females, especially Siamese, to come into season monthly if not bred. Even without the almost certain pregnancy mating brings about, heats are extremely stressful. Spay surgery is far easier on her and will allow her to live a healthier, more content life.

HOW WILL I KNOW IF MY FEMALE CAT IS IN HEAT?

Besides the busloads of tom cats yowling, meowing and brawling outside in your yard, you'll notice some behavioral changes in your temptress tabby. You may need some earplugs during the week she's in heat; she'll have increased and at times relentless vocalizations.

In her desperation to find a mate, she may present herself to neutered cats in your houschold. They'll respond with a "what do you expect me to do with it?" attitude or a flat-out refusal. She'll be constantly underfoot and rub against you. And if you pet her, especially on the neck, she'll elevate her rear end in an unladylike fashion.

If your cat is in heat, make sure it's her last heat. Get her spayed! It's better for her, better for you and better for the cat population.

SHOULDN'T FLUFFY HAVE ONE LITTER TO SHOW MY CHILDREN THE "MIRACLE OF LIFE"?

There are wonderful videotapes available through public libraries showing the gestation and birth of various species. Even if you take the time, money and energy to appropriately place the kittens you breed, there are that many more kittens in the animal shelters who will not find homes. Allowing any kittens to be born without homes means they are disposable.

WHAT HAPPENS IN A SPAY OPERATION?

First, the Vet anesthetizes the cat. Then she makes a small incision in the cat's abdomen through the skin and subcutaneous fat. The uterus and ovaries are removed. Dissolvable stitches are used to stop internal bleeding. The three outer layers are then sutured and your cat is returned to her cage and allowed to recover. She'll need to return to the Vet in seven to ten days to get her external stitches removed.

WHAT SHOULD I DO WHEN I BRING HER HOME AFTER SPAYING?

When you pick up your cat from the Vet, you'll receive a preprinted set of after-spay directions. Read them before leaving so you can ask for any clarifications.

Some cats will act as if nothing happened and some will complain and whine for a few days; it depends on age, basic personality, how the surgery went and whether she thinks she can get away with playing the invalid. Encourage her to take it easy for a few days, feed her lightly the first day and watch her. Do be careful how you lift her—no extra stress on the stitches.

Continue to watch her until the stitches have been removed; continuous grooming and chewing at the incision site can loosen or remove stitches. If all goes well, you'll have to return to the Vet in a week to ten days to have the stitches removed.

If you notice any of the following, contact your Vet:

- Fever, redness/swelling or discharge from the incision
- Loose or pulled-out stitches
- Unusual pain or tenderness

WHAT HAPPENS IN A TOM CAT'S NEUTER OPERATION?

The Vet anesthetizes the cat and makes a small incision in each testicle sack. The testicles are tied off, then cut and removed. The tiny incisions are left open, and he's then returned to his cage to sleep off the anesthetic.

WHAT SHOULD I DO WHEN I BRING HIM HOME AFTER A NEUTER OPERATION?

When you pick him up from the Vet, you'll be given a set of after-neuter instructions. Read them before leaving so you can ask questions.

Some cats will act casually unconcerned, and some will complain and tell you all about their operations. His recovery speed depends on his age, basic personality, whether the surgery had any complications and how much mileage he can get from his "weakened" condition. Try to keep him relatively quiet for a few days, give him a light meal the first day and keep an eye out for any of the following problems:

- Fever, redness/swelling or discharge from the incision
- Continual grooming and chewing at the incision
- Unusual pain or tenderness

WHAT ABOUT THOSE CLAWS?

WHY DO CATS SCRATCH ON TREES AND— OH NO!—FURNITURE?

Cats scratch for two reasons: to leave messages and to soothe and sharpen their itching claws. The scratched messages, particularly those left on outside vertical surfaces like trees, are left for other cats. He wants the opposition to know the following:

"This is part of my territory and I will defend it."
"I am this strong" (how deep he gouges).
"I am this big" (how high he reaches).
"This is me" (personal scent).

Scratching on your furniture, even if you have no other cat in the house, is still territorial behavior. It's also an effort to relieve an itch and shed the old claw sheaths. The end results are finely sharpened, cleaner claws and a shredded couch. You can stop this destruction and still let him take care of his itch. Read on.

DO I HAVE TO DECLAW MY CAT TO KEEP MY FURNITURE INTACT?

No. Cats and good furniture can coexist. It is imperative that the cat be given an alternative that is his to happily claw and shred. And for you, this item needs to be an attractive substitute for the item(s) he's using now. You have two options:

Scratching Posts or Pads

Cats can be taught to use a scratching post at any age, though it's easier to train a kitten.

Scratching post and pads come in many designs, including an inexpensive corrugated cardboard sprinkled with attracting catnip. Or you can go all out on fancy floor-to-ceiling posts with sleeping areas. If you buy ready-made, see chapter 2 for safety specifications. Or you can make one yourself; see chapter 20.

Even with a scratching post, cats without claw protectors need their front and back claws clipped regularly.

Claw Protectors

Cats that are hard to train to a scratching post no longer need declawing. There is a new product available from your Vet called Soft Paws. These are soft vinyl claw caps that are glued onto each nail and replaced every four to eight weeks as the nail is shed. Fully retractable and, more importantly, acceptable to cats, these soft caps stop all damage, and yet your cat can still enjoy the motions of a pretend shredding.

If your Vet gives you instructions and sells you the kits, you can save money by fixing the claws at home. If you have always wanted to claw your cat, here is the opportunity you've been waiting for!

MY CAT WON'T USE THE SCRATCHING POST. WHAT CAN I DO?

Since cats will scratch to leave messages, to sharpen their claws and from boredom, you will have to address all these issues.

- Put the scratching post near the place he is damaging. You can move it later, a few feet at a time, to the place you want it, after he's begun using it.
- If possible, get more than one type of post for variety and because different cats have different tastes. These do *not* have to be expensive. The inexpensive scratching pads are well received and chapter 20 has directions for making your own. Or he may like to shred a dual-purpose kitty condo.
- Clean the forbidden item he was using with vinegar to remove his scent, and once the area is dry, discourage his interest with one or more of these ideas:
  — Spray it lightly with original flavor Listerine. Reapply every few days, until he shows no interest in the location.
  — Cover the area and twelve inches beyond with plastic wrap or aluminum foil.
  — Use commercial furniture protectors.
- Add some new toys to his collection but give him only one or two toys at a time. Rotate the toys every two or three days. Consider adding "Cat TV" for interest. "Cat TV" is a bird feeder stationed outside an accessible "viewing only" window, or an aquarium with fish or with just the bubble-releasing apparatus attached to the air hoses.
- Give him *lots* of praise when he investigates and then uses the new scratching post. If he goes for the couch, distract him with a toy or gently move him to the new post and praise.
- If he will not let your furniture alone after all of the above, put a booby trap on the item.

WHAT ARE THE ADVANTAGES AND DISADVANTAGES OF DECLAWING?

Herein are lists of both advantages and disadvantages. You'll note that declawing can have disastrous effects on some cats' behavior. Unfortunately, you won't know how your cat will respond until after the fact—and then it will be too late. Almost all nations and cultures reject the idea of declawing domestic cats; the United States is the only country that declaws cats for cosmetic purposes.

Disadvantages

- According to a study by the Canadian Veterinary Medical Society, after declawing cats can develop behavior problems, including house soiling and biting.
- Some cats have a change of personality and become fearful.
- The surgery is painful.
- Some have more difficulty climbing and defending themselves.
- Generally, declawed cats cannot compete in cat shows.

- Some become less trusting of the Veterinarian—or people in general—and become harder to handle.

When you consider that declawing involves the amputation of a cat's toes to the first knuckle, it's easy to understand why both owners and Vets can end up on a feline hit list.

Advantages

- You can use a litter-box liner without the cat's making holes.
- You have fewer claws to clip.
- It is one way to protect your furniture.

INDOOR OR OUTDOOR?

SHOULD I ALLOW MY CAT OUTSIDE UNSUPERVISED TO ROAM ALONE?

No factor affects a cat's life span more than an outdoor lifestyle. The average life span of an "outdoor only" cat is tragically limited to one to two years. Cats with disabilities, young kittens and declawed cats are even more likely to become injured or killed when let outdoors unprotected.

Cats who combine both indoor and outdoor existences increase their life expectancy to an average of six to seven years. But a cat who lives inside only—with outdoor excursions in an enclosure or on a harness and leash—lives an average of fifteen to eighteen years.

"Indoor only" cats do have specific needs that can be a nuisance. But when weighed against the dangers of an outdoor lifestyle, your choice becomes simple.

Outdoor Cats (cats with free access to the outside)

- Generally live shorter lives, two to five years.
- Are sicker before their owner notices and harder to treat because they're harder to handle.
- Are exposed to outdoor dangers, including:
  - Automobiles
  - Crawling under a car's hood and being cut by the fan belt when the car starts
  - Loss or injury
  - Accidental or deliberate poisoning
  - Abscesses or infections from wounds
  - Extremes of temperature and weather—stresses of which lessen the effectiveness of the immune system
  - Recurrent parasitic infestation
  - Exposure to contagious feline diseases

— Sunburn and its complications
— Getting caught in a leg-hold trap

Note: If you still decide to let your cat roam, do a health checkup and take parasite control measures during regular weekly grooming. Check for lumps, hot spots, ulcers, sore places or other abnormalities.

SHOULD I BRING MY OUTDOOR CAT INSIDE ON COLD NIGHTS?

No, but provide free access to a wind- and moisture-proof shelter. An extreme temperature change would shock his system; he needs to live either inside or outside.

Give him access to the garage or a shed, together with a small "cat house." The house needs to be isolated and off the ground or the floor. A hooded litter box, with straw inside for a nest and straw bales outside, makes a good shelter. In really cold weather, special scratch-, bite- and wet-resistant heating pads can be used.

COULD LAWN-CARE CHEMICALS HURT MY CAT?

Yes. Chemicals, especially weed killers and pesticides, may be toxic to the cat for several hours. Pesticides can also move up the food chain and cause secondary poisoning.

HOW CAN MY CAT SAFELY ENJOY THE OUTSIDE?

Depending on your willingness to monitor your cat—and your budget— you have several options.

Commercial enclosures come in many sizes and designs, ranging from window boxes to large outdoor structures which attach to an existing fence. If you buy one of these large outside enclosures, the fence must be at least six feet tall, or higher than your cat can jump.

Generally these enclosures are meant as "playrooms." So don't lock the cat into an enclosure and leave; the weather may change or other hazards might crop up.

In much of the United States, the weather becomes too cold for a cat left outside without special accommodations. If he can't return to the house at will, the cat needs shelter, water, food and a litter box in the pen. It's best to install a pet door that you can lock; the cat can be locked in the house if needed. He can also return through an unlocked door to the safety of the house for shelter.

Two inexpensive outdoor options are a large outdoor wire dog crate and a harness with a leash. While it protects your unattended cat from harm, the crate greatly restricts freedom of movement. On the other hand, a harness and leash combination allows your pet to explore the outdoors in the safety of your company. A cat on a harness and leash must be supervised at all times for his own protection.

WHAT TYPES OF OUTDOOR ENCLOSURES ARE THERE?

There is a wide range of ready-made window and yard units that can be ordered from better catalogs.

If you want to save money and are handy, you can build your own. These make-it-yourself projects are limited in scope and cost only by your imagination and wallet. See chapter 20.

ARE BURIED ELECTRIC FENCES HELPFUL?

To understand the problems with these fences, you must know how they work. An electric wire is laid out (like a fence) and then buried. Your cat wears a special collar which delivers a shock when he nears the buried wire. Because the neck shock is "in front" of him, he acts instinctively and backs away from the fence. Of course, the wire doesn't discriminate; it will shock him whether he's going out of or coming into your yard.

While a cat with the collar can be taught not to cross the line or he'll get an electric shock, other animals can still come **into** the yard and attack your pet, whose options for getaway are limited by the fence.

If your cat survives the attack by running out of the yard and getting shocked in the bargain, he'll be turned away from your home by another shock when he tries to reenter your yard. Read the questions on outdoor enclosures and harnesses for safe outdoor excursions.

10

Pests That Go Bite
in the Night

W ITH JUST A LITTLE prevention, pests need **not** be part of
your life. **Before** moving into any new dwelling, or before flea season starts,
begin treatment and prevention. Harsh chemicals are not always needed. This
chapter offers safer alternatives for the environment and for you and your cat.

HOW WOULD MY CAT GET WORMS AND WILL THEY
HARM HIM?

Worms lower the cat's resistance, and can even kill him outright if malnutri-
tion and blood loss are severe enough. Some types of worms can also migrate
to other parts of the cat's body. Consequently, any kind of worm infestation
should be treated immediately by your Veterinarian.

Tapeworms

Tapeworms are long (from two to thirty feet depending on the worm type
and host), flat, segmented worms. Cats get two types of tapeworms—one from
ingesting fleas and the other from dining on mice and other small rodents.

The flea larva ingests only the *Dipylidium caninum* tapeworm eggs. While
these tapeworms can develop in the larva, they are also found in the adult flea.

Grooming cats inadvertently ingest the growing tapeworm along with the flea. So to eliminate these tapeworms, you must control any flea infestation.

Once ingested, tapeworms attach themselves to the cat's intestinal wall and feed on digested food. Well suited for their parasitic lifestyle, these large worms are all head (sucking or hook parts) and reproductive segments. The segments farthest from the head are the most mature and contain eggs ready to infect other hosts; segments can release the eggs, or more commonly detach intact and pass out with the cat's feces. The segments spontaneously move and spread eggs through the environment, and are large enough to be seen in the cat's litter box or around his anus. If your cat is being treated for fleas, check him for tapeworms too.

Hookworms

Hookworms are nematodes, a type of roundworm a few millimeters (one-half inch) long, which can last for the life of the cat. Happily living in the cat's bowel, hookworms gnaw on the wall of the small intestine, causing blood (their dinner) to flow. The bleeding causes noticeable black, tarry feces or blood in the cat's stool when large numbers of worms are present.

The adult worm releases eggs, which pass with the cat's feces into the environment. The eggs hatch into larvae, and in damp areas these larvae can live for some time—waiting for the opportunity to penetrate skin and migrate through an animal's body until, as adults, they can live in the bowels. In adult cats, these larvae can remain dormant in various tissues. The dormancy usually doesn't cause problems, except in an immuno-compromised cat. In most cats, hookworms can be easily and successfully treated.

While contaminated soil is one source of infection, there are others. A cat can pick up hookworms by eating infected prey—another good reason to keep your pet indoors.

This worm is also willing to snack on humans; people can become infected from egg-contaminated soil. The larvae migrating through human tissues leave red itchy "trails" called creeping eruption.

Roundworms

Roundworms, the common name for nematodes, are parasites that can be several inches long. Related to hookworms, roundworms feed in much the same way—and they're able to last, since their eggs remain viable for years in the soil, and the larvae can stay dormant in tissues until conditions are ripe for bloodletting. The most common method of infection is from mother to nursing kittens, although cats can also get these worms from eating infected prey or from contact with the eggs in the soil.

Hookworms are so named for their mouth parts by which they attach themselves to their hosts.

Roundworms are extremely common and often infect kittens before birth. Named for their tendency to curl up outside the host, they are usually easy to eradicate. Modern wormers can eliminate most internal parasites with little or no stress to the host animal.

Tapeworms are very long parasites whose bodies are composed of segments that also spread the eggs outside the body to infect new hosts. The most common means of transmission is through the ordinary flea.

The life cycle of the tapeworm begins with shed segments that spread eggs. The eggs are, in turn, consumed by flea larva which, upon maturity set up housekeeping on a warm-blooded animal (your cat). Usually by grooming, the cat can easily ingest fleas or tapeworm eggs to make the cycle complete.

When a cat or kitten is infested with tapeworm, dried segments may be frequently observed on the hairs around the anus.

Heartworms

Heartworms, another type of nematode, are thin worms that grow up to ten inches long. While heartworms are not a common problem for cats, in some areas of the United States cats do get heartworms. Check with your Vet about your area. Animals become infected with heartworms through carrier mosquitoes. Mosquitoes bite an infected animal, drawing in larvae along with blood, and then they inject the larvae into their next victim.

The larvae mature into worms that lodge in the animal's heart and blood vessels and cause the heart walls and affected vessels to thicken. The worms that die are dumped into the lungs by circulating blood, and while cats generally remain asymptomatic, most animals have reduced blood flow and difficulty breathing. Eventually the heart can no longer pump and the host animal dies.

At this time, there are no preventatives for cats, as there are for dogs. The best plan is to keep your cat inside. If your cat develops heartworms, treatment must be done on an inpatient basis at a veterinary hospital. When the worms are killed by the medication, they move to the lungs and can cause life-threatening complications.

HOW CAN I TELL IF MY CAT HAS WORMS?

All new pets and any pet with fleas should be checked by your Veterinarian. Take a stool sample in with the animal.

Diagnosis is made by lab tests on the fresh sample of feces (for intestinal worms) or your cat's blood (for heartworms). Later on, if you see what looks like a piece of rice on the cat's anus or in the litter box, your cat has probably picked up tapeworms again.

HOW DO I TREAT FOR WORMS?

The best thing to do is to take your pet to the Vet; she'll be able to determine what type of worms are bothering your cat and give you the proper medication.

Over-the-counter worm medication isn't always the best, most up-to-date answer. In most cases, worm treatment doesn't have to be difficult or expensive. To kill tapeworms, your Vet has a great, new one-dose wormer. This medication enables dead worms to be digested as extra protein without causing diarrhea.

With most intestinal worms, you'll also have to clean and disinfect the litter box. Since soil, like contaminated litter, can be a reservoir of infestation, it helps to keep your cat inside.

Heartworms are difficult and expensive to treat because treatment involves poisoning the worms over a period of time and the cat will have to remain at the Vet's for a couple of weeks.

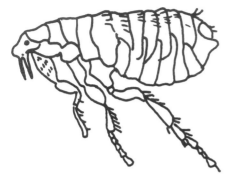

The ever-present, unsinkable flea is a major headache of every cat owner. There are a number of effective treatments to combat these pests, but care should be taken so that whatever measures used are safe for the cat.

The ear mite (left) is a common pest, but can be eradicated with a visit to the Veterinarian and the right drug treatment. A variety of mange mites (right) exists and an infestation must be taken seriously. If you suspect your cat has mange see your Veterinarian immediately.

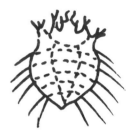

Ticks are blood-sucking external parasites that attach themselves to a passing animal, usually in bushes or high grass. One variety, the deer tick, is responsible for the transmission of Lyme Disease. Ticks by themselves are a good reason to maintain your cat as an indoor pet.

WHAT ARE MITES AND MANGE?

Mites, relatives of spiders, are segmented arthropods. Of these mighty mites, the chigger and the tick are the ones most familiar to people. The mite with which your cat is most familiar is the ear mite, whose scientific name is *Otodectes cynotis*; the damage it does in your cat's or dog's ear is officially called otodectic otitis. Living in the cat's ear canal, ear mites dine on both his skin and his blood.

If he has ear mites, your cat will probably shake his head and paw at his ears. Examine the ears. Mites will make them look "dirty" and smell bad. If you think your cat has mites, get him to the Vet. She'll prescribe ear drops to clear up the problem.

While the ear mite usually takes its pleasures in the cat's ear canal, other mite types can on occasion cause the skin problems that most of us consider "mange." Uncommon in cats and more likely to affect dogs, skin/fur-loss mange can still become a problem. Usually found on the cat's head, neck, paws and rump, these mites live on or just under the first layer of skin and suck fluids from the animal's tissues. The biting and burrowing cause some very unattractive fur loss and skin lesions (skin irritation, scaling and crusty dermatitis).

If your cat shows any of these symptoms, take him to the Vet. By examining the debris from his skin, she'll be able to make a clear diagnosis. Diagnosis is particularly important because these mites—and mange—are spread by both direct and indirect contact. The infected cat must be isolated, and to protect your other animals, you'll need to wash thoroughly after each contact with the affected pet.

Cats with skin mange are treated with prescription anti-mite medication applied by dip, powder or shampoo, and the medication must continue for two weeks **after** skin scrapings test negative. To prevent reinfection, the environment must also be treated with either a spray or a fogger, again as prescribed by the Vet.

WHY SHOULD I BE CONCERNED ABOUT A FEW FLEAS?

Fleas don't discriminate—they'll bite any warm-blooded animal, including you. If not eliminated, a few fleas rapidly become an infestation that torments everyone.

Some cats (and people) are allergic to flea bites. Allergic cats will begin to lose their fur and develop dermatitis. Because of the severe itching, cats can bite and scratch themselves raw enough to develop secondary infections.

When the cat grooms, he ingests fleas and flea debris (feces)—and fleas can carry tapeworms (see above). Also, while it's difficult to think of fleas as minuscule vampires, they can bleed very young, old or ill cats to such an extent that the animal's immune system becomes depressed. The pet is more susceptible to diseases or he may become anemic—or, in extreme cases, may die from blood loss.

WHY DO FLEAS CONGREGATE AT THE CAT'S NECK?

Fleas have the acuity of a vampire—they go for the most vulnerable, richest supply of blood. But fleas aren't drawn to the neck only by greed—it's also the safest place for them to dine because most grooming is done with the tongue, and in spite of rubber-band agility, cats still can't lick their own necks.

WHAT CAN I DO ABOUT THOSE FLEAS?

First, know your enemy. The flea season is year-round in the southern states and from March to October (after warmer days start, till the first hard frost) in the northern states. Additionally, these little bloodsuckers can become active on any day with a high temperature in the forties.

Flea research of old concentrated on rodent fleas because of their link to plague, and unfortunately, much of what we read about cat fleas is erroneously based on the rodent flea's behavior. So, contrary to what most of us have believed for years, adult cat fleas stay with their host, unless repelled by treatment. In other words, once they have begun to feed on blood, fleas do **not** spend 90 percent of their life off the cat.

You still need to treat your home for fleas, because the eggs, larvae and pupae (cocoons) survive in your carpets and in areas where your cat sleeps. You would be wasting your time and money if you treat only the animal. The entire environment must treated—all in one day. And don't forget to give special attention to the cat's napping areas. **See chapter 11 for help in preparing a new (previously owned) home *before* you move in.**

Second, know your options for treatment and how to use them. Remember that any misuse of these chemicals can be toxic to both you and your cat. (See treatment options herein.) Carefully read and follow the directions on the packages. If you use too little or do not treat for the specified time, treatments can be ineffective. If you use too much, the results can be disastrous. Some time ago, in an effort to *really* get rid of a flea infestation, an unwise fellow greatly increased the number of recommended flea bombs. The heavy gas concentration was ignited by the pilot light on his stove, blowing up the fleas—and the entire house.

Here's a list of specific don'ts to keep you and your cat out of trouble:

- **Do not** use the same class of insecticides to treat both the premises and the pet. Too much of the same ingredient can easily lead to a toxic overdose. (If you use a premises spray that was not purchased from your Vet, be sure to tell her what insecticide was used.)
- **Do not** use any product on a cat unless it is clearly stated on the label that it's specifically for cats—or unless your Vet recommends the product be used.
- **Do not** use any product on a kitten less than four months old unless the directions clearly state that it can be used on very young kittens—or unless your Vet gives her permission.

- **Do not** use any product more often, or in stronger concentrations, than directed on the package or by your Vet.
- **Do not** put flea collars or powders in the vacuum bag; the fumes can be toxic. **To kill the fleas in the bag, put the entire vacuum cleaner inside a closed-up car on a hot day.** The fleas (in all developmental stages) inside the bag will be killed, and you don't have to throw away a half-empty bag.

WHAT IS THE LIFE CYCLE OF THE FLEA?

William Kern and Nancy Hinkle of the University of Florida have been researching the complex life cycle of the cat flea. By the way, according to Mr. Kern, even the fleas on your dog are cat fleas. Dog fleas, common on Great Britain's dogs, exist here in the United States only on coyotes in the wild.

Cat fleas, even if they're on your dog, start as eggs laid in the animal's hair. Smooth and translucent, these shiny ovals are about one-fiftieth of an inch long (about the size of the period at the end of this sentence). Unable to stick to a host animal, the eggs fall off or are scratched off, usually in areas where the pet spends most of his time.

It can take from two to six days for the eggs to hatch when the temperature is between 55 degrees and 90 degrees Fahrenheit. In winter months, when household heating reduces the humidity below 50 percent, eggs will die before they get a chance to hatch. (Extreme dryness, the kind that bedding gets in a clothes dryer, is a great way to kill the eggs.)

Eggs that remain outside in your yard die with the prolonged coolness that comes with fall in northern states. Ten days at 46 degrees Fahrenheit or more than five days at 37 degrees Fahrenheit also destroy the eggs.

When an egg is ready to hatch, the larva cracks open the shell with a tooth on its head (the tooth disappears with the first molt). The eyeless, legless maggotlike larva becomes a pupa five to thirty-six days after hatching (average time is five to ten days).

The pupa stage, typically lasting between seven to ten days, starts when the larva begins to weave a silken cocoon spun from its own saliva. Inside the house, bits of carpet lint and similar debris help camouflage the cocoon. Even without food, they can remain happily inside their silken wraps for several months, depending on the temperature and humidity.

Adult fleas emerge from the cocoon when a host becomes available. These mature fleas, attracted by carbon dioxide and vibrations, will jump on the cat within seconds after they break out of the cocoon. Once on the cat, they tend to stay put. Feeding on the cat's blood triggers a physiological need for blood, and the flea can't survive more than twenty-four hours off the host animal.

Females will begin to lay eggs after this first feeding and will lay more than their body weight in eggs (twenty-four eggs) daily.

WHAT KINDS OF FLEA PRODUCTS ARE ON THE MARKET AND HOW DO THEY WORK?

Even if you passed the winter in a flea-free house, you can look forward to a new round in the flea fight when the weather warms up—if you have a pet that goes outside. One thing you can do that might help is to spray your yard (especially the shady, damp areas) with a photo-stable insect growth regulator like Torus. Another suggestion: although there is no published information demonstrating that marigolds, pennyroyal and mums repel fleas, many gardeners believe they can help.

No matter what antiflea treatment (s) you decide to use, remember that a healthy cat on a quality diet will be a less attractive target to fleas and better able to withstand the assault from the few that do bite.

The two charts below compare flea product types. Ideally, you want to combine effectiveness with safety for your cat and for the environment.

Comparison Chart: Flea Products to Be Used on the Cat

Product	Relative Cost	How It Works	Advantages	Disadvantages
Flea comb	Not expensive	Use daily to remove fleas and kill them.	No chemicals or damage to the environment; improves effectiveness of other treatments. Many cats enjoy the attention.	Time-consuming (must comb daily); more effective on short hair than long hair; elimination of fleas is difficult.
Nutritional support (brewer's yeast, garlic)	Not expensive	Fleas are repelled by the change in body odor from B vitamins and from garlic (not proven).	No chemicals; no pollution or trauma to cat; most cats love the taste; improves coat.	Value is anecdotal; research hasn't proved effectiveness.
Sulfur products	Moderate expense	Fleas are repelled by the odor of sulfur from food additives or from shampoo.	Nontoxic to pets; no pollution. Food additives are easy to use.	Works slowly; cats don't like shampoos.
Proban (brand name)	Not expensive	Insecticide is swallowed;	None.	Not approved for cats be-

Product	Relative Cost	How It Works	Advantages	Disadvantages
		flea is killed when it bites.		cause of toxicity; fleas still must bite before being killed.
Chemical flea collars*	Not expensive	They contain insecticides that kill fleas. Use collars for three-day periods only; store in airtight container.	Controls fleas at head and helps with tail; neat and clean.	See note below this chart.
Herbal collars	Not expensive	Contains herbs reputed to repel fleas. Suggested herbs: bay, eucalyptus.	No chemicals or pollution; gentle to cat, usually nonirritating. Pleasant odor.	May not be strong enough for heavy infestation. Many can be toxic if ingested. Do not use pennyroyal oil; use dried leaves only.
Dips—do it yourself	Not expensive	Cat is soaked with insecticides, which are allowed to dry on him.	Kills fleas on cat and has some residual action; only treat every six to eight weeks.	Toxic if not mixed correctly. Some cats are difficult to treat because of wetness. Once mixed, dip can't be stored; leftover dip is toxic waste.
Dips—done at groomer or Vet	Expensive	Cat is soaked with insecticides, which are allowed to dry on him.	Kills fleas on cat and has some residual action; only treat every six to eight weeks.	Some cats traumatized by the procedure; leftover dip may pollute environment.
Chemical flea shampoo— do it yourself	Not expensive	Cat is bathed with shampoo containing insecticides. Leave shampoo on for specified time.	Kills fleas on cat during the shampoo.	Some cats detest being wet. No residual action.

Product	Relative Cost	How It Works	Advantages	Disadvantages
Chemical flea shampoo—done at groomer or Vet	Expensive	Cat is bathed with shampoo containing insecticides.	Kills fleas on cat during the shampoo.	Some cats detest being wet. No residual action.
Herbal flea shampoos	Not expensive	Cat is bathed with shampoo containing herbs that repel (not kill) fleas.	Nonpolluting; rids cat of fleas for that day.	These have no residual action. Treatment can be traumatizing to cat.
Chemical insecticide sprays	Varies with brand.	Cat is sprayed with the chemical; all fur must be damp. To reduce stress to the cat, try to use a pump spray or mousse to eliminate aerosol hissing sound.	Kills fleas on cat, with residual action, but effectiveness varies with brand; best is pyrethrin based with fenoxycarb or methoprene growth regulators. Works fast.	Some are more damaging to the cat and to the environment than others. Some cats hate the sound, odor and dampness. Cat ingests insecticide because he grooms immediately; can be toxic if used too often. Some have disagreeable odor.
Insecticide powder[†]	Not expensive	Fleas are killed by the powder after it's worked into the cat's coat and spread around the house.	Kills the fleas; easy to use.	Messy. Many cats object to the mess. Cat ingests insecticide while grooming. Cats and people with lung problems should not be around powder.
Citrus oils[‡]	Not expensive	Shampoo kills fleas. Use diluted shampoo only.	Nonpolluting; kills fleas and deodorizes fur.	Never use this in spray (oil) form—toxic to cats. Shampoo has no residual effect.

*If you must use a chemical flea collar, put it on for three days and remove it. Flea-comb the cat and put it back on only if the fleas become a problem again. Store the collar in an airtight container between uses. Chemical flea collars may not kill all the fleas, especially on the tail. Some may be bad for the environment and they can cause an allergic skin reaction in some cats—particularly longhaired cats, who may even develop permanent hair loss under the collar. These collars can be inactivated by water, but while they are working, they expose the cat to constant unnecessary chemicals. Prolonged use also increases the flea population's resistance to the collar insecticides.

†See following chart for further information on active ingredients.

‡Some cats are prone to adverse reactions to citrus oil shampoos. If he begins salivating or develops evidence of nervous system involvement, immediately rinse the shampoo with lots of clear water and towel-dry the cat. Call your Vet if the symptoms persist.

Comparison Chart: Flea Products for Use in the House

Product	Relative Cost	How It Works	Advantages	Disadvantages
Sprays used on the premises†	Varies with the brand.	The house, not the cat, is sprayed.	Kills fleas on contact; residual action with some brands. Best is pyrethrin based with insect growth regulators. Cat is not bothered by sound or dampness.	Some may be damaging to the environment or have disagreeable odor. Outside the U.S., some may be ozone-damaging aerosols.
Fogger—do it yourself†	Not expensive	House is prepared (animals and plants removed; foodstuffs and equipment covered). House is sealed; fogger is started and left for time specified on label.	Kills fleas, with residual action.	All pets, people and plants must be removed till after house has been aired. Food prep equipment must be washed after treatment. Some pets and people are sensitive to chemicals. Some may be polluting.
Fogger—by pest control company	Expensive	House is prepared (animals and plants removed; foodstuffs and equipment	Kills fleas, with residual action.	You may not know the chemicals used. All pets, people and plants must be removed till after

135

Product	Relative Cost	How It Works	Advantages	Disadvantages
		covered). House is sealed; fogger is started and left for time specified by the company.		house has been aired. Food prep equipment must be washed after treatment. Some pets and people are sensitive to chemicals. Some may be polluting.
Ultrasonics	Expensive	Unit gives off high-frequency sounds that are supposed to repel fleas.	None.	Ineffective. Causes hearing loss in dogs; may cause hearing damage in cats.
Light traps	Expensive	Unit attracts fleas with heat/light; fleas drop into water or onto sticky paper.	No chemicals, pollution or trauma to cat.	Questionable effectiveness —has not been proven. Pan of plain warm water will catch fleas. Will not eliminate all fleas.
Regular vacuuming	Not expensive	Eggs and adults feces are vacuumed up. (Feces are food for larvae which are not vacuumed up.) Change bag every ten days or put vacuum in closed-up car in summer to kill eggs.	No chemicals, pollution or trauma to cat; improves effectiveness of other methods.	Useful only in addition to other treatments. If the bag is not heat-treated or discarded after use, eggs hatch in bag and adult fleas crawl out. Will not stop an infestation.
Steam-cleaning carpets (not chemical dry cleaning)	Moderately expensive	Heat from steam kills all flea stages. Eliminates larval food in carpet fibers.	Kills all flea stages. Helps prevent infestation. Effective immediately.	Takes time and physical labor to use.

Product	Relative Cost	How It Works	Advantages	Disadvantages
		(See question on nonchemical premises treatments on page 142.)		
Fuller's earth or diatomaceous earth (diatomite at health food stores)	Not expensive	It's dusted in cat's resting places; eggs and larvae are damged by the tiny pieces of shell and die from dehydration. Leave it down indefinitely. Humidity must be 50 percent or less for it to work. Never feed it to the cat!	No chemicals, easy to use.	Has been associated with lung damage from the silica and it works slowly. Can be messy (but not as bad as powders). Effective in low humidity only.
Borax, boric acid powder (EPA-labeled)	Not expensive	It's dusted in carpet and cat's resting areas; kills flea larvae. Works until carpet is shampooed. Follow directions on container.	Easy to use. Effective. Kills larvae.	Works slowly; can be messy; particle size must be correct; should be EPA-approved.** Won't kill adult fleas. Cannot be used outdoors; kills any plant!
Boric acid from pest control	Medium expensive	Applied to carpeting; kills flea larvae. Works until carpet is shampooed. Follow directions.	Effective. Kills larvae.	Works slowly; must be EPA-approved and professionally applied. Won't kill adult fleas. Cannot be used outdoors; kills any plant!
Citrus-based cleaners	Not expensive	Cleaner used in home. Kills all flea life stages.	Nonpolluting. Kills all flea life stages. Deodorizes.	Can be toxic if ingested by the cat.

Product	Relative Cost	How It Works	Advantages	Disadvantages
Insect growth regulators (methoprene and fenoxy- carb)	Moderately expensive	Kills larvae by preventing fleas from pu- pating; they never be- come the blood-feeding adult stage.	Low toxicity in mammals. Effective at low con- centrations. Kills larvae; sterilizes ex- isting adults.	Works slowly. Methoprene not photo- stable— don't use it out- side.
Insecticide powders[†]	Not expen- sive	Fleas are killed by the powder after it is spread around the car- pet and in the cat's resting places.	Kills fleas; easy to use.	Messy. Many cats and people object to the mess. Cat in- gests insecti- cide while grooming. Cats and peo- ple with lung problems should not be around the powder.

[†]See following section for further information on active ingredients.

**The EPA-approved boric acid is the safest to use because if the particles are too large, the product is not effective, and if too small, the particles become an airborne health harzard when inhaled. Borax (brand name) is a boric acid salt and its particles are too large to be really useful.

WHAT SHOULD I KNOW ABOUT THE ACTIVE INGREDIENTS IN FLEA CONTROL PRODUCTS?

The environmentally safest way to deal with fleas is to prevent the worst of the problem by keeping your pet indoors and in good health, vacuuming regularly and flea combing daily. If fleas have already invaded, stronger measures are in order. But, before buying a flea treatment, know the safety of the chemicals involved.

Many good flea treatments for your house, and some for your cat, contain a combination of an insect growth regulator (IGR) and a botanical (pyrethrin). The botanical kills the adult fleas present but most have no residual action. The IGRs stop the growth cycle of the fleas by interfering with the insect's hormones; the larva dies and the flea never becomes an adult. Insect growth regulators with methoprene (like Precor) and fenoxycarb (like Sustain, Basis, Ectogard) can be used on your cat. IRGs are incredibly effective (if used correctly). Not only do they have long residual action, but they have a very low level of toxicity for both cats and humans. For example, a cat would have to eat eight times his body weight to consume a lethal dose of fenoxycarb. Still, read labels and use appropri- ately! Some IGRs may have added ingredients and are suitable for premises use only. Better yet, buy these products only through your Vet, for uses approved by your Vet.

If you want to treat your yard, use Torus or another photo-stable IGR brand (the chemical can work outdoors in the sunlight). Many other IGRs aren't photo-stable and are effective outside for only three hours before they break down.

In the February 1990 issue of *Shelter Sense*, a newsletter put out by the Humane Society of the United States, classes of chemicals were evaluated and recommendations were made. The Humane Society of the United States does not recommend any form of the following types of chemicals for flea control on cats. (They will be listed under "active ingredients.")

Carbamates
    "Cholinesterase inhibitors"
    Bendiocarb
    Carbaryl
    Methylcarbamates
    Propoxur
Chlorinated Hydrocarbons ("sodium channel blockers")
    Lindane
    Methoxychlor
Organophosphates
    "Cholinesterase inhibitors"
    Chlorfenvinphos,
    Chlorpyrifos
    Cythioate
    Diazinon
    Dichlorvos
    Dioxathion
    Fenthion
    Malathion
    Naled
    Parathion
    Phosmet
    Ronnel
    Temephos
    Tetrachlorvinphos

The following botanicals *are* recommended by the Humane Society for use if you must use insecticides. These chemicals tend to be nontoxic to mammals and are unlikely to move up the food chain—although some people and cats can have an allergic reaction to pyrethrins. Some *synthetic* pyrethrins have residual effect. Read labels.

Pyrethrins
    Pyrethrins (from chrysanthemums)
Synthetic Pyrethrins, including
    Allethrin
    Fenvalerate

D-phenothrin
Permethrin
Resmethrin
Tetramethrin

The citrus oils linalool and d-limonene, in a diluted shampoo, are safe for cats; do not spray concentrated oils on a cat. You might also ask your Vet about a citrus oil premises spray.

CAN I IMPROVE FLEA CONTROL BY USING SEVERAL PRODUCTS?

You must treat both the cat and the environment to eliminate all fleas, and you have to be careful about what you use. While you may get toxic combinations from combining the wrong insecticides, most insecticide overdoses result when the same class of insecticide is used in different forms (home, bath, collar, spray treatments). The amount of one chemical becomes so high that the animal is poisoned. The best approach is to use different classes of insecticides which can be combined safely.

One effective approach is to use combinations of borate powders (premises only), pyrethrins and insect growth regulators. For example, you might treat your house with an IGR or boric acid to kill all the developing larvae. (IGRs, specifically for use on the cat, will sterilize the adult fleas too.) Then treat the animal with a pyrethrin product and flea-comb to remove any stunned (still living) fleas. Again, read labels, and if you are at all unsure about flea treatment, check with your Vet.

HOW CAN I SAFELY USE CHEMICAL SPRAYS?

Read the directions on the can or bottle and follow them carefully. The following are some rule-of-thumb guidelines for safe use.

- Know what kind of spray you're using and the conditions for its most effective use.
  - Some are for use on the **animal only**, some are to be used on the **premises only** and some are labeled for use on **both**.
  - Some are meant to be sprayed until the item or cat is damp and some are not.
- Spray all fabric, carpet and wood floors where fleas live and breed. Give special attention to the cat's resting places, where fleas gather.
- Wash your hands after using chemical sprays.
- If you use a premises-only spray on the carpets, do not let your cat in the area until the carpet is dry.

When Spraying the Cat

- Spray the cat on his legs, stomach, tail and back. Spray **against** the grain of his fur so the spray penetrates to the skin.

- Do **not** spray his face. Spray your fingers or a cloth and rub it on his face. Avoid getting it on his nose and in his eyes.
- If he fights the spray, you can try one or more of these ideas:
  — Change to a nonaerosol pump spray or to a different treatment option.
  — Keep the hissing spray at a distance by spraying your hand or a cloth and using that to apply the spray to the cat.
- If you must restrain the cat, try using a cat sack, described earlier.
- Wash your hands after using the sprays.

SHOULD I REMOVE MY PETS WHEN I USE SPRAYS AND BOMBS?

Yes. While the directions on insecticide bombs are clear with respect to removing pets, spray cans may indicate that animals may be inside while the house is being sprayed. After you read the directions, ask yourself if you'd like your nose and mouth near floor level when the carpets are being treated. Remove the animals—if only into a closed-off room with plenty of fresh air.

HOW DO I USE POWDERS?

Powders, like sprays, have specific uses. For example, boric acid is meant to be used **only** on the inside premises and is particularly effective on carpeting. Some commercial chemical powders can be used on both the cat and the premises. While herbal powders are meant to be used on collars or on the premises, they must **never** be sprinkled on a cat.

Read the directions on the container and follow them carefully. It's best if you use powders in a well-ventilated area. The following are some other rule-of-thumb ideas for powdering your cat:

- Do not get the powder in his nose, ears or mouth.
- Work the powder into his fur so it reaches the skin and the fleas.
- Wash your hands after using the powders.

WHAT ARE THE SYMPTOMS OF INSECTICIDE OVERDOSE?

If he shows these symptoms soon after you apply any insecticide (flea treatment), call your Vet **immediately** and tell her what product was used (read from the container). The symptoms to look for are: salivation, diarrhea or vomiting, panting or shallow breathing, loss of coordination, weakness, convulsions, severe behavioral changes and tremors.

WHAT NONCHEMICAL PREMISES TREATMENTS ARE THERE?

Steam-cleaning the carpet is one of the safest, simplest, most effective flea control strategies available. Done right, it eliminates **all** life stages of the flea, and simultaneously cleans up the larval food. So if eggs are deposited later, the larvae starve to death. Steam-cleaning also gives immediate results—there's no waiting for chemicals to work, and you get a clean-looking carpet in the bargain. The best approach is to treat your animals when you steam-clean the carpet. Then, within a week, treat the newly cleaned carpet with an IGR (Torus or Precor) so that fleas will subsequently be unable to develop in the carpet, even if they're brought back into the house. If you're moving, steam-clean and treat the carpets in the new residence before you move in!

Regular vacuuming, when the bag is heat-treated (see above) or sealed in plastic and discarded after each use, is a great help—as is keeping the cat inside. Any treatment, whether chemical or nonchemical, will work better if you combine it with a daily flea combing.

WHAT IS A FLEA COMB?

A flea comb is a small comb with thin closely set teeth. It removes fleas, flea eggs and debris such as flea feces from the cat's fur. Since adult fleas stay with the host animal, a flea comb is an important weapon in your arsenal.

Make sure you get a flea comb with metal teeth; plastic teeth are too flexible. Also, some flea combs are made for fine hair, coarse hair, etc. Unfortunately, fleas are all about the same size, regardless of the texture of an animal's coat. If the teeth on the comb are set wide apart for coarse hair, it's doubtful that the comb will do an effective job picking up fleas.

HOW DO I USE A FLEA COMB?

First, check the fur for mats and remove them. Take short, firm strokes through the fur with the flea comb, checking the comb's teeth for fleas as you go. Work with the grain of the fur, and let the teeth gently penetrate clear down to the skin. Be careful not to scrape the skin with the comb. Clean the fur, eggs and debris from the comb as needed.

When you find a flea, select one of the following methods to kill it.

- Use your fingernails to squash the flea. Wash your hands (and nails) when finished.
- Use your fingers to pull the flea from the comb. Drop the flea (with or without accumulated fur) into soapy water. Leftover dishwater will work just fine. You may need to swirl the water to get the fur to sink, and let the water set for a couple of hours to make sure the fleas are dead.

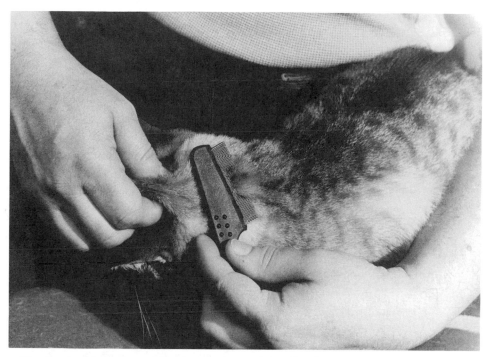

The flea comb is a specialized grooming tool that lifts fleas out of the cat's coat by means of its very fine, closely spaced teeth. It is very important to get behind the ears with a flea comb as these pests often gather there.

After checking the backs of your cat's ears, using the flea comb, go through the coat as thoroughly as possible for any other lurking fleas.

Note: For quicker killing, use rubbing alcohol, although it may offend the cat's nose. With alcohol, make sure you rinse your fingers before combing again.

- Quickly dip the comb with flea into water with liquid soap floating on it. Rinse the comb and continue. While this method of removal limits your physical contact with the fleas, there is the danger that they can jump off the comb before the comb reaches the water.

HOW DO I USE BREWER'S YEAST AND GARLIC?

While there is no published scientific evidence that these substances really work, many owners swear by the results. In any case, the yeast does help maintain a healthy coat. Read labels on yeast containers, the same as you would for any product. There are brewer's yeast powders, with and without garlic, made for dogs and cats, as well as products sold for humans. If you use a product meant for humans, use the brewer's yeast powder, not the flakes, since the flakes can contain too much magnesium, which can promote FUS.

- Use powdered brewer's yeast and/or chopped or pressed fresh garlic, or commercial yeast pills. Most cats like garlic!
- Add the yeast and/or garlic to the cat's food. Give about ½ to ¾ teaspoon of yeast per meal; give ½ small clove of garlic per meal. Sprinkle the yeast on canned food or mix it into the dry food. Moisten dry food with water and sprinkle the yeast on the dampened food—or just add it to the dry food and let the cat lick the bowl clean.

HOW DO I USE SULFUR PRODUCTS?

Use only commercial preparations specifically marketed for cats. You can find these products at your local pet store or in catalogs.

Either feed sulfur to the cat or shampoo it into the cat's fur. When adding a sulfur supplement to food, sprinkle it on canned food or mix it in. The sulfur can be sprinkled on dry food that has been dampened with water. If sulfur is added to unmoistened dry food, the cat will have to lick the bowl to ingest the sulfur, and he may not be terribly willing. Make sure that you use only the amounts listed in the package directions.

If he must be bathed to get the sulfur, you'll need to bathe him **only** in a sulfur shampoo. Other shampoos will strip the sulfur out of his hair and destroy the residual effect. Follow the directions on the container.

HOW CAN I KILL FLEAS IN PILLOWS AND OTHER ITEMS I DON'T WANT TO SPRAY?

Machine-washing with hot water will help with items you regularly wash, like bedding. But if the item can't be washed, just run it in the dryer, on high heat, for at least twenty to thirty minutes to kill the flea at any life stage. (Read labels and make sure that the item can survive the intense heat **before** you put it in the dryer.)

CAN A CEDAR-FILLED CAT BED REPEL FLEAS?

Cedar does repel fleas, but it may be unsafe to use. The House Rabbit Society has reported that the fumes from cedar can damage rabbits' livers. The final answer with respect to cats—and rabbits—is still unsettled because the rabbit studies weren't scientifically validated. Cats and rabbits do have several physiological similarities, so other cat-bed fillers may be better for your pet.

HOW CAN I SAFELY REMOVE TICKS?

With tweezers, grasp the tick close to the cat's skin and slowly and steadily pull the tick straight out. If you have some peroxide handy, saturate a piece of cotton and dab it on the wound. Don't pour peroxide or alcohol on the site, because it leaves too much to be ingested when grooming.

If you think the tick may be a deer tick and are concerned about Lyme disease, put the tick in alcohol to kill it and then take it to your Vet for identification.

WILL STINGING BUGS HURT MY CAT?

Yes! **Do not** let your cat eat, play with or hunt scorpions, brown recluse spiders, black widow spiders, fire ants, wasps, bees or hornets.

If you suspect your cat has been bitten or stung by a poisonous insect, see chapter 21. You may need to get your cat immediately to the Vet. If veterinary treatment isn't available, you can call the Poison Control Center at the numbers listed in chapter 13.

Not all bugs are dangerous, so learn what dangerous insects are indigenous to your area and find out how to recognize them. Your local public library, county extension agent and Vet are good resources.

Other than stinging and poisonous critters, it won't harm your cat to eat bugs.

If your cat enjoys "bugging," don't use any bug spray except flea sprays labeled safe for cats. Flea sprays will usually kill other household insect pests, including wasps.

11

Playtime, Travel and Pet Sitters

PLAY IS ESSENTIAL in the development of a sane and healthy cat, and it helps keep him fit and alert throughout his life. While a cat conserves his resources (i.e., sleeps) for much of the day, he'll want things to do when he's awake. If you don't provide safe and sane playthings, he'll devise his own. You may not appreciate his ideas of fun. Chapter 20 has directions for homemade cat toys.

Does your cat like to travel? This chapter will also help you reduce stress for the nontraveler and make traveling safer for the gadabout.

WHY AND HOW LONG SHOULD I PLAY WITH MY CAT?

Daily playtime helps keep your cat alert, content, slender and young. In addition, the interaction will let you catch health problems earlier; you'll notice a lack of coordination, fatigue or signs of pain when your pet tries to play. Play also deepens the cat-human relationship and reduces stress for you both.

Set aside at least five to ten minutes for daily play. For oldsters, ill, disabled or overweight cats, talk to your Vet before starting an exercise program. Most cats enjoy the activity so much that if you set a consistent playtime, they'll remind you if you forget.

WHAT GAMES CAN I PLAY WITH MY CAT?

Try the following games, but make sure you match the game to your cat's personality. Shy, timid cats will probably not enjoy exploring or taking a walk. If your cat becomes frightened or otherwise distressed, stop immediately.

UFO

In a darkened room, direct the light from a flashlight for the cat to chase.

Mouse

Get some hairy twine with a large knot in it or a large ring or a catnip mouse tied to the end. Drag it around the house, around and under things—places a mouse would run.

Bird

This game is similar to mouse, but the item is kept in the air and lands only occasionally.

Exploring

Let your cat explore closets or rooms usually closed off. Lift him up to explore the tops of doors and other inaccessible areas.

Treasure Hunt

Lock your cat in his carrier or the bathroom while you hide pieces of his dry food (as in an Easter egg hunt). Put food only where you usually allow him to go. Let him out and watch him hunt for the food. To keep him from getting fat, use some of his regular meals for this game.

Fetch

Toss a lightweight toy such as a small piece of wadded-up paper and let your cat catch and share the "prey" with you.

Walking

Using a harness and leash, take him to the park, around the block—or just out in the backyard.

WHAT IS CATNIP AND IS IT GOOD FOR MY CAT?

Catnip belongs to the mint family and is easily grown both outdoors and indoors in sunny locations. These plants can become quite large—up to two or three feet tall—if planted outside.

The scent of the plant oil nepetalactrone attracts wild and domestic cats. While some cats eat catnip, the physical effect comes from smelling it, and not all cats react to the smell of catnip. One-third of adult cats have no reaction to catnip, nor do most kittens under six months old. Also, frightened or angry cats that normally react to catnip may not be affected by the smell. However, most cats fall happily under catnip's influence, although their responses vary widely.

Reaction to catnip is hereditary, and the nonaddictive effect lowers the cat's inhibitions. The "high" usually lasts from five to twenty minutes. Most cats who react to the plant have a burst of energy and engage in their favorite activities (eating, playing, hunting, mating or even "meditating"), and then become very relaxed.

A few cats are so stimulated by catnip that they'll attack anything when they've been nipped by catnip. Because these sensitive animals react so strongly, they can be dangerous. It's better to have them forgo catnip altogether, or to confine them in a cage or crate while they enjoy.

If fresh catnip is given before a stressful event, the cat may handle the situation better. Cats will receive the most benefit from fresh catnip if it's given sparingly only two to three times a week. Too much fresh catnip can lead to long-term side effects like confusion and disorientation. It's also hard to store fresh catnip, although it can be kept like fresh-cut flowers in a vase.

Fresh catnip can be dried for storage. Rubber-band three or four stalks together and hang them **upside down** in a cool, dry, dark place. Catnip can take several weeks to dry. The idea is to keep it hanging until it's dry enough to crumble. When it's finally dry, it's ready to use or store.

Dried catnip is less potent than fresh and can be offered daily in toys and on scratching posts.

Whether you buy or grow catnip, remember that fresh catnip is the strongest, followed in descending order of potency: frozen; dried leaves; dried leaves and blossoms; dried leaves and blossoms in fine particles; finely ground leaves, blossoms, stems and sticks.

Good-quality dried catnip, of any grade, should have a clean, minty smell and a green color; dark brown or black catnip is stale. If the smell is not right, it may be moldy. Mold or mold-causing dampness can make the catnip clump. Look for dried catnip that moves freely without appearing dusty or powdery when you shake the bag, And to keep the dried catnip fresh, store it in a cool, dark place in a tightly closed jar or plastic bag. Make sure that you put it in a place your cat can't get into.

DO CATS ENJOY WALKS?

Some cats enjoy taking walks on a leash and harness, and some are too timid and feel unprotected on a leash. While cats don't learn to walk at heel like a dog, many like being outside and experience a doglike joy over the freedom a walk can bring.

Because cats won't walk at heel, you'll need to control more of his wandering. **Never** use a collar with the leash for restraint; connect the leash only to a body harness that does not put any pressure on the cat's neck. Cats have delicate necks and can be injured easily. Make sure the harness has been adjusted for a snug fit—just loose enough to allow you to slide one finger under the straps.

Some cats enjoy riding (and feel more secure) in a backpack where they can view the world from a high and safe place. If you have an old Gerry Pack for toddlers, sew some material over the leg holes and let your cat try it. Don't forget to use a harness and leash on the cat too. If he decides to jump out and explore on his own, you can reel him back in.

However your cat enjoys his walk, take along small plastic bags to pick up feces for discard in a trash can.

WHAT SHOULD I LET MY CAT PLAY WITH?

Let him play with the "good toys" in the chart below. Remember to leave toys out while you are gone and rotate them weekly, so toys stay fresh and your cat doesn't become bored. He may also enjoy it if the toys are stored in his **dry** cat food or in a bag of catnip for that special aroma.

Toy Chart

Good Toys	Toys to Avoid
Corks, unsharpened pencils, drinking straws	Objects with sharp edges
Paper grocery sack (Turn edges back for longer play.)	Small items that can be swallowed
Empty thread spool	Glass and other fragile items
Paper wads and lightweight balls	Ribbons or strings (when unsupervised)
Plastic bottle caps	Objects with small parts that can be chewed off and swallowed
Catnip mouse	Soft rubber that can be chewed
Bird feeder to watch, not a base of operations for a hunt	Anything painted
Kitty condo; see chapter 20 for this and other toy design ideas.	People parts; do not allow cat to claw or bite fingers, toes, etc.

Kitty gym (Hang toys on heavy string from doorway or crossbar of a chair so cat can attack toy.)	Plastic bags

WHY DO CATS "GET THE CRAZIES" IN THE EVENING OR LATE AT NIGHT?

Some cats will play, hard and loud, in the late evening or nighttime. Cats are nocturnal animals, and night is the time most wild cats hunt. If your cat is wound up nightly, and ready to do something or anything, it's a good time for a rousing game, especially if his playfulness is keeping you awake. If wearing him out with games makes him tired but not tired enough to sleep when you want to sleep, feed him his large meal right before bed.

VACATIONS, TRAVELING AND YOUR CAT

Before you and your cat travel, take him to a friend's home, to a public place or to a business. Unless the area has been catproofed, keep your cat on his leash and harness to protect both your pet and the host's property.

Keep in mind that the extra stress and crowds at holiday times can make traveling harder for all involved. Plan ahead! Leave yourself extra time and anticipate the unexpected. Pets do get lost, so every traveling cat needs identification. Put tags on a collar with a quick-release buckle or on an elastic collar.

It is also wise to take a travel litter box (see chapter 5) on even short trips. If you are at all unsure of your cat's acceptance of the temporary box, use clean litter from his box at home. This litter already carries his scent and, unlike new litter, will strongly attract him to the box.

WHEN SHOULD A CAT NOT TRAVEL FOR FUN?

Some cats should forgo joyriding (with the exception of regular Vet visits):

- Very young kittens (less than five months old) because their immune system is not mature enough
- Senior cats (more than ten years old), unless they have been joyriding for years, still enjoy it, and their Vet approves
- A cat or kitten who is ill or still recovering from surgery or illness
- A female who is in heat, close to heat or pregnant
- Very fearful/shy cats or aggressive cats

CAN A CAT BE TAUGHT TO BE A GOOD TRAVELER IN THE CAR?

The easiest way to teach a cat to love traveling is to start when your cat is young, take short trips and give him plenty of praise for good behavior. Short, fun excursions (a visit to a friend or to a pet store), with a treat for your cat at the trip's end, are extremely important. The cat who travels only to see the Vet won't be a good traveler, because he expects a shot or thermometer during every trip.

Any cat can learn better car manners if you're consistently gentle but firm. Do **not** reward or encourage any behavior you don't want repeated. Reward only those behaviors you want the cat to develop into habits.

Even car sickness can be avoided. Test him to see if he travels better after a meal or after fasting. This is an individual response, but many cats do better on an empty stomach.

Most states require that animals be restrained in a moving car so they can't wander, distract the driver or attempt to jump out an open window. You have two options for restraint:

- Use a carrier with the seat belt fastened through the handle. Do not open a crate in the car or outdoors; travel can stressful and any cat may take off.
- Use a harness with the leash fastened to the seat belt. (Make sure the leash is tied so it's short enough to restrict his wandering onto the driver—or out the window.) Do not use a collar or harness that puts any strain on the cat's neck; in an accident the neck can easily be injured or broken. And if you are worried about bowel or bladder accidents, cover the seat with a waterproof plastic table-cloth and lay an absorbent towel over the plastic.

Some cats prefer to travel in their carriers, closed in and safe, while more adventurous personalities prefer to travel in a harness so they can look out the window and howl at passing cars.

Whatever his mode of travel, **never** leave an animal in a standing car for more than a few minutes. The temperature can rise to a lethal level in fifteen minutes or less in the summer. Even in the spring and fall, the temperature in a car climbs very quickly. If your cat begins panting, he is in danger of heat exhaustion; see chapter 21 for instructions.

HOW FAST DOES A CAR HEAT UP?

At an outside temperature of 85 degrees Fahrenheit, with the windows open less than two inches, a car will heat up to 102 degrees in ten minutes. After twenty minutes, the temperature can reach 120 degrees. Even in the shade, the same car can heat up to lethal temperatures in a short time.

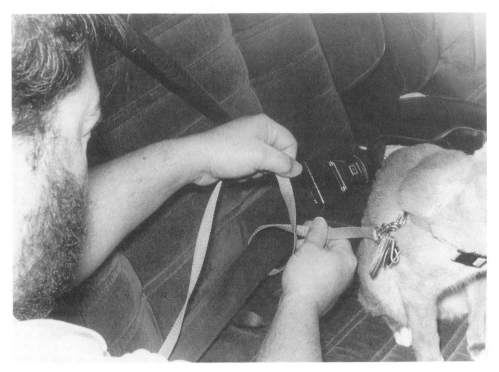

A cat may be transported in a car in its carrier or wearing a harness and the leash securely tied to a seat belt as shown.

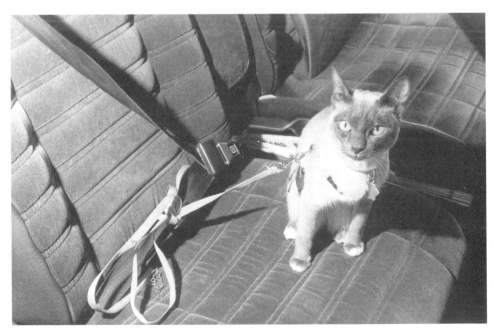

If you use the harness-leash-seat belt method in the car, be sure to tie the leash very short so the cat cannot wander.

HOW DO I DEAL WITH CAR SICKNESS?

In general, car sickness is an indication of stress. Dr. Margaret Reister, in her *Cat Fancy* column, suggests that camomile helps. One-eighth to one-quarter of a teaspoon of loose camomile leaves and blossoms, given once or twice daily, helps calm motion sickness, and the same dosage may be used for stress relief. If you don't have camomile, Calms and Bach remedies may be of some use.

HOW CAN I TRAVEL IN A PLANE WITH MY CAT?

Airlines vary widely in their policies for traveling pets—and policies do change. While we give current (1994) information and recommendations to show the variety of airline offerings, do request a rundown of specific regulations when making arrangements.

Temperature travel restrictions will probably continue to vary among carriers. With few exceptions, cargo bays are pressurized and the temperature regulated; the restrictions primarily exist to protect the animal from extremes of heat or cold on the tarmac while they wait to board or transfer flights. Even if you know your temperature facts and are safely booked, it's still a good idea to check with the airline the day before the cat travels, to ascertain the weather status.

All flying felines will need a current health certificate, and to make sure you conform to every airline's idea of "current," get the certificate within a week of your travel date. These veterinary healthy documents certify that the cat is immunized and healthy enough to withstand the rigors of travel.

When You Fly with Your Cat

Most national air carriers allow you to crate your cat in an under-seat kennel for travel with you in the cabin.

While most airlines require you to pay for a pet's "ticket" at the airport, some do allow you to prepay for your cat's passage.

Book your reservation well ahead of your flight—usually only two in-cabin pets are allowed per flight, one in coach and one in first class. To be safe, **make reservations four weeks in advance**.

It is best to check in at least one hour before flight time. Early check-in will also give you plenty of time to buy an airline crate if you need one. (Most airlines sell crates, but if you anticipate traveling, you can get a similar carrier for less by mail order through catalogs. If you need an airline crate for either in-cabin or cargo travel, be sure to tell the airline when you place your reservation.

Transatlantic air pet travel will cost more than the domestic rate, and your cat will be subject to any international quarantine restrictions. Quarantine is also a must if you're going to Hawaii. In-cabin travel isn't an option on these really long flights, so your cat travels as cargo. Call the airline, and plan ahead.

When Your Cat Travels Alone

If your pet is traveling without you, higher rates will apply, and you might want to employ a professional animal shipper. Timing and red tape can lead to unexpected complications. If you decide to ship the cat yourself, contact the airline six weeks early to get a copy of its shipping procedures and regulations.

TRAVEL GUIDELINES

Whether your cat travels in the cabin or as cargo, do **not** give him tranquilizers unless directed by your Vet, because tranquilizers can depress breathing. If you feel you must tranquilize the cat, ask your Vet to test his reaction to the drugs a few weeks ahead. Some cats don't respond well and become upset with the loss of control. Even so, there's no foolproof way to know how an animal will respond once he's on the plane.

In a Plane as Cargo

Remember, even if you are booked on the same flight, **never** ship a kitten under the age of three months, a cat older than ten years or an ill or pregnant cat without the full approval of your Vet.

We also recommend that you tape a resealable document envelope to the crate. Documents should include:

- A copy of the cat's health certificate
- Names and addresses of: owner, Veterinarian and friend/contact person at both ends of the trip
- Time of the cat's last food and water, **prior** to boarding
- A twenty-four-hour feeding schedule (in case the cat is delayed in transit)

While each airline has its own guidelines, here are some general, common-sense rules.

- Do **not** feed the cat within one hour of the flight.
- The **cargo crate**
  — Must be strong enough to withstand thrown luggage.
  — Must be shaped to allow air circulation. The center of the sides must be slightly wider than the top and bottom.
  — Must have food and water bowls.
  — Should be lined with disposable diapers, Chucks or folded newspapers to absorb accidents.
  — Should be clearly marked with "Live Animal" labels, destination address, home address and an emergency phone of a third person. You can use stick-on labels or tie-on tags. This information can be on the outside of the resealable envelope recommended above.
- Book the cat on a through summer flight in the early morning or late afternoon when the outside temperature is between 40 and 75 degrees Fahrenheit.

In a Plane Traveling with You in the Cabin

Flying in the cabin with you is the safest way for your friend to travel. For the best flight experience:

- Brush the cat to remove loose hair—and if possible, wipe the cat's fur with Allerpet/C to reduce allergic reactions to the cat.
- Do **not** feed the cat within one hour of the flight.
- Use **only** an airline-approved flight cage. This is a small box that fits under the seat. Line it with two or three disposable diapers, Chucks or several layers of folded newspapers in case of accidents. As one layer is soiled, remove and discard it; the next layer will be ready for use.
- For added security, put his harness on and tie the leash to the crate. If the crate has to be opened, he can't escape; any cat may run under the stress of travel.

WILL BUS LINES ALLOW MY CAT TO TRAVEL WITH ME?

Permission for your cat to travel is up to the individual bus company, particularly on a local basis. Inquire of the intended carrier. Almost no transcontinental bus companies allow cats on their buses. Rules do change, however. Again, call ahead for information. If you're planning to have your cat travel without you, a bus is not an option. Animals cannot be shipped by bus.

CAN MY CAT TRAVEL WITH ME ON A TRAIN?

At this time, our national carrier, Amtrak, does not allow cats on board—even in the baggage car. On other lines, if cats are permitted, they are almost always restricted to the baggage compartment. And in most cases, you won't be able to visit the animal unless there is a long stop; check with the conductor when you board. An airline-approved cargo crate would be needed for train transport. See the question herein on airline cargo crate guidelines, and also read the food and tranquilizer caveats.

Make sure you check with the rail company for the latest pet travel policies. Advance reservations are required and prices vary with the line and the length of the trip.

WILL I BE ABLE TO BRING MY CAT WITH ME ON A PASSENGER LINER?

Each shipping line has its own restrictions and regulations. Call your intended carrier and ask about their policies. If permitted, your cat will almost certainly have to travel in the ship's kennels (with the dogs), where you'll be able to visit him during the trip.

HOW CAN HE GO BOATING WITH ME?

While there may be more "boat dogs" than "boat cats," cats are out there living or vacationing on private boats. To make this a safe and pleasant experience, here are a few guidelines:

- Keep a current (within the last six months) health certificate and vaccination listing, with your other paperwork, in a waterproof pouch on the boat.
- Keep the cat inside the cabin or let him out only on a harness and lead, with someone holding the lead or with the lead attached to something. He can go overboard easily and will be next to impossible to find. If he will cooperate, have him wear a flotation vest.
- Store fresh litter (and used) in sealable plastic bags until you can properly dispose of it.
- Store dry food in airtight containers.
- Use a hooded litter box with a lid that locks to help control the spread of litter.
- Keep your cat in the cabin or let him out only on harness and leash while in a strange port of call. Make sure the cabin has good ventilation and won't become too hot or too cold. If he must go out with you, he should travel in a carrier or on harness.

WHAT SHOULD I TAKE WITH US FOR TRAVELING?

The amount of cat gear you pack will be determined by the length of time you'll be away from home. Nail clippers, combs and brushes won't be needed for a trip that lasts less than a week. (Unless you have a longhaired cat who needs grooming daily.)

When you travel in the car, make sure your cat has both harness and leash on, whether he is in or out of the carrier.

Pack the following:

- Health certificate listing vaccinations and the Vet's name and phone number
- Collar with identification tags with travel numbers
- Leash and harness
- Crate or carrier; when he must stay alone, he'll be safer if so confined.
- His usual food (dry or single-serving cans)
- Water; a sudden change can cause upset.
- Bowls for both food and water
- Litter box, scoop and litter. Flushable litter is easiest to deal with. If he's used to other types, add plastic bags for discards.
- Scratching post or boxed catnip cardboard pad
- Rug or towel for the bottom of the crate or carrier
- Toys and treats
- Dish soap to wash bowls. Don't use hotel bar soap.

WILL HOTELS, MOTELS AND AMUSEMENT PARKS ALLOW MY CAT TO VISIT?

Each establishment or chain has its own rules about animals on the premises, so we recommend the following:

- Check with them well ahead of your planned vacation and get their policy **in writing** if possible.
- Some top-quality hotels have kennels. Your pet can stay there instead of in your room.
- Pets are not allowed in amusement parks, but some, like the Disney parks, have kennels.
- Refer to *Take Your Pet USA*, a 45-page book on traveling with your pet.

HOW DO I CARE FOR MY CAT ON MOVING DAY?

Most of us hate moving day, and your feline friend will dislike it even more. Cats are territorial animals who become uncomfortable off their home turf. It's his natural inclination to run when threatened by all the confusion and strangers around him.

To make moving as easy as possible on all concerned, try the following:

- While you're packing up, put the cat in one room (an extra bathroom is good) with all his needs for two to three days. Include the following items:

    Bowls with water and food
    — Litter and litter box
    — A worn item of your apparel bearing your scent
    — Harness or carrier
    — Fresh catnip, if he responds well to it
- Put a large sign on the room's door: "Cat Inside, Do Not Open Door." This way the cat has less chance of getting out and becoming lost or injured—or getting packed up.
- Get all your belongings in the truck, and on the last load take the cat to the new place.
- In the new place, again put the cat and all equipment in one room with the sign.
- When things settle down and the outside door is closed, put his things in place and show him where the litter box, bowls and scratching post are located. Let him explore his new home. (If you moved to a much larger place, give him access to a few rooms at a time.)
- Put some butter or margarine on the top of your cat's paws to make him groom himself. The act of grooming is calming, and as he becomes more calm, he will begin to explore the house more. Once his scent is spread by his dampened paws and increased movement through the rooms, he'll begin to identify the house as his home.
- If it is your practice to let your cat out, wait for three to four weeks. By that time, your cat should understand that the new place is home.

WHAT PRECAUTIONS SHOULD I TAKE IN MY NEW HOME TO PREVENT FLEA INFESTATION AND URINE-MARKING PROBLEMS?

Unless you're moving into a brand-new structure, you should steam-clean all the carpets before you move in. Steam cleaning kills all stages of flea development and removes larval food from the carpet fibers. Within a week of the cleaning, apply an insect growth regulator (like Torus or Precor) to the carpet, to keep fleas from being able to develop if they're brought back into the house.

To help prevent house soiling or marking after your cat moves in, wipe safe surfaces (particularly the walls, one foot from the floor) with white vinegar to eliminate trigger scents.

WHAT CAN I DO WITH THE CAT DURING MY VACATION?

You have three options: your cat can stay home with a cat sitter, the cat can go to a boarding facility or he can go with you.

To determine which option is best for your feline friend, ask yourself these questions:

- *Are there quality boarding facilities in your area and can you afford to leave your cat with them?*
  See the question below for selection criteria for boarding facilities.
- *Do you have a reliable friend who would make a responsible pet sitter?*
  Does your cat have special health needs and will your friend be able to take care of them?
- *Are there professional pet sitters in your area and can you afford to hire one?*
  See the information below for guidelines to be used with professional sitters.
- *How healthy is your cat?*
  Cats with chronic health problems may become more ill with the stress of travel. If he needs special Vet care, will it be available? Does he have special nutritional needs? Will his brand of prescription food be available on this trip?
- *Does your cat enjoy traveling, going to new places and meeting new people?*
  Shy, fearful cats make poor travelers. Is he harness-trained?
- *How long will you be gone?*
  Is there a quarantine period where you are going? Will you be there significantly longer than this period to justify the expense, inconvenience and trauma to the cat?
- *Will your travel schedule allow you time to give more than basic care to the cat?*
  Locking an unattended cat in a motel room for a prolonged period can produce an unhappy pet—and a hefty bill for damages. Lonely cats confined to a carrier can yowl loudly and make everyone miserable.
- *How will you be traveling?*
  There are restrictions and extra charges for pets using public transportation. When you know how you'll be traveling, read the questions above on specific

transportation. Even if you travel in your own car, there are still obstacles to overcome. Remember, the cat can't be left in the car because of the risk of heatstroke. What will you do while you're eating in a restaurant?

- *Where will you be staying?*
  Hotels and motels may not allow pets. There are also restrictions on which public or private camping areas you can use. Many just don't want pets at their facilities.
- *Are you willing to take along all the gear and supplies you need for your cat?*
  See the question above on what to take.

WHAT DO I LOOK FOR WHEN I CHOOSE A BOARDING PLACE FOR MY CAT?

It is best to plan ahead and select your boarding facility well in advance. Good professional places are often booked months ahead in the busy season. Get recommendations before settling on a place. Ask cat-owning friends, neighbors, your Vet and co-workers for their **positive and negative** experiences with boarding agencies. Then call those who received most of the positive recommendations. Here are the important things you'll want to know:

- How do they charge? Is it by the day, or by the activities, or by cage size?
- Do they charge extra for special diets?
- What are the charges you can expect for your particular circumstances?
- How often will the cat be played with, groomed and taken out of his cage?
- Will they provide extras such as out-of-cage playtimes, walks on harness and leash?
- What written records will they keep?
- How much experience do they have with cats?
- What special facilities do they have for cats? Cats should be in a separate room away from dogs and kept in large cages in a sunny location.

After you collect this information by phone, visit the best two or three places to see the buildings and observe how pets, employees and visitors are treated by the staff.

And last but not least, when you choose your boarder, ask for a written list of their services and guarantees.

HOW DO I CHOOSE A PET SITTER?

See the question above. In addition to the applicable questions for boarding facilities, you'll need to know how often they will come to your home and how long they will stay. Will they provide extras such as watering plants or bringing in the mail?

After doing your preliminary research, interview the best two or three **in your home** to see how they interact with your pet. Do they respect the dignity and feelings of your cat? Does your cat like this person? Remember, this person will have unsupervised access to your home—will they take good care of your home and possessions?

Advantages/Disadvantages of a Pet Sitter

Advantages	Disadvantages
No cats in the next cage to expose your cat to diseases or parasites.	Cat will be alone most of the day without help in an emergency.
Cat will have less stress staying on his own territory.	Professional sitter may be more expensive than boarding.
Home will have a lived-in look while you're away. Plants can be watered and mail brought in.	You have to assume the sitter is honest and will respect the material possessions inside your home.

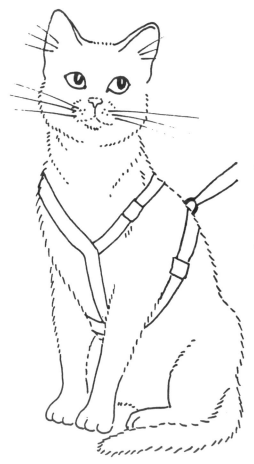

Your cat's harness and leash are its passports to freedom and the mobility to accompany you outside the home. If your cat will accept a harness, you can share many enjoyable experiences.

12

Well Cat Care

THIS CHAPTER outlines a cat's health needs and enables you to help your Vet give the very best of care, with the least stress to your pet. Following the guidelines in this chapter can extend your cat's life expectancy and enhance its quality.

WHEN SHOULD I TAKE MY CAT TO THE VETERINARIAN FOR WELL CAT CARE?

Well cat care is important for ongoing health and longevity. To start right, take him at eight to twelve weeks of age, or as soon as you adopt him. Your Vet will give him a health check and the first round of those all-important baby shots. See the vaccination schedule herein.

While the kitten can be neutered safely after the age of eight weeks, many Vets prefer to wait until later—at five months for spaying and eight months for neutering. Then your cat needs an annual health exam and vaccinations or boosters.

In addition, he'll need to go to the Vet when there is a change noted on his home health care exam, or when you see any of the changes listed in "How Do I Know if My Cat Is Sick Enough to Go to the Vet?" in chapter 13.

WHY DO I NEED TO VACCINATE MY INDOOR CAT?

Rabies vaccinations are required by law. But the most compelling reason for vaccination—all vaccinations—is to protect your cat.

Most people know that an outdoor cat has an obvious need of vaccination, but it's harder to understand why an indoor cat needs such protection. Some vaccine-preventable illnesses are infectious by indirect contact, which means you can carry it inside to your cat. Cats meeting through a window screen or door screen can also pass disease. And if you add a new pet to the household, it too may bring in a potentially fatal illness.

Also, in spite of your best efforts, indoor cats aren't always indoors. Accidents happen. Your cat may become lost and then exposed to rabies or another contagion. And if your cat is ever boarded, vaccine protection is a must; reputable boarders will insist on proof of vaccination to protect the other animals in their care.

Types of Vaccinations

Rabies. Rabies is a deadly virus that is most commonly spread by saliva, via bites from infected animals. But it can also be passed on if an infected animal licks a scratch or an open wound. Rabies is almost always fatal. The virus attacks the brain of any warm-blooded animal, including humans.

Feline Panleukopenia (Distemper). Distemper, a highly contagious virus, causes severe vomiting, diarrhea and dehydration. It has a very high death rate, particularly among kittens.

Feline Rhinotracheitis. This sometimes fatal viral respiratory disease can be very severe in young kittens. Symptoms include running eyes and nose.

Feline Calicivirus. Although extremely serious, calicivirus infection is less often fatal than distemper and rhinotracheitis. Symptoms include fever, mouth and tongue ulcers and drooling.

Feline Pneumonitis (Chlamydia). A bacterial respiratory disease with symptoms like those of rhinotracheitis, pneumonitis can be complicated by additional bacterial infections.

Feline Leukemia. Leukemia is a type of virus-induced cancer. Almost always fatal, this disease can lead to tumor growth almost anywhere in the cat's body. Damaged immune systems allow invasion by additional diseases, and the cat often dies from complications.

Vaccination Schedule

Your Vet will have her own preferred schedule for first vaccinations. Some Vets will give shots for all the diseases listed above, except chlamydia.

For the most part, vaccinations are uneventful. Your cat may be a little lethargic or tender at the injection site. Any other reactions to the injection should be reported immediately to your Vet. Some kittens and cats do react strongly to the rabies vaccine. You might see or feel a lump at the vaccination site. This usually isn't dangerous, but report it to your Vet for future reference—she may want to make adjustments in timing of the shots or in the vaccine.

Probable Vaccination Schedules

8 weeks   **Distemper-Calicivirus-Rhinotracheitis and Feline Leukemia**
12 weeks **Distemper-Calicivirus-Rhinotracheitis and Feline Leukemia**
16 weeks **Rabies**
Yearly Booster Shots for all of the above!

Or the Vet may want to give the leukemia two weeks after each distemper-calicivirus-rhinotracheitis shot. Some Vets will give the chlamydia with the distemper combo.

DOES A COLD OR WET NOSE INDICATE A HEALTHY CAT?

This is **not** an indicator of health, nor can you determine your cat's temperature from his nose.

A cold or wet nose means the cat has just licked it. A cat licks his nose to improve his sense of smell, or he wets his nose to cool off—as the saliva evaporates and lifts off into the air, it takes warmth with it!

WHAT ARE NORMAL VITAL SIGNS FOR A CAT?

Temperature: 100.4 to 102.5 degrees F.
Heartbeat (count for 15 seconds)
   Kittens: 37 to 50 beats
   Adults: 20 to 44 beats
   Older Cats: 20 to 37 beats
Breathing (count for 15 seconds)
   Kittens: 7 to 10 breaths
   Adults: 5 to 7 breaths
   Older Cats: 7 breaths
Feces: Feces should range in color from dark gray to brown; they should be soft but formed.
Urine: Urine will have a strong odor and be a clear yellow color. (Urine has a very unpleasant odor in unneutered males and in females in heat.)

HOW DO I TAKE A CAT'S VITAL SIGNS?

Body Temperature

If you have to take your cat's temperature, use **only** a rectal thermometer, because it has a blunt round end. The easiest approach is to have the thermometer ready before getting the cat. So make sure the thermometer is clean and shaken down before you lubricate it with K-Y jelly or Vaseline.

Position the cat in any way that is comfortable for him and yet still gives

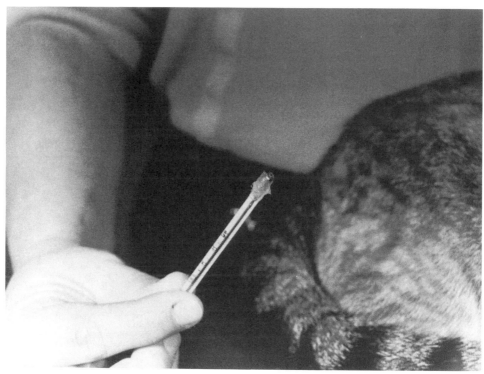

Every cat owner should know how to take the pet's temperature. In an emergency or sudden illness, it will help your Veterinarian if you can report the cat's temperature. Read carefully the instructions in the text and make taking temperature a regular part of your cat's health care.

access to his anus. Keep him under control and quiet while taking his temperature. If you think your cat will be outraged at the indignity of all this, have a towel handy—you might need to towel-wrap him to prevent injury.

To get his temperature, gently slip about ¾ inch of the thermometer into his anus. Wait three minutes, remove and then read the thermometer. Normal temperature is 100.4 to 102.5 degrees Fahrenheit. **Call your Vet if his temperature is 98 degrees Fahrenheit or below—or if it's above 103.5 degrees Fahrenheit.**

Afterward, clean the thermometer with soap and cool water, shake it down and then sterilize it with rubbing alcohol before returning it to its case.

Pulse

Place your fingers, not your thumb, over the carotid artery in his neck or the femoral artery on the inside of his leg. Gently feel for the pulse by moving your fingers slightly. When you have it, count the beats for 15 seconds. If you need to report the number to your Vet, be sure to tell her that the pulse was a 15-second count.

Breathing Rate

Watch for the rise and fall of his sides as he breathes or lightly lay your hand on his ribs and feel each in and out breath. Count **one** for each time the cat inhales/exhales during a 15-second period. Tell your Vet the number was based on a 15-second count.

WHAT SHOULD I DO FOR A REGULAR HOME HEALTH CHECK?

In addition to regular yearly checkups and vaccinations from your Vet, home health checks should be done on a regular basis. **Cats ten years and older should be checked monthly; cats up to ten years of age should be checked every three to six months.**

This health check does not replace, but rather enhances, regular Vet care. Much of this can be done weekly or daily as the cat is petted and groomed and his teeth are brushed.

- Be aware of changes in activity level, appetite (increase or decrease), water intake and personality.
- Notice any changes in the litter box or litter-box behavior (house soiling). Check for foul odors, changes in amounts or condition of urine or feces, blood in the urine or feces or straining behavior when the cat uses the box.
- Look for changes in the cat's general overall appearance. Is his fur groomed and in good condition? Are there changes in his gait or posture? Is he stiff after naps? Does he limp? Does he habitually "sit funny"—for instance, with his leg held out straight or one hip cocked?

- Weigh the cat. Because cats are not heavy enough to weigh accurately on a bathroom scale, use a baby scale, or if that's not available, weigh the cat and yourself. Then weigh yourself again. The difference is the cat's weight. An abrupt change of 1½ pounds or a pattern of continued loss or continued gain can indicate a problem.
- Run your hands over the cat's body to check for tenderness, lumps, deformities, hot spots or injuries.
- Examine the cat's anal area. Look for sores or "rice grains" (eggs of parasites).
- Look at the eyes. They should look smooth and clear and have a bright-colored iris—the eyes should not be cloudy or bulging. While the white of the eye may have a couple of red lines, truly bloodshot eyes should be reported to your Vet. His pupils should react to light and be the same size.
- Inspect his ears. They should be clean and have no odor.
- Look at the nose and mouth. His gums should be pink, not pale or bluish, and his teeth should be white. His nose should be clear, without ulcers or lumps, and should have no foul smell.
- Check the cat's abdomen for fleas. This is the easiest place to check for fleas, because the fur is thin. Comb with a flea comb and look for small black dots— flea feces. If you have any doubts that these tiny, innocuous specks are really from fleas, place one in your palm and touch it with a wet finger. You should see the red traces of your cat's blood.
- Listen to his breathing. A healthy cat is silent except for a pleasant purr.
- Check temperature, breathing rate and pulse. (Normal vital signs are listed above this question.)

Note: Photocopy the Home Health Check Form on page 167. Use the form, update and file records for each cat.

CAN I GET HEALTH INSURANCE FOR MY CAT?

Yes, but most companies cover only illnesses and accidents, not well cat care or surgical sterilization. You can expect limits or exclusions on older cats and higher premiums as the animal ages. If you are serious about coverage, call around and shop for the best deal. Your state's insurance regulatory agency has a list of companies registered to sell insurance in your state.

HOW DO I CHOOSE MEDICAL ASSISTANCE FOR MY CAT?

The first thing to do is to ask cat-owning friends, relatives, neighbors or co-workers for their **positive and negative** experiences with the Vets in your area.

Call the Vets who received the most positive recommendations and ask about their practice. What portion of their practice is devoted to cats? Do they emphasize the prevention of illness and disease? Ask about their hours, payment policy and any other items that are important to you.

Visit the practice and observe how pets and people are treated by the Vet and her staff. Are they gentle, caring and respectful with both people and animals? Do they listen to your questions—and your input? Is the Vet up to date on treatment options? Is the building clean and well equipped?

Home Health Check Form

Do home health checks **every three to six months** for cats under ten years of age and **monthly** for cats over ten years.

Cat's Name _____ **Age** _____ **Checkup Date** _____

Weight _____
(See Vet if there is a 1½ lb. change or a continued change.)

Breathing _____ (Breathing silent?)

Pulse Rate _____ **Temperature** _____

RECORD ANY CHANGES IN THE FOLLOWING:

Activity Level _____ **Appetite** _____

Water Intake _____ **Personality** _____

Bowel and Bladder Output

Amount _____ *Frequency* _____

Appearance _____ *Odor* _____

Blood in urine _____ *Blood in stool* _____

Difficulty eliminating _____

Fur _____ **Eyes** _____ **Anal area** _____

Ears _____ **Nose** _____ **Mouth** _____

Gait/posture/stiffness (after naps) _____

CHECK BODY FOR INJURIES AND OTHER PROBLEMS:

Run your hands over the cat. Record any tenderness, lumps, deformities or injuries. _____

_____

Notes _____

WHAT IS A HOLISTIC VET AND WHERE CAN I FIND ONE?

Holistic Veterinarians practice alternative health care for pets. They are licensed DVMs with further training in one or more of the following fields: herbology, acupuncture, chiropractic and nutritional therapy.

These Vets have a wider range of expertise than a traditional Vet and some animals may respond better to the holistic approach. Additionally, the wider range of treatment may, in some cases, speed up a pet's recovery.

Because there are so few of these specialists, you should expect to pay more for their services. For a list of holistic Veterinarians in your area, send a self-addressed stamped envelope to:

American Holistic Veterinary Medical Association
Department CD
2214 Old Emmerton Road
Bel Air, MD 21014

HOW CAN I HELP MY VETERINARIAN CARE FOR MY CAT?

Knowing your cat's normal health patterns and your Veterinarian's procedures will help everyone concerned. Give your cat daily attention, so you can catch illnesses early when they are easier to treat. Also become familiar with your cat's normal behavior; changes can indicate illness or injury. The most reliable approach is to do a home health check on a regular basis.

When you speak with your Vet, give concise, nongeneral information when your cat is ill.

For example:

- Cat's vital signs: breathing, temperature.
- Specific symptoms, such as: bleeding, blood in urine, limping, hot spot, drooling, foul odors, diarrhea and sudden unexplainable behavior change.

Another way to help your Vet is to become familiar with her hours, emergency policy and payment policy. It's also a good idea to keep your copies of medical records, such as rabies and other vaccinations.

Be on time for appointments and call if for any reason you can't keep the appointment or if you'll be very late. And remember, there are things she cannot and should not be expected to do. There will be times when tests are needed before she can make a diagnosis. Your Vet can't perform miracles; some diseases and injuries are not treatable. And she shouldn't be expected to make a house call or emergency office visit at 3 a.m. for a non-life-threatening problem.

WHAT IS TOOTH SCALING?

Similar to human teeth cleaning by a dental hygienist, tooth scaling is the scraping of accumulated tartar off the cat's teeth with a dental pick. Done annually to prevent cavities and gingivitis, scaling should be handled by your

Vet because most cats strenuously object and can be hard to control. In other words, the job may require anesthesia to do a good job—especially if the cat's teeth are in bad shape or if he's a behavior problem.

WHY, WHEN AND HOW SHOULD I BRUSH MY CAT'S TEETH?

You should brush your cat's teeth for the same reasons you brush your own teeth. Brushing keeps your cat's mouth cleaner and helps your cat keep his teeth longer. A mouth infection can become systemic (spread throughout his body) and can cost dearly in terms of your cat's health and your wallet. A clean mouth can also reduce your chances for infection if you're bitten.

Since Kitty doesn't eat candy or smoke, he generally needs his teeth brushed only once or twice a week. But older cats and cats prone to tartar buildup may need dental care more often. Make it part of your regular weekly grooming sessions.

Hold the cat either seated on your lap or lying belly-up on your lap. Try both positions and see which one the two of you prefer. Gently keep his teeth together with a finger under his jaw and your other fingers pulling one side of his lips back and open to expose his molars. Use a clean pet toothbrush or a soft human infant toothbrush (pet toothpaste is optional, but **never** use human toothpaste). Brush the outside surface of his molars, repeat on the other side, and then brush his front teeth. It's not necessary to brush the back sides of his teeth—the filiform papillae (Velcro-like hooks on his tongue) will keep the inside tartar at bay.

WHAT CAN I DO TO HELP MY CAT STAY COOL IN THE SUMMER?

Consider how you'd feel if you couldn't sweat to cool off and you were always wearing a fur coat. Be cool and give Fluffy a break. Here are some suggestions:

- Air conditioning is great—if it is in the budget.
- Attic fan. Run it at night to cool the house.
- Window fans. Two or more is most efficient.
  - Put one fan in a north or east window pulling air in, and one in a west or south window blowing out.
  - Place a bowl of ice in front of a fan to cool the air.
- Keep curtains closed to direct sunlight.
- Offer fresh cool water. Change the water twice a day. Try ice cubes in the water.
- Groom daily. Even shorthaired cats will be aided by daily removal of dead hair.
- Wipe the cat with a damp cloth to just moisten his coat. Do **not** wet the fur; dampen only the top layer of hair. As the water evaporates, it will cool him.

IS THERE AN EASY FORM TO KEEP
TRACK OF HIS MEDICAL HISTORY?

Yes, and the information will also help should your cat become lost. Make sure you photocopy and then update the form as needed. It's a good idea to paste a good current photograph of your cat to this form, to be used on a "wanted" poster if he gets lost.

The Form of My Cat's Life

Cat's Name (registered) _____ Common Name _____

Gender/Neutered or Whole _____ Date of Birth _____

Breed/Description (color, coat pattern, distinguishing marks, registry number ___

_____

_____

MEDICAL INFORMATION   **PICTURE (below)**

Weight _____ Height/Length _____

VACCINATIONS (original date/boosters)

Calicivirus _____

Distemper (Panleukopenia) _____

Pneumonitis _____

Rabies _____

Rhinotracheitis _____

FeLV _____

Other _____

SURGERIES (date/reason)

Neutered/spayed _____

Other surgeries _____

_____

ILLNESSES/INJURIES (date/event)

_____

_____

REGULAR MEDICATIONS (name, dose, time)

_____

_____

EATING PREFERENCES/RESTRICTIONS

_____

_____

13

Sick Cat Care

THIS CHAPTER is **not** meant to replace, but rather to enhance, the care your pet receives from your Vet. It will help you understand common health problems and how they can be treated. However, it's imperative that you **always** check with your Vet before medicating a pet. Every cat is different, with different needs and medical problems—and your Vet knows your cat's medical idiosyncrasies best.

Also, remember that "natural remedies" are not foolproof; your feline may be allergic to the product or you may not know the correct dosage or have the right chemical form of the product. Almost any of these items can be toxic when misused. For example, shampoos containing a small amount of pennyroyal may be safe, but using pennyroyal essential oil on your cat can make him very ill. If your Vet approves of using a natural remedy, there is one advantage— they're almost always less damaging to the environment.

HOW CAN I PROTECT MY CAT
FROM PARASITES AND DISEASES?

Have your cat checked for diseases and vaccinated by your Vet **before** bringing him into your home. And make sure that you keep his vaccinations up to date. It's penny-wise and pound-foolish not to do so.

To give your cat extra protection, keep him inside, and let him outside only in an enclosure or when supervised on harness and leash. Of course, if you also have a dog, you'll need to be more vigilant about fleas since the dog can bring them into the house.

Also, after touching other cats, but especially strays, you should wash your hands thoroughly with an antibacterial soap or wipe.

HOW DO I KNOW IF MY CAT IS SICK ENOUGH TO GO TO THE VET?

While **all** signs of illness and infection should be checked by your Vet, some need attention faster than others.

Call Your Vet Now

Shock Shock can occur immediately after a trauma (accident, poisoning, etc.) or anytime up to ten hours afterward. Look for **any** of the following symptoms:

- Confusion or loss of consciousness
- Inability to stand
- Involuntary passage of urine and/or feces
- Pale mucous membranes: rims of eyes, gums (paler than normal—even if pigmented)
- Feeble and rapid pulse (greater than 60 beats in 15 seconds)
- Shallow, labored, rapid breathing (greater than 10 breaths in 15 seconds)

Changes in Food/Water Intake

- Sudden change in water intake, especially unquenchable thirst

Changes in Urination/Defecation

- Change in color, frequency, amount or odor
- Bloody stool or blood in urine
- Straining to urinate and/or inability to do so

Vomiting

- Prolonged or frequent bouts of vomiting (more than just a hair ball)
- Blood in vomit or vomit accompanied by weakness, pain or fever (normal temperature: 100.4 to 102.5 F.

Change in Respiration

- Shallow, noisy or difficult breathing
- Rapid breathing (greater than 10 breaths in 15 seconds)

Abnormalities of Eyes

- Excessive tearing or discharge

- Swelling
- Third eyelid (nictitating membrane) enlarged or remaining over eye
- Cloudy appearance or film over eye

Abnormalities of Mouth

- Pale or blue gums
- Bleeding gums or lips
- Excessive drooling

Abnormalities of Ear

- Swelling

Discharge or Bleeding

- Discharge or bleeding from any body part

Indicators of Pain

- Stiffness, limping, holding a paw up, difficulty walking
- Snapping or crying when touched or when moving

Change in Body Temperature

- Temperature 98 degrees F. or below.
- Temperature 103.5 degrees F. or above.

Broken Bones

- Tail or leg at an odd angle
- Refusal to use a leg
- Broken pelvis—inability to stand
- Broken ribs—difficulty breathing

Go to the Vet Tomorrow

Changes in Urination/Defecation

- Constipation or diarrhea

Abnormalities of Nose

- Swelling
- Foul odor coming from the nose

Abnormalities of Ear

- Discharge
- Repeated head shaking or head held at an angle

Abnormalities of Skin and Fur

- Sores or hot spots

Sneezing or Coughing

- Prolonged periods of either coughing or sneezing

Fever

- Temperature between 102.5 and 103.4 F., taken rectally

Go to the Vet Within a Couple of Days

Behavior Changes

- Lethargy, less playful or less interested in exercise
- Hiding
- Neglected grooming; fur dull or messy

Abnormalities of Ear

- Foul odor
- Dirt or excessive wax

Abnormalities of Mouth

- Foul odor

Sneezing or Coughing

- Repeated single episodes

Lumps or Masses

- Any swelling, lump or mass anywhere on body (lump may or may not be warm to the touch)

Abnormalities of Skin and Fur

- Broken hairs/whiskers
- Fur loss
- Matted, greasy or dull fur
- Parasite infestation
- Excessive biting or scratching

Changes in Urination/Defecation

- Change in habits (house soiling)

Changes in Food/Water Intake

- Sudden increase or decrease in appetite
- Sudden change in weight, with or without change in appetite

WHAT IS SHOCK?

Shock can follow any trauma—an accident, poisoning, etc.—and can occur as late as eight to ten hours after the episode. Because there are degrees of shock, it can be difficult to recognize, but the cause is always the same.

Shock occurs when the cat's circulating blood drops in volume or when his blood vessels collapse. Because the heart has to struggle harder to pump, his body tries to increase blood flow by cutting off the blood supply to nonvital areas. The cat will appear weakened and shaky and have pale gums/eye rims.

As the blood supply continues to decrease, the cat may lose consciousness, lose bowel or bladder control or have any of the other symptoms described earlier.

If, after a trauma, your cat shows **any** of the signs of shock, you must call your Vet **immediately**. You may be asked to massage his legs and trunk area to increase circulation. Or the Vet may need to give the cat a blood transfusion or intravenous fluids to increase blood volume. And if the cat is in critical condition, you may have to do CPR or artificial respiration to sustain him until you get to her office.

WHAT DO I NEED FOR A FIRST-AID KIT?

You can buy a ready-made pet first-aid kit at pet stores or from catalogs— or you can assemble your own. With some minor additions, the same supplies also make good people first-aid kits with one critical exception: **Never use aspirin, acetaminophen or ibuprofen; they are extremely toxic to cats**! See the question on pain control for more information.

In a box, in a convenient location, safe from pets and children, put the following items:

- 1″-wide adhesive tape
- 1″-wide rolled gauze bandages
- 1 box 3″ × 3″ cotton gauze pads
- Rectal thermometer
- Measuring spoons or liquid medicine applicator for babies
- Eyedropper
- Tweezers
- Sharp scissors with rounded ends
- Tongue depressor for splints

- Activated charcoal capsules
- Peroxide (3%) to clean wounds and to force vomiting
- Styptic pencil or powder
- First-aid cream such as Neosporin, Topical Calendula cream or Bach Rescue Remedy cream

WHEN AND HOW DO I INDUCE VOMITING?

Induce vomiting only on the advice of your Vet; she may recommend this after *she* determines your cat has eaten something he shouldn't have.

Using an eyedropper or infant medicine applicator, give the cat one-half to one teaspoon of 3 percent hydrogen peroxide. He'll foam at the mouth and then vomit. Not a pretty sight—especially if he runs into your dining room and heaves on your best rug. So when you're going to induce vomiting, do it in the bathroom—and shut the door.

If your cat hasn't vomited with the initial dose of peroxide, call your Vet for more instructions.

WHAT SHOULD I TELL THE VET IN AN EMERGENCY?

Having information ready for the Vet will speed her evaluation. When your Vet asks for vital signs, she wants to know about body temperature, pulse rate and breathing rate. Minutes can make the difference between whether a pet lives or dies. So a word to the wise: practice taking vitals **before** there's a problem. The directions are given in chapter 12.

For a list of the most common emergency situations and information your Vet must know, see the beginning of chapter 21.

MY CAT HAS BEEN POISONED AND I CAN'T
REACH MY VET. WHAT SHOULD I DO?

If you can't reach your Vet or one of her colleagues, or if you want a second opinion, you can call the National Animal Poison Control Center.

In existence since 1978, the National Animal Poison Control Center is staffed around the clock by veterinarians at the University of Illinois College of Veterinary Medicine. Their services are available to anyone.

To help fund their twenty-four-hour service, they do charge for their assistance. Callers have two payment options:

Callers Not Using a Credit Card

- Call **1-900-680-0000**
- Charges: $2.95 per minute; average call is ten minutes. Charges are on the initial

call only, all follow-up calls are free. You will be billed on your regular phone bill.

Callers Using Credit Card

- Call **1-800-548-2423**
- Charges: $30, one-time charge on major credit card. All follow-up calls are free.

Procedure

When you call, a veterinary technician or student will take your specific information and connect you to staff veterinarian. If at all possible, have the poison container available for a list of ingredients. To assist these professionals in helping your pet, be ready with the following information:

- Species and breed of animal
- Sex, age and weight of animal
- List of substance ingredients or the name of poison
- Possible amount ingested
- Brief health history on pet. Medications? Recent surgery?
- Elapsed time since animal was exposed to poison and how long after exposure symptoms appeared.
- Symptoms animal is having and the amount of time since he became sick
- The treatment(s) you have tried and the results. Is he worse? Improved? Unchanged?
- Number of animals exposed
- Number of ill animals and which ones are ill

DISEASES

DO CATS AND PEOPLE GET THE SAME DISEASES?

There are several diseases that you share with felines. In general, keeping your cat inside, getting him fully vaccinated and following personal health and hygiene guidelines go a long way toward prevention. Here are some of these shared diseases.

Rabies

See "Rabies" under common feline diseases below.

Conjunctivitis and Upper Respiratory Infections

People can contract conjunctivitis (an eye infection also known as "pink eye") from a cat with feline chlamydia (upper respiratory infection). If your cat has infected eyes, wash your hands after handling him, and don't touch your face during or after handling the animal.

Cat Scratch Fever

Cat scratch fever is a rickettsial infection which finds its way into our bodies through a break in the skin. Sometimes severe enough to require hospitalization, the infection has mono-like symptoms in humans, and yet the cat is the only animal carrier. Some unlucky people even develop a severe allergic reaction to cat bites after recovery.

Infection from Cat Bites

Because cats bite deeply, creating a thin wound, 30 percent of all bites become infected (with a higher rate for people who are immune-suppressed and for senior citizens). Clean all wounds with peroxide. If swelling or tenderness develops, see your physician.

The best prevention is not to approach an unknown cat, and to teach your own cat not to bite. See chapter 8 for help in taking the "bite" out of your relationship.

Allergies to Flea and Mite Bites

People as well as cats can have allergic reactions to fleas and mites. And, of course, your cat can be the host for these nasty insects—and, left untreated, can be responsible for a household infestation.

The human problem is treatable by killing the fleas and mites and by taking antihistamines for the allergic reaction (check with your physician). Your cat will require additional treatment; see chapter 10 for more information.

Ringworm

Ringworm isn't a worm; it's a fungal infection (lesions are circular and crusty). Both cats and people get ringworm from direct exposure to the lesions.

The best way to prevent it is to eliminate contact with people or animals, including dogs, with open or crusted sores. Whether on cat or cat lover, the problem is easily treated with topical antifungal ointments.

Worms

Most worms dwell in the intestines in both humans and cat, but one type can worm their way only into a cat's heart. Intestinal worms are usually spread via feces, although the flea can carry tapeworm. The mosquito carries heartworm.

Cat-to-people worm problems can be prevented by keeping the cat inside, cleaning the litter box daily and washing your hands after cleaning it. It's also a good idea to wash your hands after gardening outside in areas that may contain feces. For more information on worms, see chapter 10.

Toxoplasmosis

Toxoplasmosis is a contaminant in many areas of the country, and it's present in the feces of carrier cats. See the question below for more information.

WHAT ARE SOME COMMON FELINE DISEASES?

There are several common diseases affecting cats. The following information will help you understand what may be happening to your pet.

When reading this section, remember that cats are individuals and, as such, will have their own particular reactions to disease. Your cat may or may not display all of the symptoms of the illness. And remember, any one symptom can be an indication of several diseases. Whenever you notice abnormal appearance or behavior, see your Vet. Only she can accurately diagnose and effectively treat your cat's ailments.

FUS OR FELINE LOWER URINARY TRACT DISEASE (FLUTD)

What was at one time termed FUS (feline urologic syndrome) is actually a group of illnesses which cause feline lower urinary tract disease. FLUTD, as it's now called, is a syndrome characterized by frequent urination in small amounts, avoidance of the litter box, excessive grooming of the genitals, straining to urinate and the possibility of obvious blood in the urine. The problem may progress to an emergency condition in which the cat is unable to urinate at all.

FLUTD can be a chronic or an acute problem, or it can change from one to the other over time. (Chronic conditions are ongoing medical situations needing continual care, such as medicine or special diets. Acute conditions are **emergency** medical problems that are resolved with treatment.) Without treatment, the cat with an acute attack of FLUTD can die. The good news is that, once diagnosed, this syndrome can often be controlled by a Veterinarian-recommended diet.

Any cat can have FLUTD, but overweight and inactive pets are more prone to attacks. And while both males and females can develop FLUTD, males are more likely to have a blockage because the urethra is smaller. Ten percent of all house cats experience this ailment, and once a cat has had one bout with it, additional episodes are likely.

To help prevent problems, keep clean fresh water available at all times and feed a high-quality, low-magnesium diet. Ideally the diet should maintain an acid urine. If your cat still has problems in spite of a change in food, other factors may be involved, which may require a more thorough diagnostic workup by your

Veterinarian. Also, it's a good idea to keep the litter box clean and in a quiet, easy-to-reach place. Since exercise is important to the overall health of your cat, encourage regular physical activity.

FIP (FELINE INFECTIOUS PERITONITIS)

Note the word "infectious." This fatal virus is spread by direct contact between cats in close contact (fights, mating, grooming, etc.). There's a high concentration of virus also in feces, so this may be an additional route of transmission.

FIP can survive in the environment, up to two months, and infected cats (most are three to four years of age) can carry and shed the virus for months or years before becoming ill. The best way to prevent FIP is to keep your cat indoors and away from potential carriers.

Unfortunately, there is no effective treatment for FIP, but there is now a new, controversial nose spray vaccine. Ask your Vet if it is appropriate for your cat.

Symptoms

While there are no actual direct tests for FIP, there are tests to help diagnose a possible FIP infection. Unfortunately, definite identification is often delayed until autopsy.

An infected cat is subject to secondary infections and may show the following symptoms of either *wet FIP* or *dry FIP*.

- *Wet FIP*. A fluid, ranging from clear to straw-colored, builds up in the cat's abdomen and sometimes in his chest; he experiences fever and possible respiratory failure, weight loss and depression. Wet FIP is the more severe form of FIP, and death comes soon after the symptoms appear.
- *Dry FIP*. The cat experiences fever, possible weight loss and depression. The cat's survival time depends on his general health when FIP symptoms develop. Death is always the outcome.

FIV (FELINE IMMUNODEFICIENCY VIRUS)

Like HIV (the AIDS-causing human immunodeficiency virus), FIV is a slow-acting retrovirus. The infected individual carries the virus for a long time before becoming ill. While both cats and humans can have retroviruses, only humans can be infected by HIV, and only cats get FIV—one **cannot** get HIV or AIDS from a cat!

FIV can be transmitted among the cat population through mating, veterinary blood transfusions and cat bites. A diagnosis of FIV is not an immediate death sentence, for supportive treatment prolongs life. There is still no cure, so the body will finally be unable to fight off infections by opportunistic diseases.

It's estimated that up to 12 percent of the at-risk U.S. cat population is infectious. This carrier population is composed mainly of outdoor male cats. These cats tend to be sexually active and aggressive, with a well-developed sense of territory, so they're very willing to fight—and bite.

Prevention

There is no vaccination for FIV, and the only way to prevent infection is to eliminate exposure by keeping your cat inside and having all new cats or kittens tested before they enter your household.

Symptoms

FIV has no set symptoms. What will be seen is a failure to thrive and any number of diseases which take hold in the cat's weakened condition. One common symptom is mouth/gum infections and a reduced appetite.

Treatment

To help your Vet care for your FIV-positive cat:

- Isolate him from all other cats in the household and take care not to pass infections back and forth. Thoroughly wash your hands after handling him.
- Keep his regular vaccination current, to reduce the chance of additional illnesses.
- Don't delay when you see symptoms of illness, because not only is an FIV cat susceptible to other ailments but, once ill, he'll fade more quickly.
- Keep his living area clean and disinfect regularly.
- Give him extra-good care, top-quality nutrition and plenty of personal attention.

FELINE LEUKEMIA (FeLV)

This fatal infectious disease is another caused by a retrovirus. FeLV infects by inserting its genetic material into a host cell. All daughter cells of that cell are infected and so on. The virus does not usually appear in the blood until three weeks after exposure.

After exposure, one of three things happen:

1. The cat's immune system combats the FeLV and develops antibodies that protect him; some of these cats are unaffected carriers for a short period of time.
2. The virus will become established in the cat's body and blood, and he will be at high risk for developing FeLV-related diseases. These cats are contagious to other cats. Half of these infected cats will die within six months of exposure, and after three years, 80 percent will be dead.
3. The cat will eventually enter category 1 or 2.

Prevention

The best prevention is to test any kitten or cat before bringing him into your home—and once inside, he should be kept inside. Although saliva contact is the common method of transmission, FeLV can be passed from mother to kitten in utero (during pregnancy) and, of course, later through mom cat's milk, saliva, urine, feces. However, most FeLV positive queens do not carry kittens to term.

For a cat of any age, close contact, whether through grooming, fights or shared use of litter boxes and bowls, can be deadly. After the death of a FeLV-positive cat, all that cat's equipment must be washed (use four ounces of bleach to one gallon of water) and rinsed well. Wash bedding, and generally clean the house with soap and water. Any of the cat's equipment that cannot be washed should be destroyed. Then wait at least one month before adopting another cat.

Symptoms

FeLV can cause cancers like lymphoma or leukemia, or immunosuppression, which allows your cat to contract many opportunistic diseases, including anemia and intestinal, respiratory and reproductive disorders.

Treatment

Some of the drugs used are very strong and extreme care must be taken with their use. However, there is a variety of palliative treatments to make him feel better and prolong his life. Remember, any infected cat will be shedding the virus even during remission.

HYPERTHYROID DISEASE

Hyperthyroidism is caused by a malfunction of the thyroid gland which results in the overproduction of hormones. Seen often in cats over age seven, this disease can be fatal if left untreated. The thyroid gland is located below the larynx and regulates metabolism and contributes to normal growth and development.

Symptoms

Excessive amounts of hormones cause middle-aged and elderly cats to suddenly start "acting like kittens again." They become hyperactive and have a greatly increased appetite—and yet lose weight. Other symptoms include:

- Increased water intake and urination
- Overheating easily, panting
- Vomiting shortly after eating
- Changes in feces—diarrhea, larger stools, more frequent defecation
- Coat loss or increased shedding—unkempt, greasy and matted coat

- Fever
- Fast or irregular heartbeat
- Enlarged thyroid gland

In advanced cases, the cat becomes weak and depressed. He shows less interest in food and undergoes extreme weight loss. Blood tests will show elevated levels of the hormone thyroxine.

Treatment

There are three alternatives available at this time. Radioactive iodine and thyroidectomy will permanently correct the problem. Drugs to reduce hormones will also control the disease. The treatment of choice will depend on the cat's age and general health, the progression of the disease and, of course, what you can afford in terms of money and time for home care.

Radioactive iodine is used to selectively destroy tissue in the thyroid gland. It can be used when surgery isn't advised—but only hospitals licensed to use radioactive products can do this procedure. The cat will have to be quarantined until his body wastes are clear of radioactive particles, and this can take up to a month.

Surgery removes part or all of the diseased thyroid gland. All surgery has risks, and surgery on older cats carries even greater risks. There are extra problems related to this surgery because the nerves to the larynx can be damaged. Additionally, the doctor must be careful to leave the parathyroid glands intact or the cat will have a whole new set of health problems. The surgeon must also decide how much of the gland to remove. If the whole thyroid gland is removed, some cats will have to take a daily pill to replace the appropriate level of hormones. And if part of the thyroid gland is left, it can supply the needed hormones but may eventually become hyperthyroid also.

As a less expensive approach, there are drugs that suppress thyroid hormone production. The cat will have to take the medicine daily for the rest of his life; if the drug is stopped, the disease returns. There can be side effects, however—nausea, vomiting and, less frequently, disorders of the blood or liver.

RABIES

This viral infection is passed in saliva through animal bites or if an infected animal licks an open wound. Any warm-blooded animal can carry and pass on rabies. In the wild, skunks and raccoons are the most common carriers.

Rabies is such a gruesome disease that, by law, all dogs and cats must be vaccinated yearly to prevent the disease. And if your immunized cat is bitten by any unvaccinated animal, he'll need an **additional** booster.

When humans are involved, extra caution is mandated. Even a healthy vaccinated animal who bites a human is quarantined for ten days or for the amount of time set by law in your area. While in isolation, the animal is watched carefully for the clinical signs of rabies.

Wild animals who bite a human aren't given the option of quarantine; they're immediately euthanized and their brain tested for rabies. Even **before** clinical symptoms appear, infected animals are contagious and the virus can be detected in brain tissue.

Unvaccinated domestic animals are either euthanized and tested like wild creatures or quarantined at owner expense and observed for six months—or the specific time period set in your area. The quarantined animal will have to be vaccinated before being released to his owner.

Symptoms

Rabies usually shows up in personality changes and in abnormal behavior. Common signs are aggression, restlessness, an inability to swallow, weakness or paralysis. Unfortunately, once the symptoms are evident, death is almost a certainty.

Prevention

While there is no effective treatment after symptoms appear, a five-shot series recommended on days 1, 3, 7, 14 and 28 will prevent the virus from taking hold in humans. Given in the arm (adults) and buttocks (small children), these five shots are a great improvement over the stomach shots given years ago. Rabies is fully preventable by a vaccination with a yearly booster. There are vaccines for cats and for humans who handle at-risk animals.

Treatment

Once the individual shows any clinical signs of this disease, it is fatal.

PANLEUKOPENIA (FPL) OR FELINE DISTEMPER

Distemper is an often fatal viral infection that mainly attacks kittens. While it tends to be more prevalent in the summer and fall, this hardy virus can last in the normal household for months and even years. So all sudden deaths in kittens should be checked, especially if you plan to bring another very young kitten into the household.

Prevention

This potential killer is fully preventable by vaccinations given at eight to ten weeks, followed by another shot four weeks later. If your area is experiencing an epidemic, your cat may need one more vaccination four weeks after the second dose. In all cases, yearly boosters are needed to keep your cat protected.

Before you get your female cat vaccinated, check with your Vet to see if she is pregnant; your Vet may want to postpone the distemper vaccination.

Symptoms

This disease appears suddenly. The animal experiences leukopenia (low white-blood-cell count), fever, loss of appetite, vomiting and diarrhea, dehydration and depression. Those infected in utero or shortly after birth may not show any symptoms but will die suddenly. Distemper in adult cats is mild or may not have any neurological signs.

Treatment

If the cat can be kept alive during the first week of illness, his chances of recovery are much improved. To get him through this critical period, he'll need dedicated nursing with supportive care for fluid loss. The extra attention is needed in part because there's a greatly increased possibility of secondary bacterial infections. Treated kittens (infected prenatally) who survive may develop lifelong involuntary twitching or a lack of coordination.

EAR INFECTIONS

Ear infections are caused by a variety of agents, including parasites, fungi, bacteria and foreign bodies in the ear canal. While they can occur in both the outer ear and the inner ear, inner ear infections are usually more serious and can be difficult to treat.

There is no vaccine or other preventative for these infections, but it helps to keep the cat's ears dry. It's also wise to avoid putting anything, including a cotton swab, in the ear canal.

Symptoms

The cat can have one or more of the following:

- Persistent shaking of the head
- Scratching of the ears, even to the point of bleeding
- Swollen ears
- Foul ear odor
- "Dirty" ears
- Poor balance or loss of coordination
- Loss of hearing

Treatment

Your Vet needs to see the patient for a clear diagnosis. If you're given medication, set up a medicine schedule and stick to it. Ear infections can easily resurface if they aren't fully treated.

CONJUNCTIVITIS (EYE INFECTIONS)

Conjunctivitis can be caused by bacterial or viral agents as well as by allergies. While allergies aren't contagious, the other causes are highly infectious.

Both the bacterial and viral routes of transmission can best be prevented by reducing the cat's exposure; keep him inside and quarantine any infected cats. The allergy-related cases can be prevented only by removing the allergen.

Symptoms

Look for any or all of the following:

- Runny or weepy eyes
- Prominent nictitating membrane (the third eyelid)
- Excessive blinking
- White of the eye may be red

Treatment

See your Vet. Treatment varies depending on the cause, but you will probably have to put medication in his eye.

ABSCESSES

An abscess is an infection generally associated with puncture (bite) wounds. The outer skin closes over the wound and a pocket of pus forms underneath. Abscesses usually appear on the face, legs, paws, back and base of the tail.

Symptoms

An abscess tends to show up as a warm lump, which can get quite large if left unattended. If the pool of pus is close to rupturing on its own, the covering skin will be thin and usually purplish in color. If it has ruptured, look for a wound running with pus.

Treatment

Treatment varies depending on the severity of the infection. See your Vet. The earlier the infection is treated, the better.

DERMATITIS (INFLAMMATION OF THE SKIN)

With most dermatitis, the skin is damaged by an allergic reaction to fleas or to some other allergen, although the sun can also cause dermatitis in cats with white ears and faces.

Skin-fold dermatitis—inflammation from skin-on-skin friction and moisture—affects grossly overweight cats (groin, armpit areas), "rumpy" Manx cats (rump area) and flat-faced cats (muzzle).

An even less common cause of dermatitis can be linked to behavior problems. The cat scratches or bites at his skin/fur, usually the paws or tail tip, until he's caused an inflammation. The cat may do this from stress or it may be a learned behavior.

Symptoms

The cat's skin becomes reddened and eventually breaks down (lesions), and then his fur falls out. He may groom and scratch excessively because he itches—and he's miserable.

Treatment

Treatment varies with the cause. Usually the idea is to reduce the cat's exposure to the allergen or to the sun. Of course, if the problem stems from obesity, you'll need to put the cat on a diet. And with some skin fold dermatitis, surgery may be needed to reduce skin folds.

TOOTH DECAY/BROKEN TOOTH

Tooth decay in a cat is just like the tooth decay in people; cavities show up as dark spots on the teeth. But not all cavities will be in surface locations, so look for other signs—including a reluctance to eat hard food, bad breath and drooling. Consult your Vet if you suspect a problem. And as with people, brushing teeth is the best way to prevent tooth decay.

Cats, even indoor cats, can have broken or chipped teeth. A balanced diet will help keep teeth strong. If he still needs dental work, tooth decay and broken teeth can be treated by pulling, capping or even a root canal!

GINGIVITIS

Gingivitis is a bacterial infection of the gums, and in most cases is preventable by brushing your cat's teeth regularly and by Veterinary dental care as needed. The symptoms of gingivitis are red, puffy and inflamed gums (deep pink or red gums), foul mouth odor and an often reduced appetite. Besides the obvious eating problems and pain caused by gingivitis, there's also the risk that the bloodstream will carry the bacteria from the gums to the cat's internal organs— and this makes for one sick kitty.

Your Vet can prescribe an antibacterial rinse to help with the infection, but you must brush his teeth regularly.

RESPIRATORY INFECTIONS

Feline viral rhinotracheitis, feline calicivirus and chlamydia are the three most common of the many upper respiratory diseases spread by body fluids. It is often difficult to distinguish between the various respiratory infections, and few of these illness have their own specific clinical symptoms, although lab tests can determine which disease is present.

To make matters worse, it's possible for the cat to contract more than one respiratory infection at a time, complicating treatment and adding to his recovery time. While most are viral in nature, they are often complicated by secondary bacterial infections.

Most cats recover, but some develop a chronic infection. With viral illness, cats can continue to shed the virus and may show symptoms to various degrees.

Symptoms

One to seven days after direct or indirect contact with an infected cat, the exposed animal will begin to show symptoms similar to a human cold. These all too familiar complaints include sneezing, coughing, runny nose and eye discomfort (eyes are red, watery and sensitive to light).

Treatment

Antiviral eye medications, broad-spectrum antibiotics and antibiotic eye ointments may be given to ward off any secondary infections. You'll also have to help him keep clean, since his grooming may not keep up with the drainage, or your cat may be too sick to groom at all. He'll need a warm room, dry bedding and a humidifier or vaporizer to help him recoup. **Do not under any circumstances give him any human cold medicines.**

Prevention

There are vaccinations for some of the respiratory viruses. Otherwise, good hygiene, healthy living conditions and the isolation of infected cats improve the odds for prevention.

KIDNEY DISEASES

Kidney diseases can be either congenital (from birth) or acquired. Congenital defects are associated with the formation and development of the kidneys, while acquired problems develop with aging, disease and injury to the kidneys.

Prevention

Any cat that has a genetic kidney problem or is closely related to a cat with a poor genetic history should never be used in a breeding program.

To help a cat stay kidney-healthy, petproof your home and provide the healthiest lifestyle and the best care you can.

Symptoms

There are many symptoms of kidney disease, including changes in water consumption, lack of appetite, changes in urination, bouts of vomiting or diarrhea, weight loss, deterioration of the cat's fur, foul breath, lethargy and a hunched posture from back pain. Kidney diseases can be chronic or acute; left untreated, either can be fatal.

Treatment

Treatment will vary with the cause and the amount of kidney damage sustained. In less severe cases, antibiotics may suffice, whereas more serious problems may require fluid therapy, peritoneal dialysis or surgery.

ARE THERE ANY ALTERNATIVE HEALTH TREATMENTS THAT MAY HELP MY CAT FIGHT ILLNESSES?

In addition to providing the best nutrition, daily exercise, positive social contact and thorough grooming, there are two things that may help:

- Echinacea, an herb that acts as an immune system booster, is particularity helpful for cats with chronic upper respiratory infections, FIV and FeLV. The brand Bioforce can be found at most health food stores. Give the cat one-half a tablet per day.
- TTouch, especially the ear work, can also give the immune system a helping hand.

WHAT IS TOXOPLASMOSIS?

Toxoplasmosis is a protozoal infection prevalent in many parts of the United States. But it rarely causes any problems for people unless they're pregnant or immune-suppressed. Toxoplasmosis can cause human birth defects if a woman is exposed early in her pregnancy.

While cats seem to take most of the blame for toxoplasmosis, the most common source is eating undercooked, infected meat. Feeding cats raw meat and letting them hunt rodents will expose them, and you, to toxoplasmosis.

Daily cleaning of the litter box provides protection to most people, because an infected cat's feces become contagious to humans only after forty-eight hours. However, pregnant women and immune-suppressed people should **not** be near the litter box at all. If there is no one else to change the litter, disposable masks and rubber gloves should be used. Your health care provider can demonstrate how to use and dispose of these items.

CAN CATS HAVE ALLERGIES?

Absolutely, and their symptoms are much the same as for people—watery eyes, sneezing and chronic coughing, loss of appetite, diarrhea or flatulence and breathing difficulties. Allergies that affect the skin take on added feline dimensions, with drastic hair loss and chewing both claws and fur.

Cats can be allergic to almost anything—although foods, food dyes, dust, flea bites and chemical flea treatments are some of the most common causes. Veterinarian-prescribed cortisone and antihistamines are the usual treatment for acute attacks, but long-term care must include avoidance of the allergen. A holistic Vet may be able to prescribe alternative treatment for allergy symptoms.

WHY IS HE SCOOTING ON HIS RUMP?

His anal glands may be impacted. The anal glands are located on either side of his anus. The contents are usually expelled when he is startled and during bowel movements. If the glands become impacted (blocked), your cat will lick the area or scoot across the floor on his rump in an attempt to relieve the discomfort. Take him to your Vet, and she'll empty the material from the impacted glands. For some cats, impaction and secondary bacterial infection can become a chronic problem.

CAN CATS GET ACNE?

They certainly can. Most commonly on the underside of the cat's chin, feline acne takes the form of small black dots or even reddened lumps. Unlike humans, cats can have acne at any time of life, and it isn't always related to hormone levels.

If the cat's chin becomes infected (red lumps), see your Vet for treatment. But if there are just a few black dots, try gently combing the area with a flea comb. Also, some cats develop acne from plastic food and water bowls, so try metal or glass dishes.

DO CATS DEVELOP CANCERS?

Unfortunately yes. Cancer is a catchall term for any unregulated cell growth, which may or may not metastasize (spread to other parts of the body). Nonmetastatic cancers, in general, grow slowly and, depending on location, can more safely be surgically removed because they don't spread. Metastatic cancers, on the other hand, grow quickly and, if not caught early, can invade other parts of the body. These tumors are more difficult to treat and carry a higher death rate.

Cat cancers are caused by viruses, irritants or damages to the cells that cause glitches in the cell's coded instructions. As with humans, a cat's genetic makeup can influence which cause and how much exposure it takes to start a cancer.

WHY IS A COLD SO HARD ON A CAT?

A cat with a runny nose has a diminished sense of smell, and if he can't smell food he won't want to eat—just like people. Being small animals, most cats can't stand to lose much weight for any reason.

WHAT IS THAT SMELL?

Yes, cats can expel gas, just like humans. When a cat has flatulence (gas), it can come from several sources. The culprit may be overfeeding, poor diet, allergy or illness. If the problem persists, check with your Vet.

Cats can also have bad breath. This can be from pica (eating nonfood items, which decay in the stomach), tooth decay or an infection. Again, see your Vet for a clear diagnosis and treatment.

Another odoriferous possibility may come from a startled cat. When a cat is frightened, he may express his anal glands; there will be a very strong musky smell, and you'll see (if you care to look) the greenish-gray contents on either side of his anus. Don't worry, your cat will clean up the mess all by himself.

Cats, by nature, smell good. Any foul-smelling discharge should be reported to your Vet.

HOW CAN I CONTROL MY CAT'S BAD BREATH?

Bad breath can be a sign of pica (eating nonfood items, which decay in the stomach), tooth decay or an infection. Read through the questions on these topics, and see your Veterinarian. The directions for brushing his teeth are in chapter 6.

Once the underlying cause is found, you might want to ask your Vet about using a homeopathic preparation to reduce odor during treatment.

DO CATS GET SUNBURNED?

Yes. The ears of light-colored, especially pure-white cats can get sunburned. And as with humans, repeated sunburns can lead to cancer and destruction of the ear.

Sunburn symptoms are the same as for people—red skin for mild burns and progressing to blisters and running sores for more severe burns.

Sunscreens can be toxic and are **not** an option for your cat—even if you confine their use to the ears. A cat licks his paws repeatedly to groom his ears, and the chemicals in sunscreen will end up in his mouth. Your only safe alternative is to keep your cat out of direct sunlight.

HOW CAN I GET A URINE SAMPLE FOR THE VET?

Once a cat starts to urinate, he can't stop. Most cats relieve themselves twice a day—morning and evening.

Use one of the following to collect the sample. (The container must be clean.) Slide it under his rump once he starts to urinate.

- Small jar, such as a baby food jar
- Aluminum foil shaped into a spoon
- An old spoon

If you are averse to the hand method of collecting urine, use No-Sorb, special nonabsorbent plastic beads, in the litter pan (instead of litter). After the cat urinates, the urine can be drained off.

Once you have the catch of the day, transfer it, if needed, to a clean, closable container for transport to your Vet. If the urine must be kept for more than an hour or so, refrigerate the container.

FEEDING THE SICK CAT

WHEN AND HOW DO I FORCE-FEED SOLID FOOD TO MY CAT?

Never force-feed your cat except on the advice of your Veterinarian. If forced feedings are prescribed, make sure you feed **only** the food ordered by your Vet. These special foods are either canned baby meat or a specific nutritional concentrate. To help your Vet monitor food intake, make a written record of feeding times and the amount of food your cat eats.

You may need to towel-wrap the cat during force-feeding. In that case, follow these instructions:

STEP 1 Collect the cat, the prescribed food, a small spoon (if needed), a damp washrag and two towels.

STEP 2 Seat yourself and place the towel on your lap, or sit at a table and put the towel on the table.

STEP 3 Towel-wrap the cat **if needed** and place the cat on the lap towel **or** seat the cat on the table towel.

STEP 4 Put a small dab of food on your index finger or on a small utensil like an infant spoon.

STEP 5 Gently but firmly open the cat's mouth. Place the food on the **roof of the cat's mouth near the back** and close his mouth.

STEP 6 Tilt his head up and gently stroke his throat until he swallows.

STEP 7 Repeat as needed.

STEP 8 When finished, clean the cat's face with the damp cloth. Pet him and praise him.

HOW DO I FORCE-FEED LIQUIDS TO MY CAT?

Only your Vet can decide when it's best to force-feed liquids to your cat. While forced liquids usually involve a food (thinned with water) or a prepared liquid, it's imperative that you use **only** the fluids and amounts prescribed. To get the liquid into the cat's mouth, you'll need some type of utensil like a syringe (without needle), an eyedropper or a baby oral medicine applicator. Make sure you do **not** squirt the fluid into the center of his mouth—too much liquid directly down the throat can cause choking if the cat inhales.

A written record of mealtimes and amounts will help keep things organized and enable your Vet to adjust feedings if necessary.

If your cat is hard to handle, towel-wrap him to protect you both during the feeding. Follow these instructions:

STEP 1 Collect the cat, the liquid food, a feeding utensil, two towels and a damp washrag.

STEP 2 Seat yourself and place the towel on your lap, or sit at a table and put the towel on the table.

STEP 3 Towel-wrap the cat **if needed** and place the cat on the lap towel **or** seat the cat on the table towel.

STEP 4 Draw the fluid food into the applicator.

STEP 5 Slip the applicator into the cat's mouth **between** his teeth and cheek and squirt out a small amount of fluid.

STEP 6 Tilt his head up and gently stroke his throat until he swallows.

STEP 7 Repeat as needed.

STEP 8 When finished, clean the cat's face with the damp cloth. Pet him and praise him.

WHY DOES MY CAT GET DIARRHEA OR LOSE HIS APPETITE WHEN TAKING ANTIBIOTICS? WHAT CAN I DO?

Particular antibiotics can kill all bacteria in the gut, both bad (those that make him ill) and good (those that help him digest food). It's the lack of good bacteria that can cause diarrhea.

Call your Vet—she may want to change the antibiotic to one that is less damaging to digestive system bacteria. While you have the Vet on the phone, you might ask her if you can feed a little plain yogurt, with live cultures, to help your cat redevelop his supply of good bacteria.

SHOULD I BE CONCERNED ABOUT LOOSE STOOLS/ DIARRHEA AND HARD STOOLS/CONSTIPATION?

Changes in bowel movements can be caused by any of the following:

- Antibiotics (see the question above)
- Parasites
- Sudden change in water or food
- Milk intolerance
- Bowel blockage
- Stress or emotional problems
- Allergies
- Certain diseases
- Physical changes due to aging

One bout of diarrhea in an adult cat, with no indication of pain or blood, is most likely no cause for concern. If the problem returns or happens with regularity, see your Vet.

While diarrhea is easy for most people to recognize, constipation can be a harder problem to diagnose. If the cat strains without producing a stool, if there is nothing in the litter box or if the feces are small, hard, dry—your cat is probably constipated. If he has not passed a stool for more than a couple of days, it's time for a trip to the Vet.

The treatment for either diarrhea or constipation will vary with its cause. Sometimes these conditions become chronic and are very difficult to treat. In this case, it's vital that you keep a complete written record of treatments given and the results, to help your Vet monitor his care.

WHAT SHOULD I DO WHEN MY CAT VOMITS?

If your cat vomits occasionally, consider it normal behavior; he may be getting rid of hair balls or reacting to quickly gobbled or spoiled food. And there are some finicky felines who will throw up if their food is too cold.

Recurrent vomiting, however, can indicate illness. Prolonged vomiting (more than three times in one hour or vomiting hour after hour), retching without bringing anything up and bloody vomit are all signs of illness. Take the cat to the Vet **immediately**.

IS MY CAT DEHYDRATED
(NOT GETTING ENOUGH WATER)?

Gently pinch and lift the skin on the cat's side or back. If the skin springs back into place, he's not dehydrated. If the skin returns to its place slowly or not at all, your cat is dehydrated and must be seen by the Vet **immediately**.

HOW CAN I GET MY CAT TO DRINK MORE WATER?

Consult your Vet before you encourage your cat to drink more water—a medical problem may be involved. For example, **never** force water on a cat in the acute phase of feline lower urinary tract disease. If he's already having difficulty urinating and his bladder is full, additional water can put a severe strain on his kidneys. But if your cat has recovered, he may benefit from extra water. Only your Vet will know.

If the Vet approves, here are two suggestions that work well without any trauma to your cat:

- Add one tablespoon of water to your pet's canned food. Start with little and gradually, over a few days, increase the amount of water.
- Add a few drops of flavored water to his water bowl—such as the water from water-packed fish and meat, broth or any other interesting flavors OK'd by the Vet. Be sure to change his water regularly, because the flavoring can quickly spoil at room temperature.

FIRST AID

For emergency first-aid instructions, see chapter 21.

WHY WOULD I HAVE TO RESTRAIN A CAT?

It's much less stressful for all concerned to work with your pet from an early age so he can be handled and groomed with ease. Cats unused to handling haven't learned to relax when they're medically treated or groomed.

These unsocialized cats not only can shred you, they can also injure themselves as they struggle for freedom. So when you have to give medical treatment, clip claws, flea-treat or groom such a cat, towel-wrap him—to protect you both from unnecessary harm.

HOW DO I TOWEL WRAP A CAT?

As the term implies, you use a **large** bath towel to cocoon the cat so he can't hurt you or himself. There are other alternatives such as the cat sack or pillowcase, but towel wrapping gives far more protection against sharp claws.

Partial Towel Wrap

You may be able to cover only the offending body part. For example, you can drape the towel over his hind feet so he doesn't scratch you, or put the towel over his face to stop biting. These partial wraps will **not** stop a cat that is really fighting you.

Full Towel Wrap

A full wrap should be a last resort. It's far less traumatic to hold the cat gently and accustom him to being handled.

Full wraps are usually effective without covering the cat's face. But if you have a biter, leave about six inches of a second wrap loose over his face. This will leave part of the towel as a shield for your arm. (If you're working alone, use a safety pin to keep the towel closed at his neck.)

HOW DO I GIVE LIQUID MEDICINE TO MY CAT?

It's easier to give medicine with food (ask your Vet). Measure the dose, mix it in the cat's food—and hope that he doesn't notice. And, of course, if you have more than one pet, make sure that the correct animal eats **all** the food. Letting him eat in his carrier will keep other animals and toddlers out of his meal.

Sometimes medication is less effective when combined with food, and while most cats are fairly cooperative when it comes to liquid medicine, there is the occasional cat who needs restraint. You may have to towel-wrap him to protect yourself and to get the medication down his throat.

If the medicine cannot be given with food or if he won't eat the food, follow these steps:

STEP 1   Using a dropper or other measure, prepare the medicine.
STEP 2   Gather the cat, the medicine, a damp washcloth and a heavy bath towel.
STEP 3   Fold the towel on your lap and get the cat into a sitting position on the towel **or** towel-wrap and hold him on your lap.

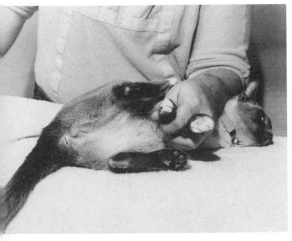

The photographs on this page illustrate the technique of towel wrapping as described in the text. Towel wrapping protects the cat and the handler from stress and injury when veterinary attention is required.

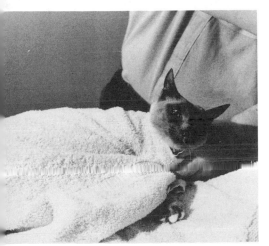

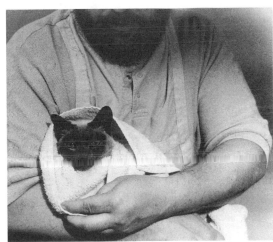

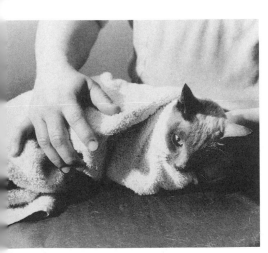

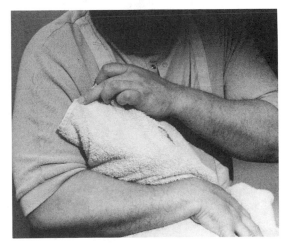

STEP 4 With one hand, gently hold his muzzle at his upper lips. (Use your forearm to hold the cat close to your chest.)

STEP 5 Tilt the cat's head up at a 45-degree angle.

STEP 6 With your free hand, angle the dropper **between** his teeth and cheek and slowly express the medicine in. **Do not squirt the medicine down his throat; he may accidentally inhale the liquid.**

STEP 7 If the cat does not automatically swallow, stroke downward on his throat till he does.

STEP 8 Wipe his face to remove all traces of the liquid; sick cats often don't groom well, and once the medicine dries, it's very hard to remove. Pet him and praise him.

HOW CAN I GET MY CAT TO TAKE A PILL?

If the pill can be finely crushed and mixed with food (ask your Vet), your job will be easy. Make sure that only the patient gets the food. As mentioned previously, feed him in his carrier.

When the pill is prescribed or when you check with the Vet, ask if a **light** coating of butter or margarine will adversely affect the medicine's ability to work properly. Greased pills slide down more easily, and your cat won't be bothered by a pill's bitterness. If your cat gets residue from a bitter pill on his taste buds, you'll know right away, because he'll have streams of drool flowing out of his mouth.

A hard-to-handle cat may require restraint; you may need to towel-wrap him.

If the medicine can't be given with food, or if he won't eat the food, follow these steps:

STEP 1 Butter the pill, but **only** if your Vet approves.

STEP 2 Gather the cat, the pill and a heavy bath towel.

STEP 3 Fold the towel on your lap and get the cat into a sitting position on the towel **or** towel-wrap and hold him on your lap.

STEP 4 With one hand, gently hold his muzzle at his upper lips. (Use your forearm to hold the cat close to your chest.)

STEP 5 Tilt the cat's head up.

STEP 6 With your free hand, touch the pill to the cat's mouth; if the cat does not open his mouth, use one finger to gently push down on the lower jaw.

STEP 7 When his mouth is open, put the pill in the back of his mouth as far back toward his throat as possible.

STEP 8 Gently close his mouth and stroke downward on his throat till the cat swallows. (He may stick out the tip of his tongue when he swallows.)

STEP 9 Release the cat's head when you see him swallow the pill. Pet him and praise him.

If all else fails, you can use a ''pill gun'' to pop the pill into a cat's throat; they are available from a Vet or a catalog.

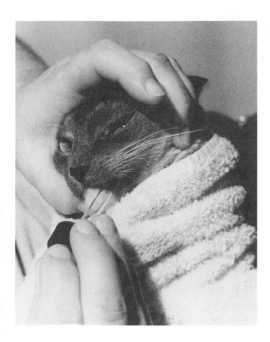

Administering liquid medication via eye dropper to a towel wrapped cat.

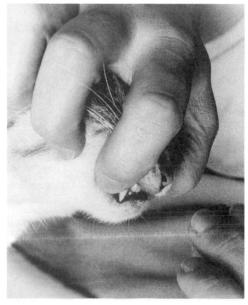

Prepare food-wrapped pill or capsule in advance and calmly position cat and medication to make administration as smooth as possible.

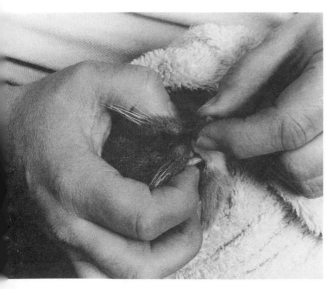

To insert pill or capsule, gently pry cat's jaws apart with thumb and forefinger, push dose to back of cat's throat, close mouth and stroke cat's throat to induce swallowing.

199

WHAT CAN I GIVE MY CAT TO EASE PAIN?

All pain medication should be closely monitored by your Vet. Pain control is difficult with cats since they cannot tolerate many common analgesics. **NEVER give your cat aspirin, acetaminophen or ibuprofen—these medications are toxic to cats!** Steroids or narcotics are the most commonly prescribed pain medications for cats. Unfortunately, both can have serious side effects if continued over a long period of time.

Alternative health care can provide additional treatment for pain. In her June 1990 column in *Cat Fancy* magazine, Dr. Margaret Reister indicates that one tablet of SOD (superoxide dismutase) per day will help with pain. Sold in health food stores, SOD works by ridding the body of toxins caused by chronic pain. Remember: check with your Vet before medicating—even with SOD.

Another alternative resource is Tellington TTouch, developed by Dr. Linda Tellington-Jones. TTouch is helpful as a nondrug, noninvasive treatment. The intent of the gentle TTouch is to activate cellular function and to release fear and pain.

Ask your Vet if Bach Rescue Remedies may also help. These natural medications are very dilute infusions from flowers.

TOXINS AND POISONS

WHAT ARE SOME COMMON TOXINS AND POISONS?

Toxins and poisons are materials or substances that when inhaled, absorbed through the skin, eaten or groomed off the fur cause illness or death. Some substances are more deadly than others. For example, it takes less than one-fourth teaspoon of antifreeze to kill a cat. Alcohol, on the other hand, can make your cat very ill—or dead, if enough is ingested.

Secondary poisons are poisons in the food chain—e.g., the mouse eats a poison and then the cat eats the mouse, or you spray general insecticides and the cat eats the roach. Secondary poisoning is harder to diagnose but can be just as deadly.

Any product that is labeled as hazardous, toxic or poisonous to humans—or labeled "keep away from children"—should be considered unsafe for a cat. The list below shows some of the common items in your home.

Common Toxins and Poisons

- Acetone
- Acetaminophen and aspirin
- Alcohol
- Algae toxin

- Amphetamines (speed)
- Antifreeze*
- Arsenic
- Bleach
- Carbon tetrachloride
- Chlordane
- Common commercial household cleaners (read labels for warnings)
- Cosmetics
- House plants (see chart in chapter 3 for dangerous species)
- Insecticides (except those clearly labeled for cats)
- Lead salts
- Over-the-counter human medicines
- Paints, specifically lead-based paints

DO CATS GET POISON IVY?

No. Your cat won't react to poison ivy, but he can give it to you. If he goes out, brushes up against the plant and gets the oil (urushiol) on his fur, the oil is transferred to your skin when you pet him. If you react to poison ivy, you, not your cat, will develop the blisters.

To get the oil off his fur, wash him with a cat shampoo—and don't forget to protect yourself with rubber gloves at the same time.

GROOMING AND HEALTH PROBLEMS

MY CAT IS GROOMING OFF HIS FUR. WHAT DO I DO?

The condition of a cat's coat is an indication of his physical and emotional health and the quality of both his nutrition and his grooming habits. A healthy coat is clean and shiny with an even, full texture.

Cats will chew and groom off their fur because of fleas, allergies, pain, injury, emotional distress or even because you accidentally taught him to do it through your attention.

Overgrooming is a frustrating problem because it can have so many causes. First, see your Vet to be sure a medical problem is not the cause. If the excessive grooming has created skin irritation or infection, he'll need immediate medical treatment anyway.

Regardless of the reason for the overgrooming, it's important to treat the source of the problem to correct the behavior. If medical treatment, adjustment of diet and more effective overall grooming don't help, an animal behavior consultant or pet therapist may be the answer.

There are two things you can do to help your cat recover while the problem

*Traditional antifreeze is made with ethylene glycol.

is being treated. First, use an Elizabethan collar. Second, **after checking with your Vet**, give your cat nutritional (low magnesium) yeast to sooth the skin irritation and to aid fur regrowth. Sprinkle ¼ to ½ teaspoon on his food at each meal.

WHAT IS AN ELIZABETHAN COLLAR?

Elizabethan collars are funnel-like devices that prevent the cat's mouth from reaching any part of his body. Used to stop self-mutilation, pulling off bandages or pulling out stitches, these collars can be borrowed from your Vet or made from poster board or plastic milk jugs. See chapter 20 for construction tips.

While he wears the collar, you'll have to help your cat with grooming. After meals, wipe his face with a warm, wet cloth and once a day give him a damp bath.

WHY DID HIS FUR CHANGE COLOR?

When the fur of some cats is damaged, it regrows in a different color. Siamese usually regrow darker fur, and other breeds tend to regrow white or lighter-colored fur.

MY CAT IS PULLING OUT STITCHES. WHAT DO I DO?

The first thing to do is to call your Vet. The stitches may need to be replaced. If your cat won't leave the sutures alone, you may need to use an Elizabethan collar.

WHY AND HOW SHOULD I CONTROL HAIR BALLS?

Hair balls form from groomed fur that has been ingested and should be treated before problems develop. At the very least, cats with hair balls will chew on house plants to make themselves vomit, and you'll have to clean the mess up. But plant eating has its dangers too. In extreme cases, the hair balls themselves can cause death; bowels, blocked by chunks of hair, may require emergency surgery. Any way you look at it, an ounce of hair-ball prevention can definitely be worth the cost of the cure.

To help prevent hair balls, groom your cat regularly. You can also give a commercial hair-ball preventative weekly (the dosage is listed on the package). More frequent doses will be needed during the spring and fall shedding seasons and year-round for a longhaired cat.

MENTAL HEALTH

CAN MY CAT BE AFFECTED BY MY EMOTIONAL STRESS LEVEL?

Yes. Cats can be extremely sensitive to human anxiety and mood swings; like dogs, they can "read" or understand your paralanguage. If you're stressed by illness or in an uncomfortable predicament, the situation itself can add to your cat's discomfort. Before handling a tense, frightened or ill cat, get a handle on your own stress and fears. Stress also decreases the body's natural defenses against illness. So stress management is an important part of staying well for both you and your cat.

HOW CAN I REDUCE MY CAT'S LEVEL OF STRESS?

First, become calm **before** interacting with your cat. And for everyone's increased comfort, try to reduce the level of noise and confusion in your home.

To help soothe your cat, set aside ten to twenty minutes for daily aerobic play. Exercise helps him relax just as it does humans. It's best to start slow and easy with any exercise program, and you might want to get an OK from your Vet, particularly if your cat is elderly or has health problems.

Your cat also needs some quiet time with you. You might brush him (if he enjoys it), or sit and talk to him, using his name in a positive message. Relaxation and this "almost" meditation will help compose you both.

Catnip is a great relaxer for most cats. Give him dry catnip daily **or** fresh catnip two to three times a week—unless he's a "mean drunk" or his Vet says no. (See chapter 11.) Two other medicinal products are helpful in reducing stress—camomile tea (⅛ to ¼ teaspoon of the loose tea leaves, once or twice daily) and Calms or Calms Forti tablets (one tablet given once or twice daily; do not use the tinctures).

Just as important as mental refuge and medicinal relaxers is a quiet, safe physical place your cat can escape to when things are busy in your home. In his quiet place, especially when you have to be away, you can still comfort an ill or anxious pet. Here are three ideas that work:

- Leave an unwashed shirt for bedding. It will have your comforting scent on it. Cats use their sense of smell to identify individuals.
- Tune the radio to an easy-listening station and leave it on low in your absence.
- Make a soothing continuous-play audiotape of your voice to play while you're gone. See chapter 20 for instructions.

14

Disaster Preparedness

DISASTERS can take many shapes and forms, ranging from potential dangers to your cat in connection with the holidays, to the anguish of a missing cat, to life-and-death situations during a storm or an earthquake. This chapter tells you how to deal with these situations and more. It's a chapter to read *before* there is a problem. See chapter 21 for first aid.

WHAT SHOULD I DO DURING SEVERE WEATHER OR AN EARTHQUAKE?

Your cat's survival depends in large part on your survival. Being prepared can help both of you weather the glitches Mother Nature deals us.

General Survival Guidelines

- If you usually let your cat out—don't.
- Keep ample supplies of nonperishable food on hand. Rotate this reserve so the food stays fresh.
- The safest places are a bathroom without windows and a basement away from windows.
- Learn what the common weather problems are in your area and how to deal with them. Then develop an emergency plan.
- Plan ahead for alternative placement for your animal(s). People may be urged to go to public shelters. Pets are not allowed, and animal shelters and Vets will be crowded or unreachable.

- Keep a battery-powered radio ready for use in your safe room and check the batteries regularly.
- Learn where the main connections are for water, gas and electricity—and know how to turn them off.

After the Disaster Has Hit (After the All Clear)

- If your home has sustained damage, turn off the main water, electricity and gas connections until the house has been checked for structural problems.
- If the house is undamaged and the power is out during cold weather, close off as many outer rooms as possible, and stay together to keep warm; a cat under the covers is a great space heater.
- If you search for your cat after the disaster, be very careful—buildings can be unstable. Check the animal for injuries before moving him. Be careful! Cats who are injured or traumatized may bite. See chapter 21 for instructions.
- If your cat has been so traumatized that he will not let you near him:
  — Use a humane trap to catch him. These food-baited traps don't harm the cat. They are available from animal shelters.
  — Do **not** touch the cat after he has been trapped. Take him to a small, safe room with his water, food and litter. Release him, and leave him alone for an hour or two.
  — After he has calmed down, make friends with him again.

WHAT SHOULD I DO IF THERE IS A FIRE?

While we understand your love for your cat, don't jeopardize your own life in a fire in an attempt to save him. If you can quickly find your cat, put him in his carrier or an emergency carrier and follow these guidelines:

- If there is smoke, keep low and crawl. There's less smoke at floor level.
- Touch doors before opening them. If a door is hot, do not open it.
- Call for the firefighters from a neighbor's (911 in most urban areas).
- Have your Vet check the cat for smoke inhalation, burns or other injuries; see chapter 21.
- Should your cat become lost in the confusion, see the lost-cat instructions below—but also check and recheck your house and property in case the cat tries to return to a formerly safe place. Be very careful when you search burned-out buildings; they can be unstable. And never enter a fire-damaged building until firefighters have given permission.

HOW WILL EMERGENCY PERSONNEL KNOW PETS LIVE IN MY HOUSE?

Many shelters, catalogs and pet shops carry stickers you can put on windows and doors. The sticker states that pets will need assistance in an emergency and usually provides space to write in how many of each species live in the house. Put one sticker on each door and bedroom window.

HOW CAN I PROTECT MY CAT IF I, THE SOLE CARETAKER, HAVE AN ACCIDENT?

Carry identification that asks authorities to call the person listed who has agreed to care for your animals. This person can be a friend or relative you trust or a professional pet sitter on a contingency arrangement. Ideally, this individual should have a key to your home—or in the case of a professional sitter, they should know where to get a key.

Put another copy of the identification in your car where it's easily seen, and add this information to any medical ID you must carry.

If your cat has special dietary restrictions or other medical needs, it's a good idea to post clear instructions on your refrigerator or in another obvious location. (Special-order tags can help identify animals by name and medical problem.)

WHAT SHOULD I DO IF MY CAT GETS LOST?

Every day that passes decreases the chance that your cat will be found. Don't waste time waiting for him to return home, but don't act out of panic. Follow these suggestions and try to keep up your spirits.

Immediately

- During the first hour: Check your yard and the neighbors'. Check your closets and any other area that's closed off inside the house. Call the cat, shake a box of cat food and look under things and in high places; cats can hide in very small spots. Listen for his cry; he may be trapped inside something or stuck in high branches.
- When you're sure he's not on your property, search the neighborhood. Enlist the help of neighbor children, the mailman and regular delivery people. Without listing a specific amount, offer a reward for information leading to his recovery. Rewards don't have to be a lavish amount; five dollars is enough at this stage.

Later That Day

- Go to the local animal shelters and check the cages. Leave a picture or description of your cat at each place.
- Widen the search to cover a six-block area in each direction.
- Give restaurants, homes with an intact female cat and other interesting places to the cat special attention. Leave your name and phone number with the people at each location.

After Dark

- Put his litter box outside. Do **not** clean it out; the scent may lead him home.
- Make a poster and photocopy it on bright, easy-to-see paper. The poster should include an objective description of your cat with the following information:
  — In large print the words LOST and REWARD (Do not list amount; it can still be a token amount.)
  — Your phone number **and** a friend's phone number
  — A recent photo of your cat
  — A description of the cat's color and identifying marks, breed, gender, age and size (height and weight).

Second Day

- Recheck the neighborhood. Tack up posters as you go.
- Go to the animal shelter and **personally** check the cages. Leave a poster.
- Take posters to all the Vets, pet stores and groomers in your area. Also leave posters at local veterinary or medical schools, labs or research complexes that use animals and any other places in your area that deal with pets.
- Place an ad in your local paper. Notices in the "lost and found" column are usually free, but ads in the "pets" space may not be free.
- Call the local radio and TV stations and ask if they announce lost pets. (Don't forget the public-access and alternative stations.) Take posters to the stations that will be making the announcements.

Following Days

- Daily recheck the local shelter and the neighborhood.
- Check the ads in the newspapers, both to see that your ad is correct and to read the "found" ads and the "pet" column.
- Mail posters to delivery businesses and give one to your mailman.
- Replace any posters as needed.
- Have someone at the phone numbers on the posters at all times or use an answering machine.
- Follow up on all leads and DO NOT GIVE UP.
- **Report any attempt to ransom your cat** to the police.
- Before you go to meet anyone who calls concerning your cat:
  — Take a friend with you, and even if you're taking along a friend, tell a family member or another friend about the meeting. Tell them who you will be meeting and give the location of the meeting and the times you expect to leave and return.
  — Call the family member or your friend when you return.

When You Find Your Pet

- Report this to your local shelter and any other place you often checked.
- Write a letter to the newspaper editor thanking people who helped you with the search.

HOW DO I KEEP MY CAT FROM GETTING LOST?

More than 15,000 pets disappear outdoors every day and are never found. A good way to prevent your cat from becoming another statistic is to never let him roam outside alone.

Even an indoor cat needs his ID, since you never know when an emergency will happen. Use one of the high-tech ID systems or keep a breakaway or elastic collar (with his rabies tag or an ID tag) on your cat at all times.

To make the best use of an identification tag, include the following information:

- Your name and phone number
- Phone number of a friend or relative
- Abbreviated summary of ongoing medical problems

ARE THERE ANY ALTERNATIVES TO USING TAGS FOR ID?

Tattoos are another option. While your name and address might seem to be an ideal identification choice, addresses—and names—do change. A much better tattoo option is your social security number or a cat registry number. Cats are small animals with limited writing space on the inside of their back thighs—so try to keep the tattoo short. Ear tattoos are **not** recommended because those who steal pets to sell to research labs have been known to cut off animals' ears to remove IDs.

The tattooing is quick and relatively painless. These feline IDs are not etched as deep as traditional human tattoos and as the years pass they may fade enough so that they need to be done over.

While the tattoos are considered a ''permanent'' fixture, they still need to be seen. You'll have to clip your cat's fur short—and keep it short—so the number remains visible. Many of the shelters in large cities are regularly checking each new animal for tattoos, but unfortunately not all shelters follow the procedure. If the hair over the tattoo is kept short, the number may be noticed during routine handling.

Microchips are the newest entry in the pet ID field. A very small microchip is injected under the cat's skin at his shoulder. Regarded as permanent, microchips can be detected and read only by a special electronic reader—which, at this time, is not widely available. Another drawback is that the technology has not settled on standards—so a microchip reader can't read all chips. And as with other identification registry companies, these microchip shippers can serve your cat only if they stay in business.

MY CAT IS UP A TREE. WHAT DO I DO?

Your cat's out on a limb because his curved claws enable him to hook his way up the tree. Unfortunately, that same inward curve prevents the cat from climbing down headfirst. So he must back down if it's too far to jump. Like most people, cats don't like to lead with their posteriors. Not only can't they see where they're going, but putting their backs into the descent leaves them vulnerable to attack.

First, remove other pets or children from the area. Wait for an hour or two; the cat may come down unaided when he is less stressed. If he is still in the tree after two hours, lean a long board or ladder against the tree at a 45-degree angle—and wait again.

Your next option, if he's still up the tree, is to entice him down the board or ladder with his favorite smelly food. Eventually, your cat will come down when he gets hungry enough—the instinct for survival far outweighs fear.

Waiting for the cat to come down can be harder on you than on him—especially if your friend isn't the strong, silent type. After hearing two or three days of plaintive meows from a particularly high tree, you'll be tempted to call the fire department or the police. Don't. They can't be expected to (and won't) tie up emergency equipment rescuing a cat, who will come down anyway when he's good and ready.

Only as a last resort, for the cat in danger or in need of medical treatment, use a ladder to climb up after him. Because he may attack from fright, it's best to wear heavy gloves and a long-sleeved jacket. Protective covering for your face isn't usually an option, so handle the cat accordingly. Don't cradle him near your neck or face as you come down the ladder.

WHAT EXTRA PRECAUTIONS ARE NEEDED AT HOLIDAYS?

Holidays and other special days are stressful to us, but we can understand what's happening. To a cat, these days can be even more unnerving. In general:

- Give the animals a quiet place to retreat to in order to get away from your guests.
- Watch out for the cat's stealing unhealthy or toxic foods.
- Do not share harmful holiday foods or overindulge him with good foods. A little treat is fun; too much can lead to a tummy ache and an extra mess to clean up.
- Do not let animals drink alcohol, eat cigarettes, cigars or their butts or get into food wrappers or other trash that accumulates with parties.
- Be sure pets are not stepped on or let out accidentally. If there is a great deal of in-and-out traffic, isolate him in a room with his litter, food and water or put his harness on for safety and tie his leash to an out-of-the-way table leg.
- Keep all candles on an open shelf out of the reach of curious paws and whiskers. Yes, fur will burn. See chapter 7 for training cats to avoid specific areas.
- Ask your guests to adhere to these guidelines.

Some holidays have additional hazards. Consider the following:

Fourth of July

- Do not use fireworks around your pets; the sounds are frightening and panic may lead to biting—or escape.

- Clean up the yard before allowing pets in it. Leftover gunpowder may be toxic.
- Give the animals as quiet a place as possible to retreat to, such as a closet or basement.
- Be careful of the grill.
- Watch for heat prostration.

Halloween

- Keep cats, especially black cats, inside during this holiday. Cats are favorite animals to use in misguided Halloween rituals because of their perceived connection with the occult.

Christmas

- Place breakable ornaments high on the tree out of reach of curious paws and put unbreakable ones where he can play with them safely. Origami, Japanese paper folding, makes excellent ornaments. Food, such as popcorn strings, do **not** make good ornaments from a safety perspective.
- Check the balance of the tree. Use extra tie-downs so it can't be knocked over if a cat climbs it. Fishing line won't really show and can be tied from the top of the tree to cup hooks in the window frame. If you use fishing line, make sure it is high enough or close enough to the wall so that humans can't be injured by the invisible string.
- Cover the tree's water bowl; sap and water additives can be toxic to small children and animals.
- Be careful with tinsel and package ribbons; if swallowed they can block the intestines.
- Keep real mistletoe, holly and Jerusalem cherry out of reach; they're toxic and can poison your cat. Poinsettia is not as dangerous as once believed but this plant is still not good for snacking. Keep it inaccessible.
- Be careful when using decorative sprays, such as spray-on snow. While you may enjoy the look on the evergreen or window, Kitty won't enjoy the effect on his fur.
- Discourage pine tree nibbling and electric cord chewing; spray the lower branches and cords with white vinegar or original flavor Listerine; reapply every few days.

Your other tree option is to use a nontraditional tree with nonbreakable ornaments. Here are some choices:

- Decorate a firmly secured artificial tree. (Make sure it can't tip over.) For added stability, fasten the tree stand to a $2' \times 2'$ or $3' \times 3'$ piece of plywood.
- Decorate large nontoxic potted plants and trees. Choose plants that aren't fragile and can't be damaged by extra attention from your cat. Trees with large thorns will discourage climbing, but keep an eye on it. While cats are likely to avoid the thorns, small children can be hurt.
- Decorate a large branch from a deciduous tree. In some areas, people also decorate Easter trees this way.

15

Cats and the Law

IN MANY WAYS, the law considers a cat, or any pet, to be a possession—the same as a chair or car. There are, however, laws which govern minimum standards of care (food, water, shelter, vaccinations) and are enforced by local animal shelters or humane associations.

In reality, pets don't have many legal rights, and you have few rights with respect to keeping pets. One notable exception: if you are elderly or handicapped, and qualify for federally subsidized housing, you may have the right to have a pet.

Needless to say, you can avoid problems for both you and your pet if you know your legal obligations.

WHAT ABOUT CATS AND THE LAW?

State laws vary, and each community has the right to set certain standards regarding domestic animals. If you have a problem and are concerned about your legal position, consult your attorney.

In almost all cases, a cat is considered property, valued only according to his "resale" price. Sentimental value rarely enters the picture, although if the pet was deliberately injured or killed, you may be able to collect something for emotional distress.

Conversely, you are almost always responsible for damage to people and property caused by your cat. Bites, scratches and other injuries to a human can carry a heavy price tag. And depending on the circumstances, you can also be held financially liable if your animal injures or kills someone else's pet.

While your local animal control facility is the most visible enforcer of animal law, most states establish and enforce animal regulations. The amount of regulation and enforcement varies from state to state, but all states have laws requiring rabies vaccinations. Other than that, the most in-depth laws regarding any animal in human custody usually regulate the minimum level of care in terms of food, water and shelter.

City and county ordinances vary widely and can be shaped by local animal problems. Some cities or counties have leash laws pertaining to cats; most, however, don't. In cities where licenses are required for dogs, a cat probably needs to be licensed too. And if you own several cats and dogs, you may be breaking another city ordinance; most cities can specify the number of animals you can legally keep. To have more animals on your property, you might need a zoning variance and/or a kennel license.

ARE THERE ANY SPECIAL ARRANGEMENTS TO CONSIDER DURING A DIVORCE?

Even the most amiable divorce will cause some disruption in the household, as property is divided and someone moves out. While most adults can understand these changes, your cat will have a more difficult time.

For the cat, any change can be disconcerting. He likes his routines—the same spot for sunbathing every day, the same person to scratch his ears and fill his bowl. He becomes upset with the increased level of tension and human mood changes. The added stress can lead to cat behavior problems.

Who gets what can be a thorny problem. Here are some things to consider when preparing the pet section of your divorce agreement:

- Who was the animal adopted by? When? Before or during the relationship?
- Can/should the children and the animal stay together?
- Who has been the primary caregiver to the pet?
- Will there be visitation rights? Can the cat tolerate this arrangement? (It takes an easygoing cat to handle joint custody.)
- Will the noncustodial spouse help pay for care?
- Will the animal be used by one person to manipulate the other or to prolong unwanted contact?
- Will one party be moving in with someone, and will that person or their animals want the cat?
- Is it better for all concerned—cat, children, parents—for the cat to go to a temporary home? Or should he be returned to the breeder, put up for adoption or euthanized (in the case of an ill or very elderly pet)?

Whatever is decided, include provisions for the family pet in the formal divorce agreement so there are no misunderstandings. Include a description of the pet, the estimated cost of pet care, who will be responsible for the cost of temporary care, the length of temporary care and what happens to the cat if the temporary care or adoption doesn't work out.

This is also a good time to assemble pet medical records and a description of the pet's diet for the caregiver.

MY CAT WAS STOLEN. WHAT DO I DO?

If you didn't actually see a theft occur, the animal may have gotten out by himself. A cat can easily disappear into small holes or through partially open doors and windows.

Sad to say, but if your cat was really stolen, he'll probably not be seen again. Thieves steal nearly two million animals annually. Household pets become experimental animals for laboratory testing—and purebred animals are stolen to resell.

If you have evidence that your cat was stolen, do not disturb the "crime scene" in any way. Report the theft to the police and your local shelter and let them follow up.

The more information you can give the police, the better chance you have for recovery. You'll need to describe your cat in detail. A recent photo and "The Form of My Cat's Life" (see chapter 12) will be great helps in the search. Also be prepared to describe any strangers and unfamiliar cars in the area.

There is a national information clearinghouse concerned with pet theft. In Defense of Animals has an automated Pet Theft hot line: 1-800-STOLEN PETS. Or you can speak with staff people based in the San Francisco Bay Area at 1 415-453-9984.

WHAT DO I NEED TO KNOW ABOUT INSURANCE?

First, read your homeowner's or renter's policy carefully; coverage—and premiums—will vary according to company. Additionally, your state's insurance regulatory agency may have set specific insurance standards. If you're looking for insurance, it pays to comparison-shop. Learn what different companies have to offer and at what price.

Most homeowner's policies will exclude coverage for damage done by an animal living in the house and for recovery of the monetary value of the animal if he's lost, stolen or dead. Renter's policies are handled the same way as homeowner's with respect to liability and contents. They are not going to cover damage to the apartment—or the shredded couch or the pet-stained wall-to-wall carpet.

There are ways, however, to broaden coverage in homeowner's and renter's policies. Keep in mind that additional coverage will cost more—but if you have a problem pet or special circumstances, the peace of mind may be worth the extra cost. For example, you may be able to purchase extra insurance to cover the accidental death of a purebred show cat. To prove his value, you'll have to keep careful records of his breeding, purchase price, registry and show achievements. Discuss options with your insurance agent. In any case, the provider's total liability is the limit of the policy.

Insurers are particularly concerned about aggressive animals and personal injury liability. A well-socialized, trained cat will save you money and legal problems in the long run. The insurance company may tolerate one cat bite. At two bites, you'll probably find that your policy won't be renewed, and you'll be considered "at risk." Insurance companies share information on bad-risk clients, and you may have trouble getting household insurance in the future.

If you breed and sell kittens, most insurance companies consider that you are conducting a business. Homeowner's policies exclude coverage for any claim arising from an in-home business. So if your cat or her kittens bite or claw someone looking to buy a pet, you—not the insurance company—will be liable for damages. To be covered, you would need to purchase business insurance. And if you run an in-home business in which you have another person's animal in your possession, you should look into a "care, custody and control" policy.

Always be up-front with your agent and insurance company. If you lie to them about anything, including information concerning ownership of an animal, they not only can refuse to pay the claim in question, they can retroactively cancel your policy.

IS THE LAW INTERESTED IN CAT BITES?

There's nothing like an animal bite to get people interacting. The law, your insurance company and the victim all have a serious view of cat bites. While the victim may forgive, where the law is concerned there can be no compromise— all cat bites are to be reported to local public health authorities. The cat will have to be quarantined at the animal shelter or a veterinary hospital for ten days (with proof of up-to-date rabies vaccine) or for six months (if there is no proof of current rabies vaccination).

The quarantine may seem harsh, but these laws are for **everyone's** protection. By the time rabies symptoms appear, the disease is fatal. If the cat is isolated and diagnosed early enough, preventative shots can be given to the bite victim.

WHAT SHOULD I DO IF I AM SOLD A "DEFECTIVE" CAT OR KITTEN?

During your new cat's first health appointment, the Vet may find a genetic problem, signs of abuse, parasites or disease. Ask her to document the problem and explain the ramifications to you. Minor, easily treated ailments, such as worms and fleas, may be an expense covered by the purchase agreement. To know what you're getting into, be sure to discuss the following with the Vet:

- What is the problem? How serious is it in terms of the cat's quality of life and life expectancy?
- What would need to be done to correct or control the problem now? Later?
- What ongoing changes would you need to make in your life to cope with the pet's special needs?
- If the condition is contagious to humans or to other animals in your household, what can be done to protect the other household members?
- How much will this care cost now and in the future?

After speaking to the Vet, you'll need to decide whether to keep and treat the pet. Usually the decision comes down to three considerations: Will the cat have a reasonable quality of life? Can you, now and in the future, deal with the lifestyle changes needed with a handicapped cat? Can you afford the cost?

Before making a final decision, check your sales contract, if you received one, for policies concerning "defective merchandise." Pet stores are covered by "puppy lemon laws" on the federal level, and in some cases on the state and local levels. These laws are concerned with the health of any animal sold; the store must refund the money or replace the pet.

When dealing with the seller, remain calm and report the facts as documented by your Vet. Don't make critical comments to the seller or about the seller to other people. In other words, don't compound the problem by antagonizing the seller or by giving him a basis for filing slander charges.

Your next step will depend on the circumstances. You can report the problem to the local Better Business Bureau and/or to the newspaper or magazine which carried the seller's advertisement. If the animal shows signs of abuse or neglect, consult the local humane association, the local animal control facility or your lawyer. **In all cases, make sure you stick to the facts in the Vet's report to keep yourself out of legal hot water.** It's also a good idea to keep copies of all correspondence and reports for your records.

What happens to the animal if you return him to the seller? After refund or replacement, several things can happen. The pet may be resold locally or sent to another store in the chain to be resold. He may be given away or euthanized. You might want to ask your local humane association about licenses or permits that apply to the sellers. There are many variables, but the end result should be humane treatment of pets.

Returning a pet and not knowing how the animal will be disposed of can give most of us a bad case of the "guilts." But to knowingly buy (and keep) a "defective" cat out of pity and a perceived need to protect him from harm isn't usually the best answer for you, the cat or the seller. Keeping the cat will do nothing for the seller's other ill or abused animals—and you can't adopt them all. The best thing to do is to document the cat's return and immediately report the facts to your local humane authorities to protect animals in the future.

CAN A LANDLORD STOP ME FROM HAVING A CAT?

Yes. It's imperative to check your lease for pet clauses **before** signing an agreement. Pets may be prohibited or restricted by number, size or species. Even if pets are allowed, you may have to pay a higher rent, an additional deposit or even a nonrefundable deposit.

If you qualify for federal assistance in housing and are elderly or handicapped, you are covered by Section 227 of the Housing and Urban Rural Recovery Act of 1983 (12 USC 1701 R-1). Check with HUD and the landlord; you may be able to keep a cat. Under this provision, the landlord or manager of the building can limit the number of animals you may have, the size of your animal and where the animal is allowed outside of your apartment.

After you've read and signed a lease, but **before** moving into any dwelling, **document in writing, with both your signature and the landlord's,** any pet damage or flea infestation. Hold on to your copy of the report and use it, when you are ready to move out, to settle the return of the damage deposit.

Bringing a pet into a no-pet rental can bring big problems. The landlord may evict you or require you to remove the pet from the dwelling and/or yard. If evicted, you may be responsible for court costs and for the remaining balance of the lease.

If your pet is well behaved, you may be able to negotiate a pet clause with a landlord. See the question below.

HOW CAN I CONVINCE A LANDLORD TO
CHANGE HIS/HER MIND ABOUT ANIMALS?

This can be difficult, especially if the landlord has had previous bad experiences. But it may be worth a try when you have found that perfect place to live. Here are some ways to show your dedication to responsible care:

- Take the animal with you when you visit the place. Keep him on a leash or in a carrier and ask the landlord to meet him.
- Write a résumé for the cat. Introduce him by name, age and birthplace and list everything special about him. Give your Vet's name and phone number. List references from past landlords who can vouch for his good behavior and for your responsible care of both the pet and the premises. (Ask these references for their permission before using their names and phone numbers.)
- Write an animal care résumé for yourself to show that you have experience and are responsible. List any training you have had or have given to others. Also include animal experience (number of animals, species and how long they lived), a statement from your Vet and other references.

ARE THERE LAWS GOVERNING
HOW MANY CATS I MAY HAVE?

Yes. Your city will most likely have ordinances limiting the number and/ or type of animals you may have in your home.

These ordinances were written to protect the animals involved, your neighbors' physical safety and sanity and public health.

WHAT HAPPENS TO MY CAT WHEN I DIE?

Unfortunately, all pets, including your cat, are considered property by law, without rights—and unless you provide for your pets in your will, they're at the mercy of whoever clears up your estate. They may find your cat a home, euthanize him, or he could end up at a shelter with little chance of a home.

You can bequeath your pets to a responsible person—a friend or relative— who has agreed to take them. If you bequeath the cat, to prevent mix-ups leave your executor a complete description of the animal, including a registration number and a photo.

You can provide money for the care of your cat, a trust for the cat or an inheritance for the person to whom the cat is given—but you **cannot** name your animal as your beneficiary. Your attorney can best advise what's legal in your state. He'll also know how to set up the will, what limits there may be on trusts and in general what the best plan of action is for your particular circumstances.

ARE THERE ANY LEGAL RESTRICTIONS
ON PLACES PETS CAN TRAVEL?

Yes. All foreign countries have their own regulations. The most stringent restrictions are usually in the United Kingdom and its former colonies. (Canada is an exception because of our shared border and common exposure to rabies.) The quarantine required by rabies-free countries can be up to six months and is designed to prevent the import of rabies.

Plan ahead and plan carefully. Even a new rabies vaccination can play havoc with the incubation period. The best approach is to write for information or call the Area Vet in Charge (AVIC), Federal Veterinarians, located in nearly all states. The AVIC also issues the health certificates for foreign travel. They tend to be a better source of help than foreign embassies, because you may get inconsistent information from different staff in an embassy. To avoid problems, make sure you contact AVICs well in advance of your travel date.

The following states do not have an AVIC: Connecticut, New Hampshire, Maine, Rhode Island, Vermont and Alaska. To get a certificate in the New England states listed, use the AVIC in Massachusetts. In Alaska, you'll need to contact the AVIC in Washington State.

TRAVEL INSIDE THE UNITED STATES

With a health certificate from your Vet, your cat is welcome to visit any state but Hawaii—it's the only state that is truly rabies-free, and they want to keep it that way. Like Britain, Hawaii requires a quarantine for all incoming animals. You must pay the boarding fees and can visit the kennel only during specified hours. And if your cat is on a special diet, you'll need to provide food during the quarantine. Contact the AVIC in Hawaii for more information.

The only other governmental restrictions you may run into inside the United States are in state and national parks, both of which set their own policies. Write or call ahead and ask for the most up-to-date regulations.

16

Strays and Ferals

UNFORTUNATELY, not all cats have good homes. Some are born wild (feral) and some are turned out of homes and become strays. With few exceptions, these animals live short, harsh lives. Most cats dumped out on the country roads will not survive; they'll be hit by cars, be attacked by dog packs or starve to death. Not all cats know how to hunt!

Stray and feral populations are fast becoming an unmanageable problem in many communities. There are things that you and your humane shelter can do to help.

HOW DO FERAL, STRAY AND HOUSE CATS DIFFER?

The differences between feral and house cats (and strays) are the result of domestication. Stray cats, with a house cat tendency to play and remain kittenish into adulthood, will thrive as a pet but not in the feral cat's wild environment.

Feral Cats

Feral cats are born in the wild, and as kittens haven't interacted with humans. Tending to bite and slash on first contact, these cats are fearful and suspicious of people. Biologically driven, they fight to defend their territory, mate as their hormones dictate and hunt when they're hungry. Feral cats have fewer vocalizations than house cats; they are loners in the true sense of the word, coming together only to mate or to protect their turf.

Each feral female will have her own hunting territory (often as large as three acres). The male will defend an area that encompasses a portion of each female's territory, where, as a couple, they meet and breed.

While the freedom of nature makes their life sound idyllic, these cats live an average of eighteen months to two years and almost always die violent deaths.

House Cats

House cats live with people and depend on them for their care. Because of their close association with humans, these cats live longer, healthier lives and retain their carefree, kittenish behavior longer into adulthood. More vocal than ferals, they keep their kitten calls and add adult sounds for a wider range of voices.

The kind and amounts of good food make house cats larger than ferals. For these bigger, heavier cats, hunting is unnecessary—it is a matter of play instead of survival.

The other basic animal behavior is affected too. Since most house cats (hopefully) are neutered, they aren't driven to mate by hormones, and they tend to display less aggression and territoriality. Gentler in their interactions, house cats are more social. They enjoy the company of people and other animals.

Stray Cats

Stray cats are homeless house cats. While some avoid people because of abuse, others will walk up and demand a place to live.

More vocal and social than feral cats, these homeless animals tend to cluster in colonies—particularly in food-abundant locations like garbage dumps and grain-storage areas.

Colonies made up of intact (nonneutered) stray cats are less stable than the neuter-and-release colonies described later in this chapter. All the pheromones floating around bring a heightened awareness of the other cats. Intact females draw wandering toms into the colonies, and even though food is abundant, old and new males fight (sometimes to the death) for breeding rights.

The constant arrival of new toms brings ongoing violence and instability to the community. If young kittens are left alone, a new intact male will instinctively kill the babies to hasten the female's heat, allowing him to begin his own bloodline. In response, colony females, usually related, will share the rearing of the young—so that one can care for and protect the kittens while the other hunts.

Even if strays are neutered, where food is scarce it's every cat for itself. Each must establish a hunting territory and struggle to keep the area free from invaders. Without abundant food, play becomes secondary to survival. The sparser the food supply, the greater the territory each cat needs to defend for hunting.

In spite of their strong instinct to survive, hungry strays may have a hard time learning how to catch their food and guard their territory. Some may not learn to hunt before their desperate lives and starvation catch up to them.

WHAT IS THE BEST WAY TO INTERACT
WITH A STRAY CAT?

Be very careful when approaching strays. And make sure you tell your children not to go near stray cats and kittens at all. If a cat needs help, your kids should seek out an adult.

For strays, an outdoor existence can be cruel. Many will scratch or bite on first contact. So it's generally not a good idea to greet strays as you would a pet. You wish him no ill will, but he doesn't know it.

In addition, strays often carry diseases and parasites. For whatever the reason you come into contact with a stray, after touching him wash up (if possible, with an antibacterial soap) to avoid spreading disease to your own pets.

If the cat needs to be relocated or captured for treatment, borrow a humane trap from your local shelter, bait it with food and leave the area. (These traps don't harm the cat.) Check the situation every few hours from a distance until the animal is caught, and then use the trap like a carrier to transport him. (Protect your car seat by putting waterproof material under the trap; a frightened cat may release urine or feces, or the leftover food may spill from the trap.)

If you are attempting to win his trust so you can adopt him—once, twice or more times daily, take food and water to him. Gradually move closer as he eats. Always remain calm, quiet—and move slowly; it may take days or even months to win his confidence. Let the cat approach you and slowly move your hand (fingers curled in to protect the tips) to the cat's level, then close to his nose so he can smell you. You can present either the back side of the hand or the palm side to the cat. Once the cat is comfortable, reach out and scratch him under the chin or behind the ears. Never drop your hand unannounced onto the cat. While your goal is to show affection, he'll see a move that is both powerful and threatening.

HOW DO I KEEP STRAY, FERAL OR
OTHER CATS AWAY FROM MY HOME?

Having unwanted outdoor cats using your petunias for a litter box or marking your house with urine can be very upsetting to your cat and unpleasant to your nose. The sight and scent of another cat can also cause your pet to begin marking inside your home. When this territoriality takes the form of indoor spraying, the intruder needs to move on. To discourage outdoor cats from using your yard:

- Clean the outside sprayed areas on your house with plain distilled vinegar. Pour it on the surface and then hose it off.

- Outline the perimeter of your property with one of the following items:
  — Feces from your cat's litter box
  — Citrus peels (orange, grapefruit or lemon)
  — Ammonia-soaked rags

Note: The repellent of choice needs to be replaced weekly, for at least two weeks after the intruder's last visit.

- Reinforce the message of the repellents by tossing a rattle can near the visitor, or hiss at him. An aluminum soda can with a few pennies inside and a taped-up opening makes a great rattle can.

WHAT ARE THE COMMUNITY OPTIONS FOR DEALING WITH STRAY AND FERAL CATS?

While stray cats are more easily reintroduced into a home, feral cats over the age of four months are difficult to domesticate and can rarely be trusted. There are two views on dealing with stray and feral cats:

1. Humanely trap the cats and evaluate each one. Those that are healthy, calm and able to live in a home are neutered and put up for adoption. Those that do not fit the criteria (unfortunately, this applies to most) are euthanized. The idea is that the **only** appropriate place for these cats to live is in a home.
2. Humanely trap all the cats in the area and take them to a Vet for evaluation. If the animal is ill, old or injured, he is euthanized. If healthy, the cat is anesthetized, neutered, vaccinated and examined for parasites and other easily fixed problems. The Vet then marks only the females. (Neutered males are easy to identify because of the absence of their testicles.) The spayed females have the top one centimeter of the tip of their left ear clipped and cauterized when they're still under anesthesia.

   After a short recovery time in a cage, each cat, whose stitches will dissolve by themselves, is released where it was found or in another safe place where people routinely feed the population.

The first option destabilizes the existing cat colonies. As one cat is trapped, another moves in to take its place. The second option is popular with businesses and large residential schools because it stabilizes the cat population and yet keeps the number of rodents reduced. The idea is that these neutered cats do not add to the overpopulation. They can assist man and yet live as they had before capture.

WHAT CAN I DO TO HELP A STRAY OR FERAL CAT?

It's impossible for any one individual or group to save all the homeless animals. But if you want to try to help that one little cat pathetically trying to win your heart, here are some guidelines to help you.

A rabies vaccination is certainly a good idea if you're going to make a habit of animal rescue.

To Handle the Occasional Rescue

Keep supplies on hand. Provide a towel for a bed, and a litter box (any cardboard box with a plastic bag liner will do in a pinch). The animal will also need bowls for water and food, and toys to play with.

To Catch the Cat

If the cat is really terrified, he may be feral. Call animal control to help you catch the animal, and make sure when you call that you explain that the cat is wild. Their rescue strategies and equipment will likely include special padded gloves, a cat grabber and a humane trap. (A cat grabber is a long-handled instrument with padded "hands" that can safely grab the cat around the neck.) Your other option is to borrow a humane trap from the shelter. If, however, the cat appears to be a friendly stray, you might be able to entice him into a crate.

Once you have the cat either in the trap or in a crate, take him to the animal shelter, or make the decision to care for him until a home can be found.

Again, care must be taken in handling any strange cat, because these fellows may have had to fight or kill to survive. Wear heavy gloves and a long-sleeved jacket, and by all means, keep him away from your face!

To Protect the Health of You and Your Pets

Always assume the cat is contagious and wash your hands well with antibacterial soap after contact. Until you can get the animal checked out by your Vet, keep him separated from your other cats in a secure space.

Just as important—until disease and parasites can be ruled out—before letting your other cats near any equipment used by the newcomer, **clean it with one part bleach to ten parts water**. Anything that can't be cleaned must ultimately be thrown away or given with the cat.

To Try to Locate His Owner

- Place an ad in the newspaper's "lost and found" column (usually free) and in the "pets" column.
- Read the "lost" ads in your paper.
- Check with the shelter and nearby Vet's for lost-animal notices.
- Talk to the neighborhood children and regular delivery people, like the mailman, to see if they know of a lost cat.

If no one claims the cat within a week, you must decide how much responsibility you want to take.

If No One Claims Ownership

You can take the cat to the animal shelter, where the cat will either be adopted or euthanized after a specific period. If he is feral, ill or injured, most shelters will not allow the animal to be adopted.

You may choose to keep the cat until you find him a home; that decision can only be yours. No matter how long he is to stay, make sure the animal is thoroughly checked out by your Vet **before** you let your other pets come in contact with him.

A trial period with the cat may help you decide to keep him, especially if your existing pets seem to adjust to the newcomer. If you make a commitment to the animal, make sure that he or she is neutered immediately.

Unless a stray cat has been abused, the readjustment to home living should be relatively easy. But don't expect too much from a feral cat. They are very difficult to domesticate. For help in introducing a new pet to the household, review chapter 3.

THE STRAY MAY BE PREGNANT. HOW DO I CARE FOR HER?

So how do you determine if she is pregnant? At three to four weeks, a Vet can palpate her abdomen and tell you if the cat is expecting. At this time her nipples will change color from a light pink to a deeper rosy pink. And yes, as in humans, the pregnancy can be determined by ultrasound.

By about forty days, you should be able to feel the kittens kick and move around. If there is any possibility the cat is pregnant, tell your Vet. Vaccinations are not usually given during a pregnancy.

The expectant mother must be in good health. If she's not, or if you don't want to add to the overpopulation problem, your Vet can terminate the pregnancy and spay the cat at the same time.

Prenatal Care and Preparation

If she is to keep the kittens, you should know that gestation lasts sixty-one to seventy days (with an average of sixty-five days), during which time she will gain between two and three pounds.

While she's pregnant and later when she is nursing, she'll need larger meals of a high-protein, quality diet. (Check with your Vet for the amount. The general rule of thumb is to feed her about ¼ cup more than what you normally feed your other cat, or ⅜ cup twice a day.) But don't let her overeat; an overweight queen can have a more difficult delivery. The water in her bowl must be fresh and she must have constant access to it. And while she will be able to continue her normal activities, she shouldn't be allowed outside.

In the last week before the kittens are due, the mom-to-be will search for her own delivery room. Put the nesting box (described below) in the area she's selected—if possible. And make sure all closet doors and drawers in the room are closed, or she may use them instead of the box. If the room is normally kept cool, you might want to turn up the thermostat; the temperature in the room should be about 72 degrees Fahrenheit. If she has long hair, this is also a good time to clip it short around her nipples and genitals.

The cardboard nesting box should be ten to twelve inches high and as long as the cat's body (not counting the tail) plus three to four inches. The width can be a little shorter than the length. It should be cozy but large enough for family comfort. Line the bottom of the box with an old towel and cover this with several layers of newspaper topped with soft paper toweling; the paper layers can easily be removed after the births to furnish a soft towel nest.

The Birth

Keep water available during delivery but don't offer food. Try to give her some peace and quiet; frisky dogs and noisy kids should be kept away. As labor starts, she will be restless, may cry or call repeatedly, and then she'll go to her choice of nesting place.

Within an hour, the first kitten should appear, and if all goes well, the last one will be delivered within four to six hours. As she delivers, she'll most likely take a posture similar to that of having a bowel movement. As each kitten is born, the mom cat will bite the umbilical cord and clean the embryonic sac off the kitten. The vigorous licking stimulates the kitten to breathe and to begin moving.

Other than checking on her health, do **not** disturb the queen during delivery. If you bother her, you will disrupt the bonding process with the new arrivals and stop her from continuing the normal delivery sequence—possibly causing her to kill and eat her own kittens.

How fast the delivery goes depends on her mental and physical health and the number of kittens. The queen should be able to deliver the kittens without any help. Breech births (backward presentations) are normal and occur about 40 percent of the time. But if she goes longer than two hours with strong contractions **without** producing a kitten, call your Vet for advice.

After the Birth

When all are delivered, the queen eats all the afterbirths—a normal response. With this action, she gets a meal, cleans up the nesting area and, as an evolutionary holdover, protects the kittens. In the wild, blood in the afterbirths would bring predators, maggots and disease to the nesting area. In nature's often perfect way, the exhausted mom cat eliminates the potential problem and gets iron-rich nutrition without leaving the nest unprotected. In spite of this unusual nutritional snack, it's a good idea to leave clean bowls with fresh food and water next to the new mom's nest.

When she's finished with her cleanup, change the paper lining in the box. She'll enjoy the soft warmth of the towel underneath. Most queens recover without problems and are content to be left alone with their new brood. You can keep a parental eye on her and still respect her need for quiet. If she has a foul-smelling vaginal discharge or hemorrhaging or doesn't eat, call your Vet.

As long as she is nursing, continue the high-quality diet. And to start the babies out right, review the kitten sections elsewhere in the book.

Some moms are more protective or less trusting than others, so review the section on making friends in chapter 7. Unless medically necessary, do not disturb the kittens till they are a week old.

HOW DO I PLACE A KITTEN OR CAT UP FOR ADOPTION?

First, place ads in the newspaper classified section. It also helps to make a poster-type ad with a photocopied picture of the cat for distribution at veterinary offices in your area.

When you call in your ad, **never** offer a free cat, because some people collect free animals to sell to experimental labs. If you charge at least five dollars for the cat or kitten, they won't want the animal. Also, the people who adopt the cat will tend to value their charge more because they had to pay for him.

The more particular you are when screening applicants, the better home the pet will have. Test the cat to find out if he would adjust to living with other pets, including dogs. If the answer is no, you can eliminate everyone who already has a pet.

Your humane shelter has a policy for adoption similar to the questions we are suggesting you ask. Right now, you're the only advocate the animal has, so when people call, ask these questions and listen for the right answers.

- Do they have pets now? Find out how much space they have and ask what kinds of personalities their existing pets have. Too many cats in a too small area leads to stress, and if their pets are extremely territorial, they may not accept the newcomer.
- What happened to their last pet? If the animal was left outside and became injured or lost, or if the pet unnecessarily died young, these people may not be appropriate adoptive prospects.
- Are their present or past pets neutered? If the answer is no, and their pets are over six months old, these people may not be appropriate.
- Where will the cat live? The answer should be that they live inside.
- Are there two people who can be called as references? If they are unwilling to give references, or if the references can't be verified, look for another person. If they have pets already, one of the references should be their Vet.
- Do they have children or are they planning to have a child? Meet the children. Are they gentle with animals? Will this cat enjoy children?
- Do they plan to declaw? The best answer is no.
- What will they do with the cat if it doesn't work out? They should be willing to bring the cat back, and you can try again to find him a good home.

- Do they own their home or rent? If they rent, they should have permission from the landlord to keep a pet.

If their answers sound good, go to their home for a visit with the cat. This step also screens for people who are buying for labs. Is everyone, including the cat, happy?

To screen out impulse adoptions, tell the people to think it over and call you back in two days if they still want the cat. When everything is set, have them sign a written agreement to do the following:

- Spay/neuter within a stated period.
- Take the cat to a Vet within 24 to 36 hours for screening.
- Allow you to have at least two return visits to check on care.
- Agree that if the conditions are not met, you will take the kitten back.

Follow up! You won't be adopting out many cats during your lifetime. Be a responsible advocate and make the visits to see that the written agreement is kept—and if it is not, take the cat back and start again.

17

Special Cats—
Special Needs

THE VERY YOUNG, the disabled and the senior cat need special care to survive and thrive. We tend to be more at ease with the trials of kitten care and less comfortable with the needs of the old. And the idea of daily coping with a disabled pet can panic the most capable pet owner.

A disabled cat can live a long, full life with some extra effort and adjustment on your part. Because cats do not intellectualize about their lives, they do not feel disabled. As long as the cat is not in great pain and can eat, drink and groom, he's content. In other words, the disability is more in your mind than in your cat's mind.

The questions in this chapter have been selected to help both you and your cat adjust to his special needs, accept his life changes and share a loving relationship.

KITTENS

HOW DO KITTENS DEVELOP?

A kitten's early experiences with humans, his littermates, adult cats and other species have a great impact on his later trust and ability to accept living with others. The kitten who widens his experience with the world at a later date

228

may still become acclimated to people and other animals, but he'll need more love, time and support to become adjusted.

The developmental descriptions given below offer a general idea of what to expect. Remember, they're based on average growth patterns. Breeds like Siamese and Burmese may develop faster than other breeds, whereas Persians tend to develop at a slower-than-average rate.

One Week

Kittens weigh between three and five ounces and respond only to warmth, touch and smell. Their sense of smell is already so keen that each kitten can locate its "own" particular nipple to nurse from. To protect their immature sensory nerves, nature provides them with ears and eyes that are sealed shut. Both will open later on their own—don't try to force the eyes open or unfold the baby's ears.

While they have no trouble taking in milk, they can't eliminate on their own. The mother cat grooms the kitten's anus and genitalia to stimulate elimination, and then she eats the feces—to keep the nest clean. By day five, what remains of the umbilical cord will be dry enough to fall off.

Don't handle the kittens unless they need to be moved for safety reasons. Mom cat needs to feel secure and in control with her new babies.

Two Weeks

The kittens can eliminate independently. Their eyes are open. Irrespective of breed, all young kittens will have baby-blue eyes. The tiny ears begin to straighten out and take a more catlike form. The kittens begin teething.

Daily, **gently** pick up each kitten and quietly talk to him for a couple of minutes. This will teach him to trust people. Do **not** carry him away from the nesting box. Mom cat may resent it, and the kitten will become upset.

Three Weeks

The kittens can pull themselves up into a shaky standing position. They have almost no control over their little needle-sharp claws, so keep some distance as you begin playing with the kittens. Use a piece of string or an unsharpened pencil.

By this time, the kittens are either climbing over the sides of the nesting box or close to making the jump. So it's a good idea to kittenproof the area. Block off doorways or other forbidden areas with cardboard high enough to stop the kittens but low enough to let mom cat in and out. You also need to provide a small, low-sided litter box for the kittens. Put the box near the nest. Mom's already getting tired of cleaning up after the babies—she'll quickly teach them how to use the box.

Continue holding each kitten and talking to him daily. If you're accidentally clawed, **gently** disengage his claws and praise him when he isn't hurting you. **Never** hit or otherwise discipline a kitten this age.

Four to Six Weeks

Already sixteen ounces, these growing kittens can securely stand, walk and groom themselves. They play easily with each other and with people. Siamese kittens begin to show their points (darker fur on their extremities).

At this stage, kittens should begin taking solid food. Offer them kitten food softened with warm water or broth. See chapter 4 for help with the feeding schedule.

Continue holding them and increase playtime. **Never** play rough or let them use you or your clothes as toys. It's now time to begin teaching the kittens good manners. A well-socialized cat will be easier to handle for grooming and medication—and easier to love.

Unless mom cat objects, introduce the kittens to other species. Show the kittens that a dog can be friendly. Pre-screen the dog to be sure that she's calm and well mannered.

Six to Eight Weeks

Their eye color changes from baby blue to their adult color. By this time the kittens weigh about two pounds, and mom is already cutting down on nursing time. She'll wean the kittens all by herself and on her own schedule. In most cases, they should be weaned by the eighth week and eating nothing but kitten food.

In spite of this reduced dependence on their mom, the kittens are **not** yet ready to adopt out. They still have a great deal to learn.

Lengthen your daily interaction with the kittens. Hold them and pet them. **Gently** tap the kitten's paw or nose while saying "No!" for biting or scratching. Continue to play with them, using toys—not your hands or other body parts.

Nine to Ten Weeks

The kittens continue to grow and explore. Lengthen your handling and training time with the kittens. This is a prime socialization opportunity for the youngsters. They're learning how to interact and communicate with other cats too.

Twelfth Week

The kittens' coat patterns fully develop, and they begin to lose their baby teeth.

Thirteen Weeks Through One Year

The kittens grow and gradually become adults. By six months, they will have all their permanent teeth. They play, and learn what is expected from both their mom and you. At the beginning of the thirteenth week, they are ready to be adopted into permanent homes.

HOW DO I RAISE AN ORPHANED KITTEN?

Hand-raising kittens can be both rewarding and frustrating. The reward is seeing a totally dependent little creature survive and grow. The frustration comes from the medical fragility of these tiny babies and from the enormous amount of commitment it takes to do the job right. The younger the orphans are, the lower their chance of survival and the more time they'll require. Following the guidelines below will give these youngsters the best chance of survival.

Immediately

- Dry off the kittens, if needed, and keep them warm. Wrap them in a towel or blanket or put them in your coat.
- Determine, if possible, why they are orphaned. If the mother was ill, they may also be ill.
- Take the kittens to your Vet and report what you know about their circumstances. Discuss with her the litter's health, age, care needed and other issues you both feel are important. You'll need to decide whether to euthanize the kittens or to attempt hand-raising the litter.
- Try to find a lactating queen (female cat with milk) who can and will adopt the kittens. Check with Vets, breeders, friends, co-workers or your local animal shelter.

  To get the surrogate mom to accept the kittens, use a cloth to wipe her and her own kittens. Then use the cloth to transfer their scent to the new kittens. Put the orphans in her nest. Wear heavy gloves—they may need rescuing if she violently rejects them. Your best chance of success is to find an experienced mom cat whose kittens are close to the orphans' age. These conscientious moms have been known to make a second nest for the younger kittens and include the runt from their own litter.

Long-Term Care if You Must Hand-Raise the Kittens

The Nesting Box

- Use a cardboard box big enough for all the kittens, with sides at least twelve inches high. Look at the amount of space the kittens take up, then double the area for the right-sized box.
- Put a heating pad, set on low, under half of the box so the kittens can move on or off the heat source.
- Lay a couple of sections of newspaper in the bottom of the box and cover the

newspaper with two towels. The newspaper is insulation so the kittens aren't burned by the heating pad. Have lots of washable snuggly towels on hand so the layers can be changed at least once a day.

Feeding Equipment and Formula

- Get nursing bottles from a pet store or your Vet, or use an eyedropper or a syringe without the needle.
- Have a heavy pan for sterilizing the bottles after **every** use. Warm the formula to body temperature; do not use the microwave to heat formula, because it produces hot spots in the liquid.
- Use a commercial kitten-milk replacement formula—available from your Vet or pet store.
  Note: If replacement formulas are not available, the May 1992 issue of *Cat Fancy* suggests this formula: Mix 1 cup of whole milk, 2 egg yolks and 2 teaspoons of light Karo syrup. Store the leftovers in the refrigerator in a clean, airtight container. Discard any formula not used within 48 hours.
- Use bath towels, cotton balls or washcloth and a small container of warm water for feeding cleanup. The high sugar content of the formula makes it set up like cement if it's not wiped off the kitten's fur.
- Weigh the kittens weekly to check growth. Consult your Vet if any kitten has feeding problems or does not thrive.

Feeding Schedule

For the first couple of weeks, you'll have to feed the kittens through the night. The kittens' weight and the amounts of formula listed in the table below are reasonable estimates.

Age of Kitten	Weight of Kitten	Formula per Kitten per Meal	Feedings per Day
Birth to 1 week	4 ounces	1 to 1½ teaspoons	6 (every 4 hours)
2 weeks	7 ounces	2 to 3 teaspoons	4 (every 6 hours)
3 weeks	10 ounces	1 tablespoon	3 (every 5 hours, daytime only)
4 to 5 weeks	13 ounces	3 to 4 tablespoons; begin to offer kitten food.	3 (every 5 hours, daytime only)
6 weeks	16 ounces	4 to 5 tablespoons	3 (every 5 hours, daytime only)

Feeding Instructions (one kitten at a time)

This is, at best, a messy process. Protect your clothes and furniture with a towel!

Note: If the kitten cannot independently suckle, consult your Vet.

STEP 1   Lay the kitten belly-**down** on a towel on a table, your lap or other convenient surface. Don't lay him belly-up like a human baby; the kitten will choke!

STEP 2   Carefully put the nipple into the kitten's mouth and hold the bottle at a 45-degree angle. Keep a gentle pull on the bottle. The bottle positioning and slight pull encourages the kitten to suckle. If he coughs, hold him head-down to drain the excess milk. Keep him in this position until he can breathe easily again.

STEP 3   While he is suckling, gently stroke his head and his back as his mother would when she grooms. Quietly hum or speak sweet nothings to him— it's the closest we can come to purring.

STEP 4   Let him nurse till he's full and refuses to swallow the formula. He'll have milk bubbles around his mouth and his stomach will be nicely round.

STEP 5   When he is finished, burp him as you burp a human baby. Hold him over your shoulder and gently pat his tiny back.

STEP 6   Wash his face and any other sticky places. The formula is sugary, and after it dries, it's nearly impossible to remove.

STEP 7   For the first two to three weeks, until he can urinate and defecate independently, you will have to stimulate his elimination reflexes as his mother would. Gently but firmly wipe his anus and genitalia with a warm, wet cotton ball. The light pressure will help the kitten eliminate. There won't be much—the cotton ball should take care of the mess.

STEP 8   Clean up the feeding mess, wash the towels and grab forty winks, because it all starts again in a few hours.

Feeding Older Kittens

After the kittens are three weeks old, with Vet approval, they can be switched from bottle feeding to a gruel.

Directions for preparation: Soften kitten food with formula until it's the consistency of cooked cereal. Warm the mixture to your body temperature and pour a small amount (one tablespoon per kitten) into a saucer or shallow plate.

Directions for feeding: To feed the kitten, dip a finger into the gruel and then wipe it on his lips. Then, to draw his attention to the saucer of gruel, move your dipped finger to his lips and then gradually away toward the saucer. Never shove a kitten's face in the food to show him where it is.

Extra Care Instructions

Environment

- Keep the kitten(s) in as quiet a room as possible. That room should be off-limits to all other animals and to the children in the household. The room temperature should be kept constant (around 72 degrees F.) because young kittens can't regulate their own body temperature.

- **For the "only" kitten:** as much as you can, keep him inside your shirt. If he is left alone in the nest he won't thrive. Kittens need contact and shared warmth.

Health Checks

- Consult your Vet. Find out how often she should see the kittens. Check with her if a kitten fails to eat well, gain weight or thrive.
- Hold and pet the kittens—and check their bodies daily. The need to suckle is very great, and the hard nipples on bottles don't meet the need. Orphaned kittens often suck on—and do damage to—littermates' tails, ears or other convenient body parts. Encourage the kittens to suckle on your finger or on the corner of a damp cloth.

Handling

- Do not disturb a sleeping kitten for anything but a meal. For the first two weeks, about all the babies do is sleep and eat. After that, they'll spend more time playing and learning how to use their bodies.

Litter Training

- At about three to four weeks, introduce the babies to the litter box. After each meal, instead of stimulating their reflexes by wiping them, place each kitten in the litter box. If after a few minutes he hasn't eliminated, stimulate his reflexes and try again at the next meal.

WHY DOES MOM CAT MOVE THE KITTENS FROM PLACE TO PLACE?

Female cats are usually excellent mothers. They are concerned that their young, vulnerable kittens have a protected environment. If mom cat feels that the kittens are being bothered—or are not fully safe—she'll move the nest to a better location.

HOW DOES MOM CAT TRAIN HER KITTENS?

Mom cat teaches her kittens by example. They watch and copy her actions in play—practicing hunting skills, litter box rituals and colony hierarchy.

WILL MY KITTEN OUTGROW BITING?

Unless you take corrective measures, cute little kittens who claw, bite and attack grow into big cats who claw, bite and attack. Most often kittens learn aggressive behavior because their human has entertained them with a hand or a foot moving with the stealth of a large, dull-witted rat under a blanket. It shouldn't take more than one or two "accidents" to convince a person that human body parts are unacceptable toys for cats of any age. With some patience on your part, the problem can be solved. Chapter 8 has easy-to-follow instructions for taking the bite out of your relationship.

WHEN CAN A KITTEN GO TO A NEW HOME?

While kittens are usually weaned by two months, they need one more month for early socialization. During that last month, the kittens are taught how to be successful cats, both by their mother and by interacting with their littermates. Among other things, they learn not to bite nonprey animals (including you). They also discover the importance of keeping their claws in, and how to share space with another cat.

An orphaned kitten raised with no other cats or kittens doesn't fully learn how to be a cat and is less conversant in "cat speak." These animals tend to be strongly bonded to their human parent and may have behavior problems when teamed up with another pet.

DISABLED CATS

HOW CAN I TELL IF MY CAT IS DISABLED?

Listed herein are major disability categories and their most common symptoms. If your cat displays any of these characteristic signs, see your Vet. Even temporary health problems, if not treated (irrespective of your cat's age), can quickly become permanent disabilities. If your Vet diagnoses any of these disabilities, consult the specific topics in the questions that follow.

Deafness

- He doesn't respond to the can opener, opening of the refrigerator door or cupboard doors or food box rattling.
- Violent head shaking (possible ear infection, mites or other damage to the ear that can lead to deafness).
- He startles when touched; he doesn't know you're near until you touch him.
- He doesn't respond to birds singing, other cats "talking," nature noises or sudden sounds.

Blindness

- He bumps into things that are not in their usual place.
- He has many broken whiskers.

- His eyes no longer glow in the dark, or they look cloudy in the light.

Vision Problems

- He doesn't jump or is very clumsy when jumping.
- His eyes are crossed (common in Siamese).
- His eyes jerk back and forth (strabismus—common in Siamese).
- He loses toys even when they are in plain sight.

Physical Problems or Pain

Note: If you think your cat is in pain, **do not under any circumstances** give him any human painkillers. Aspirin, acetaminophen and ibuprofen are extremely toxic to cats and can kill.

- He limps or holds a paw up.
- He snaps or bites when you touch a certain body part.
- He no longer engages in an activity he used to enjoy.
- He overgrooms a body part, to the point of fur loss or skin damage.
- He's slow to start moving after a nap.
- He doesn't jump or climb.

WHAT SPECIAL CONSIDERATIONS DOES MY DISABLED CAT NEED?

Diabetes

Diabetes is common in older or obese cats. Your schedule needs to accommodate your cat's medical needs because insulin dosage and food have to be constantly monitored. Here are some of the things you can expect to do if you have a diabetic cat:

- Follow the feeding schedule recommended by the Vet.
- Inject insulin daily.
- Check weekly or, if necessary, daily the sugar content in urine. (The frequency will be recommended by your Vet.)
- Check regularly for sores and infections.

Blindness

Although common in old age because of cataracts, blindness due to injury can be found in a cat of any age. If you have a blind cat or kitten, follow these guidelines:

- Do **not** let the cat out unattended.
- Do **not** rearrange the furniture, the water and food bowls or the litter box if at

all possible. Your cat has learned to get around by means of his sense of smell and by feeling his way with his whiskers. If the furniture or any of his own equipment must be moved, you'll need to help him relearn where things are.

- Watch where you're walking and warn visitors to do the same.
- Check the cat's whiskers regularly, because he needs them to help locate things. If they are badly broken, you may want to make "curb feelers" for whisker protection; see chapter 20.

Deafness

Deafness is common in white cats with blue eyes and in older cats. Here are some suggestions to keep your cat safe from harm.

- Do not let the cat out unattended.
- Watch where you are walking and warn visitors to do the same.
- Stamp your foot hard on the floor or flick the lights on and off to get the cat's attention. If you startle him by touching him without warning, he may attack. This is not a personal attack on you; it's a natural response.

Physical Disabilities

Arthritis is very common in old cats and affects them in much the same way it affects us. Disabilities from injuries can occur in cats of all ages, and of course the severity of the disability will vary with the type of injury. If your cat still has a good quality of life, the following guidelines will help you both cope:

- Watch where you are walking and warn visitors to do the same.
- Arrange the essentials of cat life (water, food, litter box, sunny spots, napping places) so that they are accessible. Ideas include:
  — Steps leading to window ledges.
  — A litter box with a low edge at the entrance and large enough to turn around in (without bending). Its sides should be high enough so the cat does not need to "aim."
  — An uncovered nesting box for napping (low entrance, and big enough to stretch out in). **Note:** Some special-order catalogs have "egg crate" foam-rubber beds for disabled cats.
  — A pet heating pad, set on low with several layers of towels over it, in the nesting box or in a nest type of bed.
- Ask your Vet if she has any recommendations for pain relief. Drugs? Acupuncture?
- Consider learning how to use TTouch to ease his discomfort.

AGED CATS

WHAT HAPPENS AS A CAT AGES?

The natural process of aging is influenced by the cat's genetic heritage, his lifestyle and the quality of care received throughout his life. Even the best-preserved oldsters, however, will experience physiological changes as they age.

A cat is considered a senior citizen by about age ten. Older cats sleep for longer periods and may have stiff joints when they get up from a nap or when they exercise after periods of inactivity. Fur may thin out and become gray on the muzzle. Thinning fur and decreased circulation often combine to make the cat less tolerant of both heat and cold, a situation which compounds problems in an arthritic cat. Consequently, he may need help with his grooming because of increased stiffness—and a good brushing daily to stimulate his skin and improve his coat.

His diet will probably need adjusting too. He may need a special diet or a simple change in the amount of food. He may not want to eat because he can't smell the food. Tartar, loose teeth or infections in the mouth can make eating difficult. It's not unusual for aged cats to lose weight because of lack of appetite, a sore mouth or increased fussiness. The loss may be severe enough so that his skin hangs and the backbone, hips and shoulders become prominent.

There may be other behavioral differences. He may be less tolerant of changes in his environment, such as the movement of his litter box or food bowls or the introduction of a new pet into the household. Some physical impairments, such as vision problems from cataracts or increased deafness, may require environmental adjustments.

These cats can suffer from additional, more serious health problems like chronic constipation, partial or total incontinence, hyperthyroidism, kidney disease, diabetes, heart disease and cancer. These are the complications which make most pet owners afraid to take on the care of an older cat. In many cases, these disabilities can be manageable for both your cat and you. Working closely with your Vet and setting up a well-organized schedule can take the fear out of caring for a severely impaired pet.

WHAT CHANGES MAY I NEED TO MAKE FOR MY SENIOR CAT?

An older cat will most likely need some adjustments in lifestyle, equipment setup, grooming, diet and health care. While the amount of change will, of course, depend on the cat's individual needs, here's an idea of some of the things you may need to do to make his life easier:

Lifestyle

- Do not let the cat outside. He will be less able to cope with weather changes and far less able to defend himself.
- Encourage physical activity with daily play sessions.

Equipment Setup

- Fix one or more sleeping areas that are warm, draft-free and easy to get to. A lidded box with an entrance hole on one side and lined with a blanket makes an excellent bed. Half of the blanket or towel can be laid on a special pet heating pad, set on low, to help him keep warm. Catalogs carry heated and "egg crate" foam-rubber beds.
- Add more litter boxes so one is always nearby.

Grooming

- Help the cat with grooming. In addition to the usual care (see chapter 6) do the following:
  - Wipe his body with a warm, damp cloth every few days. Gently wash his face and anus with a warm, wet cloth and pat dry. Do not let the cat become chilled.
  - For longhaired cats, clip the long hair around the anus to help with hygiene.
- Your Vet may need to clean or repair the cat's teeth.

Diet

- Give him stronger-smelling food and warm it to body temperature to tempt the reluctant eater.
- Feed soft foods or even baby food if your cat has a sore mouth or throat or if he is missing some teeth. Check with your Vet to make sure the diet is complete.
- Offer three to four smaller meals each day.
- Follow your Vet's recommendation for changing to one of the prescription diets or to a senior formula.

Health Care

- Be willing to make a commitment to take care of a disabled cat.
- Make frequent home health checks and trips to your Vet to catch/treat health problems as soon as possible. Check with your Vet for a schedule.
- Monitor water and food intake if necessary, particularly for terminally ill cats and for cats with kidney and bladder problems.
- Be willing to make a decision about euthanasia if your cat needs to be relieved of his suffering.

HOW CAN I HELP MY CAT AGE GRACEFULLY?

While we can't stop the clock, we can ease the process. Train him while he is still young and healthy to accept grooming (brushing, tooth brushing and nail clipping) and handling (holding, gentle restraint and touching him everywhere). Here are some other tips to prolong his life:

- Always feed him a nutritious diet.
- Take him to the Vet for regular yearly checkups. Have blood work done before he is ten years old for a baseline guide. After the age of ten, he should have his blood work checked yearly.
- Play with him daily.
- Have a quiet place for him to nap where other animals and people won't bother him. Senior cats need more sleep than younger cats.

18

The Inevitable Equation

WHILE THIS IS NOT the most cheerful topic, it is one we'll all have to face. This chapter will help you evaluate your particular situation, decide what needs to be done without guilt and deal with the inevitable sorrow.

MY CAT IS DISABLED/ILL. SHOULD HE BE EUTHANIZED?

Before you consider making any decisions, remember the disabled cat care advice in chapter 17 and the related questions in chapter 13, including the section on giving medicine. You and your cat may be able to adjust enough to give him a life worth living.

Remember that euthanasia is never an easy decision to make, but it can be a way of saying that you love your pet too much to let him suffer.

Ask these questions to help you decide what is best for your cat:

- Is my cat in chronic pain? (It is difficult to medicate a cat for pain.)
- What is his quality of life? Will he be able to maintain his dignity?
- Does he have control of his bodily functions (eating and elimination)?
- What is your cat's personality? Will he reject the extra attention of treatments and be repeatedly terrorized by constant trips to the Vet?
- How old is he and is this a chronic, terminal or acute problem?
- How much money and time will this cost? How much can you afford? Be realistic.

WHAT HAPPENS WHEN HE IS EUTHANIZED?

Your Vet may give him a tranquilizer injection so he'll be relaxed and it will be easy to find a vein. Then she'll give the animal an overdose of an intravenous anesthetic. The cat will become unconscious and die painlessly within minutes.

WHAT SHOULD I DO IF I DON'T KNOW WHY MY CAT DIED?

If you don't know the cause of death, you may want an animal autopsy (necropsy) done by your Vet. Other pets may need treatment if there's a contagious disease involved, or they may need protection from a poison or other danger. Expect to pay a base fee of from $15 to $20, in addition to the cost of any lab work. When tissue samples from various organs need to be studied, the cost can be quite high. Check with your Vet.

HOW WILL MY CAT'S BODY BE DISPOSED OF?

Several choices are available, and most Veterinarians will keep the body in a freezer to give you time to make a decision. To discover your options, consult the yellow pages, the local public library, local animal organizations, or ask your Vet.

Burial

Lined coffins are available for cats. One company we called offered handmade twenty-inch galvanized and copper caskets ranging in price from $129.95 to $169.95 plus the cost of shipping. Overnight shipping was available for an extra fee. Obviously, costs will depend on what you get and where you get it. Take some time and call around; costly decisions are easy to make when you are upset. See ads in cat magazines for more options. If you don't want to wait for a coffin or don't wish to shoulder the extra expense, you can use a box or other material you have at home.

Pet cemeteries exist in some areas, and again costs will vary depending on the services you want. Personalized markers can be ordered from your local monument company or from specialty firms advertising in cat magazines. A stonelike aluminum-alloy plate (with stake) can be engraved and shipped by one company for about $25. Shop around and you should be able to find something that will fit your budget.

Home burial may be prohibited; your local health department will be able to explain local ordinances. If you bury your pet at home, dig a hole at least one foot deep. If the grave is in an unprotected area, lay heavy stones over the top of the grave so it won't be dug up by dogs or scavengers. And never bury an animal near a well.

Cremation

Your Vet can arrange an individual cremation. The ashes will be returned to you by mail in a small wood or metal box, although you can purchase fancier boxes. Another option your Vet can arrange, mass cremation, is less expensive but you won't be given your cat's ashes.

Freeze-drying

Freeze-drying is available through specialty companies featured in cat magazines. If you make inquiries, you'll find it's fairly expensive. Nevertheless, shop around; you may find a price that fits your budget. With this process, your pet is dehydrated to preserve his body. The result looks somewhat like a stuffed toy and keeps indefinitely at room temperature.

Taxidermy

Taxidermists have shops in many communities. Look in the yellow pages. When an animal is taken to a taxidermist, he is skinned and his fur is placed on a form. The result is not as lifelike as freeze-drying but it's less expensive and can often be done locally.

IS THERE ANYTHING THAT WILL HELP ME DEAL WITH THE DEATH OF MY CAT?

What you feel, and how you deal with these feelings, is a personal and individual response. The process is additionally influenced by the level of stress in your life and how much social support you have.

You may feel many different things—such as shock, depression, denial and guilt. You may even feel relief that your cat is no longer suffering, or relief that you no longer have to wait for his death or have to plan your schedule around his treatment. There are no "wrong" feelings; you feel what you feel.

It's all right to mourn; it is normal to be bereaved at the loss of a family member and constant companion. It may take quite some time for you to come to terms with the loss of your furry friend. But try not to let things turn to grief and get stuck there.

There is a difference between mourning and grief. Mourning is working through the loss; grief is mourning turned inward. The important thing is to acknowledge your heartache or "get in touch with" your feelings. Here are some ideas to help you through your mourning:

- Give yourself time and permission to mourn.
- Acknowledge or "get in touch with" your feelings by talking to someone—friends, support groups, switchboard.
  - The Delta Society has a comprehensive listing of nationwide resources, including pet bereavement specialists and support groups. Contact them at:
    The Delta Society
    P.O. Box 1080
    Renton, WA 98057-1080
    206-226-7357
  - You might want to dial the Pet Loss Support hot line at 1-916-752-4200. The service, open 6:30 p.m. to 9:30 p.m. (PST), is run by the veterinary students of the University of California at Davis.
  - For consumer information, you can write the Pet Loss Foundation, 1312 French Road, Suite A23, Buffalo, NY 14043. This is a chartered not-for-profit organization.
- Make a photo album of the pet who died, or you can include all your pets—past and present—in a collage.
- Write your pet's biography—for yourself.
- Make a donation to an animal welfare group in your pet's name.
- Be good to yourself—eat right, exercise and find time to play.

HOW CAN I HELP MY CHILD TO ACCEPT OUR CAT'S DEATH?

Although it may be difficult, experts all agree that the best course of action is to be truthful. Don't tell the child the cat went to sleep or went on a trip or use other euphemisms for death. The cat died.

Remember, children do not fully understand death. In their efforts to accept death, they may ask to see or touch the animal. They may be very curious about what will happen next to their pet, or they might playact the event. These behaviors are normal and natural, and they can help a child understand death. If, however, the cat had anything contagious to humans, it's best not to let your child hold the body.

Your job is to acknowledge the child's feelings and to give permission to feel the hurt and mourn.

The following books may help you explain death to your child:

- *The Tenth Good Thing About Barney* by Judith Viorst, paperback, ISBN 0689712030
- *Lifetimes: A Beautiful Way to Explain Death to Children* by Bryan Mellonie, ISBN 0553340239
- *Mustard* by Charlotte Towner Graeber, ISBN 0027366901
- *Ramona Forever* by Beverly Cleary, ISBN 0688037852
- *Goodbye My Friend* by Miriam L. Elias, ISBN 0873064917

- *Coping with the Loss of a Pet* by Christina M. Lemieux, paperback, ISBN 0962215813

HOW CAN I HELP MY REMAINING PETS?

Set aside additional time to encourage them to play. Time should also be spent grooming them and relaxing with them. Animals can sense your distress, so try to be calm before interacting with bereaved pets.

WHEN SHOULD I GET ANOTHER PET?

If your cat died of a contagious disease, check with your Vet before you make any decision. Wait the time required for the house to be safe, and follow your Vet's directions for disinfecting your home and all the cat supplies and equipment.

It's important that you give yourself time to mourn and accept your companion's death before you bring another animal into your life. When you're still mourning it's easy to resent a new pet for not being like the one that just died.

If you're ready for another pet, don't make snap decisions—take some time to think about what species and breed you want to share your home with.

WHEN SHOULD I SEEK PROFESSIONAL HELP?

Mourning has several stages: denial, anger, bargaining, depression and acceptance. It's natural to move from one stage to another over a matter of minutes, hours or days. Gradually, over weeks or months, your emotions will focus more on acceptance.

People differ in how long they take to mourn depending on their beliefs, support systems, the level of stress and their other experiences with death and mourning. A general rule of thumb is to expect between six and eighteen months to pass before one completely accepts the death of a loved one.

Sometimes, however, grief can be overwhelming. When someone gets stuck at one stage of mourning or becomes very depressed for months, professional help may be needed.

WHAT CAN I DO TO HELP A FRIEND WHOSE CAT HAS DIED?

The best thing to do is to give the person permission to mourn. Because this is uncomfortable territory, use the following guidelines:

Some Things to Say and Do

- "It is hard to lose a friend."
- "I am sorry _____ died."
- "Tell me what happened."
- Tell the person a funny or touching story of an interaction you had with the pet.
- Send a sympathy letter. In this letter, write a sentence or two about how sad it was that the pet died. Then add a little funny or touching story about an experience you had with the cat, or recount a story your friend had shared with you.

Some Things Not to Say and Do

- "It was only a cat."
- "You can get another cat."
- "You will get over it." One does not "get over it." The pain becomes less intense and you spend less time thinking about your loss after a while. But it can take months or even years to reach a point when you can think of your pet without crying or feeling sad. Everyone needs their own amount of time to come to terms with a death.
- Change the subject when the cat's name or the topic of death is mentioned; your friend needs to talk about what happened and express how he or she feels.

19

I've Always Wondered . . .

T HIS CHAPTER has the kind of trivia that keeps you awake at night. Are cat innards really used to make violin strings? How can I get good photographs of my cat? And much more.

WHAT CAN I DO TO SUPPORT SHELTERS AND HUMANE ASSOCIATIONS?

Maintaining a well-run shelter and humane association requires various skills and many levels of involvement. Working with the animals is not the only volunteer job. If work inside a shelter is too hard on you emotionally, you can:

- Donate occasional work time to your humane association's education program by sharing your knowledge of pet care, designing posters or other displays or doing anything else your local program needs.
- Donate volunteer time to the shelter's other ongoing programs. Edit the newsletter, work with fund-raisers or serve on the board of directors.
- Donate money.
- Donate pet food, litter, cleaning supplies, washable toys, newspapers (no glossy inserts), general office supplies or other needed items. It's easy on your budget to pick up one or two items every time you go food shopping. Then once every month or two, take everything to the organization.

DO CATS EVER WORK?

Yes. In ancient Egypt, the cat's job of guarding the stored grain was so appreciated that killing a cat was punishable by death. Today, cats enjoy more varied work—and far less protection under the law.

- Outdoor cats hunt for a living.
    - They kill the young, old and ill.
    - They protect grain stores and barns.
- Indoor cats have more job variety.
    - Some live in stores to mouse, to protect merchandise and to entice people to come into the shop.
    - Some live at the Vet's as blood donors.
    - Some live in nursing homes to cheer the residents.
    - Some work with therapists to help clients' emotional growth.
    - Some work with physical and occupational therapists to assist relearning physical skills.
    - Most share our homes to bring us joy and comfort.

Note: If you are interested in having your cat work in a visitation/therapy program, contact:

The Pet Partner's Program
The Delta Society
P.O. Box 1080
Renton, WA 98057-1080
Phone: 206-226-7357

I HAVE ALLERGIES. CAN I HAVE AN INDOOR CAT?

It may be possible to have an indoor cat. The allergy is most likely to the cat's saliva on his groomed fur, not the fur itself or the dander. Before getting a cat, visit a friend's cat and stay overnight, and then evaluate your reaction.

Generally, if your reaction is mild and your other allergies are under control, you can live with a cat if you take the following precautions:

- See an allergist for tests and investigate the possibility of desensitization shots. Also, eliminate other possible allergens, such as:
    - Flea control products (pyrethrin-based sprays may be *less* likely to cause allergies)
    - Household dust and mites
    - Pollen
- Bathe the cat every three or four weeks with distilled water. Or use Allerpet/C (allergen reducer) on the cat weekly; it won't damage the cat's fur and will be less objectionable to your cat than a bath. Estimated cost for Allerpet/C is $24 per year. To use, dampen a clean sponge with Allerpet/C and wipe the cat's fur (similar to a damp bath).

- Do not touch your face after touching a cat or after touching a fur-covered object; wash your hands first.
- Wear a mask when grooming your cat and cleaning the house. Better yet, have someone else in the family do it while you are out of the house.
- Keep the house clean by vacuuming every few days with a good-quality vacuum and change the bag regularly. ''Spring-clean'' at least twice a year and don't forget the heating/cooling ducts.
- Change the filter on the furnace and the air conditioner every month.
- Wash your cat's bed or special sleeping places weekly.
- Redecorate. Carpets, drapes, pillows and other fabrics trap allergens and concentrate them for increased exposure. Hard, smooth surfaces are easier to clean and help reduce the amount of airborne allergens.
- Use an ion fountain that puts out negative ions. Cost will vary depending on size, which ranges from single-room size to whole-house size. These fountains remove allergens from the air by changing the electrical charge on hair and other particles so they fall from the air.
- Use an air filter system that cleans the air by drawing it through filters. The cost varies with size.
- Keep your bedroom door closed and don't let the cat in at any time. Between work and sleep time, you can cut your exposure time by almost two-thirds.
- Don't try to take in every stray that comes calling. The fewer the cats, the milder your allergic reaction.
- When selecting a new companion cat, remember that all cats can cause problems but a small cat, with less fur, may be less problematic. Cats vary by breed and even by individual with respect to allergy potential. You may find that special cat by sniffing his fur. The best approach is to:
  — Adopt a cat with a short, thin coat such as a Siamese, Rex, Wirehair, Abyssinian or domestic shorthair.
  — Avoid longhaired or dense-coated cats like the Persian, Russian Blue and Korat.
  — See a good breed book for breed descriptions.

DO THEY REALLY USE CAT GUT FOR VIOLIN STRINGS?

According to the nineteenth-century writer Edward Heron-Allen, the ancient Egyptians used cat gut for their stringed instruments because the cat was sacred to them. (The cat-headed figure Bast was one of their goddesses.)

In more modern times, instrument makers and musicians discovered that a docile lamb made better strings than the highly strung cat. In fact, any carnivore's small intestines played second fiddle to the intestines of the lamb who grazes on dry grass.

In the 1960s, Perlon (a synthetic) was found to be as technically good as lamb gut and far safer. The gut strings broke easily and had been known to put out eyes.

A cat preparing to pounce will often wiggle his or her entire rump. This is for the purpose of building momentum to get more into the jump.

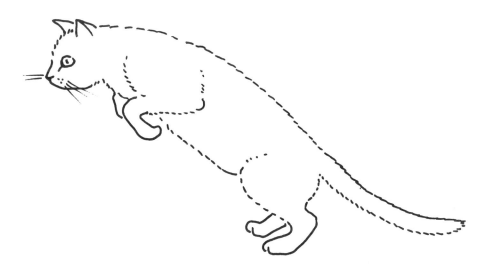

WHY DOES A CAT WIGGLE HIS RUMP BEFORE HE POUNCES?

He's building up momentum to be able to jump higher and pounce a longer distance.

HOW DOES A CAT DRINK?

A cat uses the Velcro-like hooks (filiform papillae) on his tongue to scoop the liquid into his mouth.

WHAT ARE SOME MYTHS OR OLD WIVES' TALES ABOUT CATS?

Cats will hurt babies.

Even a newborn is loud enough and physical enough to keep your cat at a distance. If you're still worried about your newborn, you might keep the cat out of the baby's room when the baby is alone and sleeping. When the baby can turn over unassisted, any fears about injury should be directed to your cat's welfare. See chapter 7.

Black cats are bad luck.

Superstitions vary from country to country. In fact, in England a *white* cat is connected with bad luck.

Cats always land on their feet.

No. They don't **always** land on their feet. How cats land depends on several factors. For a full explanation, see chapter 1.

A cat's mouth is clean or sterile.

No. Despite the old wives' tale, you can get a nasty infection from a cat bite. The antibacterial substance in the cat's saliva is strong enough to keep the cat's groomed fur smelling good, but not strong enough to prevent infection.

A male calico is valuable.

Since this color/sex combination is rare, as is a male tortoiseshell, this is a common belief. However, most males of these colors are sterile. Even so, there's still no particular financial value attached to those males who are fertile.

There is no need to groom a cat.

All cats need extra help with grooming. This is discussed more fully in chapter 5.

Cats are evil and familiars for witches.

Cats are not inherently evil but they do misbehave at times, like all pets. This myth itself is evil, because misguided, ignorant people have used it to justify killing cats and kittens.

All cats become fat after spay/neuter surgery.

Cats become fat when **you** overfeed them, irrespective of whether they are intact or altered.

Cats are sneaky.

Cats do tend to do their own thing, but they're usually open about it.

Cats cannot be trained.

Not only can cats be trained; if you don't train your cat in everyday good manners, you're doing both of you a disservice. See chapter 7 for training guidelines.

Cats can survive when dumped.

No! Both kittens and adults are the prey of other, larger animals. And even as adult cats, unless their mother had a chance to teach them how to hunt, they won't have the skills to survive.

Cats are loners.

Strays and occasionally ferals will form large colonies. Most cats will enjoy having other cats, dogs or lots of people for roommates. Kittens who are shown love, and are touched and handled gently, will grow up to be cuddly, loving cats.

The female should have one litter before spaying.

No! The surgery is easier on her when done before her first heat (at five months of age). The early surgery is also more beneficial to her overall health and longevity.

Cats should routinely be declawed.

No! Declawing your cat means amputating part of his toes. There are far better alternatives with far fewer negative consequences. See chapter 9 for more information.

Cats have nine lives.

No. But cats seem to be able to land on their feet (literally and figuratively) more than most other species.

A cat's whiskers are the same width as his body.

No. The wide-load cat doesn't always have long whiskers. The length and curliness of his whiskers are determined by the gene for coat length—longhaired cats have long whiskers.

Cats need very little care.

If cats needed little care, this book could be a small pamphlet. Cats are clean, easily trained to use a litter box and do not need to be walked—but to be happy and healthy, they do need care and lots of attention.

WHY DOES MY CAT DROOL WHEN I PET HIM?

Unless there is a medical problem, your cat drools because he is *so* relaxed.

WHY DOES MY MALE CAT GO NUTS OVER HAND CREAM?

Some hand creams contain methylparaben. This chemical smells like a female in heat!

CAN SECONDHAND SMOKE HARM MY PETS?

Yes. Secondhand smoke is no better for animals than for us. But because their life span is shorter than ours the results are not likely to be seen, unless the cat already has respiratory problems.

20

Make It Yourself

WHILE THERE are many great products on the market, it can be fun to make it yourself—and you can save money. Some items may be hard to find or unavailable through commercial channels. So this might be your chance to have the first cat whatsit on the block. Relax and have fun with it, even if you do smash your thumb once in a while.

HOW DO I MAKE TOYS FOR MY CAT?

This chapter has instructions for a number of toy projects. Some, like the catnip mouse, are projects grade-schoolers might enjoy doing—if they can handle a needle and thread. Other projects are more difficult and would require adult supervision. Better yet, involve the entire family in the design, building and decoration of these toys. Even very young children can participate because you use nontoxic materials throughout.

To get an idea of what to avoid in toy design, see the toy chart in chapter 11. The idea is to use materials that won't cause external or internal injury. **All** materials must be nontoxic.

Even the simplest oddments—cardboard boxes, paper wads, paper bags—make great toys. If you need more ideas than we've been able to give, look for a book titled *187 Ways to Amuse a Bored Cat.*

Fishing Box

This is a closed box with holes, through which the cat "fishes" for objects.

Materials

- Box (with top) about 12″ to 18″ on each side and no more than 3″ to 4″ deep
- Knife
- Sealer and paint, or Con-Tact paper (optional)
- Treats or small toys

Procedure

STEP 1   Position the box so you can mark where you want to cut the holes.

STEP 2   With a pencil, mark the hole locations. The holes need to be spaced so the cat can stand on the box and put a paw in the holes and "fish."

STEP 3   Cut a few small holes (1½ ″ × 1½ ″) in the **top** and **sides** of the box.

STEP 4   Decorate the box, if desired, by sealing the cardboard first (spray with acrylic sealer or cheap hair spray) and then painting; or you can use colorful Con-Tact paper.

STEP 5   Put a catnip mouse, a few pieces of dry food or a ball inside the box— and watch Kitty go fishing.

Catnip Mouse

Materials

- Old sock (no holes in toe section)
- Old nylon stocking
- Sewing needle and thread
- Two teaspoons of dried catnip

Procedure

STEP 1   Turn the sock inside out.

STEP 2   Cut the toe off the sock. You should have a piece about two inches long.

STEP 3   Stitch the cut edges together, leaving a finger-size hole you can later push the stuffing through.

STEP 4   Turn the toe right side out by pushing the material back through the hole. Make sure you get all the raw edges pushed inside.

STEP 5   Cut the leftover stocking into small pieces. You'll need enough to "stuff" the mouse.

STEP 6   Stuff the stocking pieces into the hole, along with two teaspoons of dried catnip.

STEP 7   Tuck in any raw edges and sew up the hole.

Note: If your cat likes rats better than mice, use the whole foot part of the sock to make the toy.

Prize in the Bottle

Put a few pieces of dry cat food in a clean plastic pint-sized bottle. (The mouth of the bottle should be the width of your cat's paw plus a half inch.) Lay the bottle on its side on the floor and watch him try to get to the food. Some cats will work the food out of the container by spreading their toes apart over the food and then closing the pads around the food to pick it up.

HOW DO I MAKE A KITTY GYM?

To give your cat a great solo workout, try the following idea. Attach (sew) a catnip mouse to the end of a piece of heavy string, twine or, even better, a length of half-inch elastic. Hang the mouse three or four inches off the floor in an area where it can dangle freely. The back of a wooden chair or an out-of-the-way nail at the top of an open doorway works well.

HOW CAN I BUILD AN OUTDOOR ENCLOSURE FOR MY CAT?

Whatever your approach, make sure that the cat has access to the house through a pet door or via an enclosed ramp. If he can't get back into the house in an emergency, the cat will need constant supervision. Make sure you add play and exercise items to the enclosure.

It's also important to provide shelter from weather and sun with shade trees or an enclosure roof or at least a partial roof. Your cat also needs access to water at all times, whether in the enclosure or inside the house.

You may be able to make an enclosure with a little effort and some extra money if you have a porch or an existing fence (six feet high). Try the following:

- Screen in a porch and install a pet door leading from the house onto the porch.
- Add an eighteen-inch overhang to existing (six feet minimum) fencing. Use two-by-fours, chicken wire, nails and staples. The addition should be at an upward 45-degree angle.
- If you have a tree or another interesting feature in your yard, build a small enclosure around it. Use two-by-twos and chicken wire to fence the sides, and for the top bring the chicken wire up around the tree trunk.

If you aren't intimidated by the idea of building an entire structure, two options exist:

- Using two-by-fours, heavy-duty chicken wire, nails, door hinges, hook-and-eye and staples, build a box with five sides (four sides and top). Assemble a cube frame with one side hinged for a door, and then cover the frame with chicken wire. You can build a cube of any size. Six feet by six feet is big enough not to give your cat a caged-in feeling. If he's a tunneling escape artist, you'll need a floor in the cube.

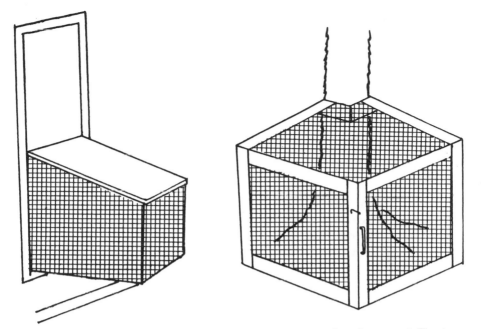

There are a variety of ways to provide safe outdoor access for a house cat. The two enclosures illustrated here are easy to construct and are fully described on the facing page.

The Elizabethan collar is commonly used to pre vent cats from damaging surgical sites, ingesting topical medication or other need to limit a cat's freedom in touching its own body. The collar here is made from the bottom of a plastic milk jug.

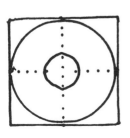

A poster board Elizabethan collar before final assembly.

The most familiar Elizabethan collar is crafted from a circle of poster board.

- Attach a small box (three screen sides, solid top and bottom) to the outside of an open window. Use paint or weatherproofing stain on half-inch plywood for any exposed parts. The roof extension outside the window should be slanted down at 25 degrees, and if possible protected with shingles. Cover the floor with tile or linoleum. Brace the hanging portion of the box with two-by-fours. To cut down on heat loss, you can add a commercial pet door to a closed window.

HOW DO I MAKE AN AUDIOTAPE?

Audiotapes of your voice and one of your unwashed shirts can soothe an ill or stressed pet when you can't be there. The audiotape idea, developed by Carol Wilbourn, appeared in her *Cat Fancy* magazine column.

If your tape player has a continuous-play function, use a regular audiotape; if not, use the longest outgoing answering machine tape you can find. On a day when you have time and are relaxed, collect the cat, tape recorder and tape, along with whatever your cat will enjoy, such as catnip, toys or a brush. Sit or lie down with your cat where you will both be comfortable. Turn on the tape player and have quality quiet time. Talk to your cat using his name and positive messages while you pet or brush him or play with him to get him relaxed.

HOW DO I MAKE AN ELIZABETHAN COLLAR?

The primary function of an Elizabethan collar is to prevent the cat from chewing itchy skin, biting healing wounds or removing stitches or bandages. You can easily make a collar in one of two ways:

Method 1

Materials

- Plastic gallon jug
- Scissors
- Three paper fasteners
- Cloth or duct tape

Procedure

STEP 1 Measure your cat from side of neck to nose (length of cat's head).
STEP 2 Measure the width of the cat's neck (approximate diameter) and **add** one inch (neck measurement).
STEP 3 From the bottom of the jug, measure up each side and mark the distance equal to the length of the cat's head.
STEP 4 Cut the jug, using the four side marks as a guide, and discard the top section of the jug.

STEP 5 Cut from the raw side edge to the center of the jug bottom and then cut (from the center of the bottom) a circle with a diameter of the neck measurement in Step 2.

STEP 6 Fold duct tape over all rough or cut plastic edges.

STEP 7 Place the collar around the cat's neck, overlap the cut edges and mark the width of the overlap. **Remove the collar.**

STEP 8 Using a hole punch or scissors, make three evenly spaced holes (through both plastic layers) in the overlapped area.

STEP 9 Place collar around the cat's neck and attach through the holes with paper fasteners.

Method 2

Materials

- Three paper fasteners
- Large piece of poster board
- Cloth or duct tape

Procedure

STEP 1 Cut a poster-board circle sixteen inches in diameter.

STEP 2 From one side of the circle cut a straight line to the center of the circle.

STEP 3 Measure the width of the cat's neck (approximate diameter) and **add** one inch (neck measurement).

STEP 4 Out of the center of the poster-board circle, cut a circle with a diameter of the neck measurement in Step 3.

STEP 5 Fold tape over all cut edges to reinforce them.

STEP 6 Place the cardboard cone around the cat's neck, overlap the cut edges and mark the width of the overlap. **Remove the collar.**

STEP 7 Using a hole punch or scissors, make three evenly spaced holes (through both layers) in the overlapped area.

STEP 8 Place Elizabethan collar around the cat's neck and attach through the holes with paper fasteners.

HOW DO I MAKE "CURB FEELERS" FOR MY BLIND CAT?

These curb feelers will protect a blind cat's whiskers from breaking as he feels his way around the house. As he gets used to the feelers, he'll come to depend on them.

Materials

- Nylon web cat collar with safety release buckle (do not use an elastic collar)
- Three-foot length of $1/16$" flexible acrylic dowel (available at hardware stores)
- Glue suitable for plastic
- Monofilament fishing line and sewing needle

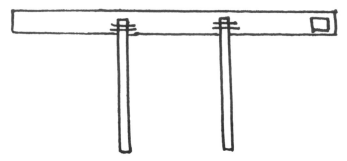

Curb feelers are an ingenious refinement in making life more comfortable for a blind cat and they are easy to make.

Curb feelers in place.

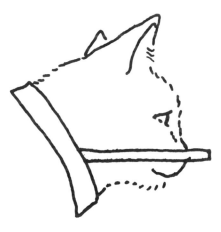

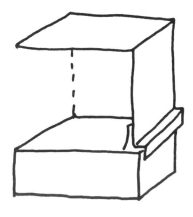

A drip seal will prevent the cat box from leaking when the occupant stands and sprays.

Procedure

STEP 1   Measure from the side of the cat's neck to his nose and **add** a half inch.
STEP 2   Cut two lengths of the dowel to that measure.
STEP 3   Put the collar on the cat, with the fastener under his chin.
STEP 4   Mark both the right-side and the left-side locations for the acrylic curb feelers. The end of the dowel should run from just below your cat's ear to his nose, in line with his whiskers.
STEP 5   Take the collar off the cat and lay the bottom portion of a dowel on one of the marks (at the angle described above) and then glue it in place. Repeat on the other side.
STEP 6   Overstitch the ends of the dowels through the collar with the monofilament.
STEP 7   Let the glue dry completely before you put the collar on the cat.

HOW DO I MAKE AN HERBAL FLEA COLLAR?

You can make these collars with herbs or essential oils. Equally effective, they are both safe for the environment and your cat and will be far more pleasing to everyone's nose than commercial flea collars. See chapter 10 for more information on flea control.

Herb-Filled Collar

Materials

- One or more of the following herbs: pennyroyal, eucalyptus, citronella
- Nylon panty hose
- Sewing needle and thread

Procedure

STEP 1   Measure the cat's neck, and then measure and cut a length of hose (without stretching it) twice as long plus two inches. (Use the toe, and you'll have only one end to sew.)
STEP 2   Put two or three tablespoons of herbs in the open end of the hose.
STEP 3   With the herbs at the bottom end, twist the hose at the midpoint and fold the nylon back onto itself. You will have two layers of nylon over the herbs.
STEP 4   Stitch the open end closed. (Sew through all layers of nylon.)
STEP 5   Spread herbs evenly in the collar and stitch across the collar in several places to keep the herbs in place.
STEP 6   Stitch both ends together to make a circle.
STEP 7   Slip the collar over the cat's head.
Note: If you want a fancier collar, cover the hose with ribbon or fabric.

Essential Oils Collar

Materials

- Essential oils of one or both of the following: eucalyptus, citronella (available at many health food stores) **Do not use pennyroyal oil; it can be toxic to cats.**
- Quarter-inch elastic cord or a ready-made safety collar (see collar suggestions in chapter 2)
- Cooking oil
- Sewing needle and thread

Procedure

Note: If you use quarter-inch elastic rather than a ready-made collar, measure the cat's neck and **add** one inch. Cut the elastic to that length and stitch the ends together to make a circle.

STEP 1   Mix the essential oil and cooking oil (one part essential oil to ten parts cooking oil). Mix enough to fill a small pill bottle—it will keep well in a cool, dry place.

STEP 2   Dip the collar in the oil mixture.

STEP 3   Squeeze out the excess oil; run the collar through your fingers as you pull it out of the oil.

STEP 4   Put the collar on your cat.

Note: To recharge these collars, add a drop or two of the mixed oils every two or three weeks.

THE HOODED BOX LEAKS WHEN MY CAT SPRAYS. WHAT DO I DO?

With many older hooded boxes, the lid fits against the outside of the box bottom. When the cat sprays (stands and sprays urine on the side of the box), the urine runs down the lid into the joint and out of the box. To repair the problem, make a "drip seal," so that the spray drips down into the box.

Materials

- Litter-box lid
- Cloth duct tape

Procedure

STEP 1   Clean the lid.

STEP 2   Cut four strips of duct tape two inches longer than each side of the lid. (Handle it carefully so it does not twist and stick to itself.)

STEP 3   Lay the tape sticky side up.

STEP 4   Along the length of the tape, fold one edge to the center so each strip has both a nonsticky part and a sticky part on the same side.

262

STEP 5   Starting one inch before a corner, press the sticky edge of the tape to the inside perimeter of the lid's edge.

STEP 6   Overlap the previous tape strip by one inch when you apply the next strip. Repeat until all four edges are taped. The overlaps should cover all gaps in the tape.

STEP 7   Make sure the drip seal is tucked inside the box when you put the lid in place.

HOW CAN I STOP A COLLAR FROM FRAYING?

If your cat frays his collar when he grooms, you can prolong the life of the collar with clear Con-Tact paper. If you follow the directions below, the collar will still be able to stretch if it gets caught on a branch.

Materials

- Clear Con-Tact paper
- Safety collar

Procedure

STEP 1   Measure the length of the collar **minus** the buckle parts.

STEP 2   Cut a clear Con-Tact paper rectangle 3¼ " × collar length.

STEP 3   Peel the backing off the Con-Tact paper, and along the length of the tape fold one and a half inches of a sticky side back on itself. (You'll have a quarter inch of sticky edge left.)

STEP 4   Wrap the nonsticky side around the collar once and secure with the sticky quarter-inch edge of the tape. Make sure both parts of the buckle are outside the wrap.

MY CAT SLIDES AROUND IN HIS CRATE.
WHAT CAN I DO?

You have several options, all of which are effective. The more padding you use, the more comfortable for your cat. Here are three ideas you can use:

- Cut a carpet remnant or rubber tub mat to fit the bottom of the crate. Replace as needed.
- Sew two towels together. See the next question on making a flat bed for your cat. (Dish towels will fit most crate sizes, or you can use a bath towel folded in half.) Wash the pad as needed.
- Cut foam rubber to fit and wrap in a towel or pillowcase. Replace as needed.

IS THERE AN EASY WAY TO MAKE A SCRATCHING POST?

One of the easiest scratching posts to make is one that cats naturally choose—a log. Choose a large log (18" to 24" long and 7" to 10" thick). Spray the outside of the log with insecticide before bringing it into the house. Make sure you let it air for a few days before bringing it inside. Set it up in a box or in a tray to collect the chips—and let your cat enjoy. Turn the log as the bark is removed.

Another no-fuss scratching surface is a cardboard box. You'll be surprised how much Fluffy will like shredding the surface, especially if you've peeled a corner to get him started. If he still seems reluctant to use the cardboard box, rub it with a little catnip.

COMMERCIAL-GRADE SCRATCHING POSTS ARE EXPENSIVE. IS THERE ANYTHING I CAN MAKE AT HOME?

If you are handy, you have practical options. The easiest project is a covered flat board with a rope handle that can hang from a doorknob. If you place catnip under the covering, your cat will be immediately attracted to the board.

The ideal sizes for the boards are 12" × 6" and 18" × 12". Coverings include burlap (two layers thick), low-nap nylon or wool carpet and sisal rope. Glue or staple enough rope to form a 10" handle on one end. **No matter what you choose for a covering, make sure the handle is in place before you apply the covering.**

The burlap and the carpet can be secured with tacks or heavy-duty staples. Before the material is fastened, all edges must be tucked under to prevent busy claws from pulling the material loose. If you use the sisal rope, wind it around the board so that the ends are caught securely. A glue gun works well with the rope.

Short Carpeted Post

This is a slightly more ambitious undertaking. The major concern is the stability of the post. If the base is too small, the post will tip and scare your cat. He won't return to the post and will find other, safer places to scratch—places you may not like. Nudge the post to test for stability as soon as it's attached to the base. If it tilts at all, enlarge the base.

Tools/Hardware Needed.   L brackets, wood screws, carpet tacks, hammer, staples, staple gun, screwdriver, utility knife, ruler.

Post Specifications.   The post should be 4" × 4". You can use two-by-fours screwed together. Two and a half feet is a good height. Make sure the post is centered on the base for stability.

Base Specifications.   For a 2½-foot post (depending on the floor surface beneath it), a base of 15 square inches to 20 square inches may be sufficient. Half-inch plywood is ideal for both the base and the top shelf. Use L brackets to attach the post to the base.

Shelves.   The top shelf should be large enough for the cat to lie down on with no danger of falling off—12 square inches should suffice. If you decide on a top shelf, attach it with one L bracket on each side of the post.

Covering.   Use low-nap jute-backed nylon or wool carpet. To measure the carpet, add two inches to the height of the post, four inches to the circumference of the post, twelve inches to the length and width of both the base and the shelf. Use one piece of carpet for the base, one for the post and one for the shelf. Keep the number of carpet pieces to this minimum; the more pieces you use, the greater the danger of unraveling.

Make sure that there are no carpet edges for claws to catch. When you finish with the post, rub the carpet with fresh catnip to attract your cat (reapply the catnip every three days). You can also put dried catnip under the carpet.

Tall Carpeted Post

Follow the suggestions for the short post except use a post one inch (plus the depth of the base) shorter than your ceiling. Folded cardboard or carpet wedged tightly between the top of the post and the ceiling will help stabilize the post. It's also a good idea to tie the post to a fixed object to prevent any movement. Keeping in mind that a falling post can damage your furniture, give the post a test nudge. It should not move at all! Put three to five shelves at different heights along the post. The shelves should be large enough for your cat to sleep on.

Carpet the Walls

Watch your cat climb the wall! Cover part of wall with low-nap jute-backed carpet. Add carpeted shelves using L brackets and drywall screws. If the wall space is beside a door, a shelf over the door frame can be fun. Again, use catnip to encourage use. **If you decide later to remove the carpeting, expect some wall damage.**

HOW CAN I MAKE A FLAT BED FOR MY CAT?

This pillow can be machine-washed and dried on low heat.

Materials (estimated cost $10)

- Two dish towels or larger towels
- Ten to twelve pairs of clean, used panty hose cut into 4″ to 6″ pieces, or one small bag of kapok

- Sewing supplies

Procedure

STEP 1   Place towels with right sides together and pin with half-inch seam allowance.
STEP 2   Sew seam, leaving an opening for stuffing.
STEP 3   Turn the towel (sack) right side out.
STEP 4   Stuff the sack. Do not overstuff—leave room for the material to shift so that it can conform to the cat's body.
STEP 5   Tuck in the edge and sew up the hole used for stuffing.

HOW DO I BUILD A KITTY CONDO?

A kitty condo is a cardboard playhouse for your cat. It's low maintenance and there's no grass to mow.

Materials

- Two to six cardboard boxes, each larger than the cat
- Glue gun or white glue
- String
- Knife
- Sealer, paint, Con-Tact paper (optional)

Procedure

STEP 1   Stack the boxes (sides should touch). Try different arrangements until you find a way they fit best.
STEP 2   Mark and cut matching areas for doors (holes through the top, sides and/ or bottoms of the boxes to make entryways from one box to another box).
STEP 3   Use the glue gun or white glue to attach the boxes and tie the boxes together with string to hold them till the glue is dry.
STEP 4   After the glue dries (two hours or more), the condo can be decorated any way you want. Here are some suggestions:
- Spray it with a sealer (acrylic spray from craft store or cheap hair spray) and then paint it with nontoxic paints.
- Cover it with Con-Tact paper.
- Put decals on the boxes.
- Let your children color designs on the boxes.
STEP 5   Put some catnip, toys or dry food in the box, and watch the fun. Treats may not be needed and won't be needed after the first fun romp through the condo.

HOW DO I KEEP THE CAT FROM STEPPING ON THE BUTTONS OF THE ANSWERING MACHINE?

Unfortunately, you won't think this is necessary until Fluffy has turned off the machine when you were expecting an important message. If the problem does arise, go to your hardware store and buy a transparent vent hood designed to direct the heat from a floor heating vent. Since the vent is clear, you will be able to see all the function lights. And if you follow the installation directions below, the hood will also be easy to remove.

STEP 1 Center the hood over the answering machine and mark where the hood magnets are. Adjust the size of the hood to make sure the buttons on the machine are covered.

STEP 2 Glue or tape a paper clip at each mark so that they overhang the sides of the machine by the width of the magnets.

STEP 3 Set the hood cover on the machine so that the magnets stick to the paper clips.

Note: If the hood vent won't cover enough of the buttons, use a clear box over the entire machine. Upside-down plastic storage boxes will work. Cut a notch out of the box lip for the wires.

HOW DO I KEEP HIS BOWLS FROM SLIDING ACROSS THE FLOOR?

Try one of the following:

- Feed him in a corner to block the bowl.
- Change to heavy crockery bowls.
- Put the bowl on an upside-down plastic place mat; the nonskid side will hold the bowls.

21

In an Emergency

WHILE THIS CHAPTER is meant to assist you during a medical emergency, it would be helpful to glance through it **before** anything happens. All emergency care is meant to be supervised by your Vet.

Note: When your cat is in pain and frightened, he may bite or scratch—no matter how loving and gentle he usually is. He is not mad at you, nor is he trying to hurt you.

WHAT SHOULD I TELL THE VET IN AN EMERGENCY?

Accident

- Where is the injury?
- What is the injury?
- How did it happen?
- Is the cat in shock?
- What are his vitals?
- What treatment have you already given?

Burns

- What burned the cat—heat or a chemical? What chemical? If a chemical, take the container or a sample with you when you take the cat to the Vet.
- Is the cat in shock?
- Treatment given?

Illness

- What are the cat's vitals?
- What are his symptoms (vomiting, unable to urinate, etc.)?
- How long has he been sick?
- Treatment given? Results?

Poisoning

- What was the poison? If unknown, take a sample of the vomitus with you when you take the cat to the Vet.
- How long has it been since the cat was exposed to the poison?
- What are the cat's vitals?
- How much poison did he eat?
- Treatment given?

SHOCK: DIAGNOSIS AND TRANSPORT INFORMATION

Shock Symptoms

Shock can occur immediately **or** up to eight to ten hours after a trauma (accident, poisoning, etc.). Excessive thirst can be a sign of shock; if any of the following signs of shock are present, **do not** give water to the cat; he can involuntarily inhale the fluid.

Call your Vet immediately if ANY of the following symptoms appear.

- Confusion or loss of consciousness
- Inability to stand
- Involuntary passage of urine and/or feces
- Pale mucous membranes (gums, rims of eyes)
- Feeble and rapid pulse (greater than 60 beats in 15 seconds)
- Shallow, labored rapid breathing (greater than 10 breaths in 15 seconds)

Treatment

- Wrap the cat in a blanket.
- Hold him so his head is lower than his hips.
- Go directly to the Vet; the cat may need to be transfused to increase blood volume.

Transport to the Vet

- Lay him on his side.
- Elevate his rump with a folded towel.

POISONING

Poisoning Symptoms

If any of the signs below are evident, call your Vet immediately or rush the cat to treatment. Take the container of suspected poison and a sample of vomitus with you.

- Evidence that the cat has been into forbidden items—e.g., open containers or spills
- Toxic or poisonous material on the cat's fur or paws, or burns on his mouth
- Change in behavior or in body functions, such as:
  — Drooling and gagging
  — Vomiting
  — Diarrhea
  — Breathing problems
  — Weakness
  — Convulsions
  — Shock

Treatment

Do not treat the cat until you have spoken with a Vet. Forced vomiting of a caustic substance can do additional damage to the throat and mouth. **If your Vet suggests forced vomiting, give one teaspoon of hydrogen peroxide per ten pounds of body weight.**

If you can't reach your Vet or one of her colleagues, or if you want a second opinion, you can call the National Animal Poison Control Center (twenty-four-hour service). See chapter 13.

CHOKING AND THE HEIMLICH MANEUVER

Choking Symptoms

- Pawing at the mouth and gasping
- Labored, noisy breathing
- Crying from pain
- Drooling
- Eventual loss of consciousness

Treatment

Open the cat's mouth and look; if the object can be seen, use your finger to hook it out, **but not** if it is string, a needle, a fishhook, thread or a similar object.

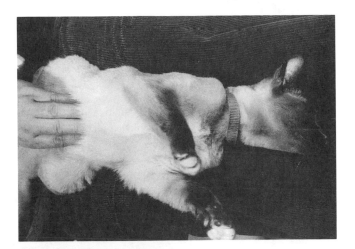

This photo shows one of the steps in the Heimlich maneuver as applied to cats.

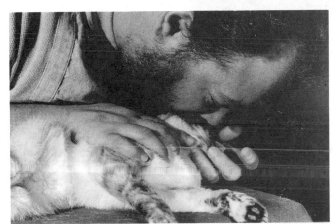

The technique of artificial respiration involves mouth to mouth resuscitation.

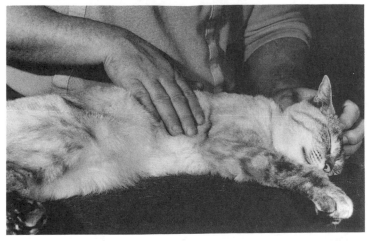

CPR is performed on an unconscious cat when a heartbeat or breathing cannot be detected.

If it cannot be removed yet, use the Heimlich maneuver.

STEP 1   Place the cat stomach-down on your lap.
STEP 2   Keep his head lower than his body.
STEP 3   Sharply slap the cat on the back.
STEP 4   Turn the cat over belly-up.
STEP 5   Push in and up on his stomach, toward his ribs.
STEP 6   Look in the cat's mouth and remove the object if possible.
STEP 7   Repeat these steps until the object is loosened and removed.
Note: Watch the cat for a few hours, and if he continues to show even mild distress, coughs up blood or loses his appetite, get him to your Vet.

CPR AND ARTIFICIAL RESPIRATION

First, touch the cat to arouse him. **If there is no response and his body is still warm:**

- *Check breathing.*
  — Put your hand near his nose/mouth to feel for moving air.
  — With your hand on his chest, look and feel for movement; no movement means no air.
- *Check pulse* at front of neck or inside of rear leg; no pulse means no heartbeat.

<table>
<tr><td>YES HEARTBEAT</td><td>NO HEARTBEAT</td></tr>
<tr><td>NO BREATHING</td><td>NO BREATHING</td></tr>
<tr><td>DO</td><td>DO</td></tr>
<tr><td>*ARTIFICIAL RESPIRATION*</td><td>*CPR*</td></tr>
</table>

Artificial Respiration Procedure

STEP 1   Place the cat on his side.
STEP 2   Open the cat's mouth by inserting fingers at the mouth corners, and cover both his mouth and his nose with your mouth.
STEP 3   Breathe one short, tiny breath into his nose and mouth. Pause for two to three seconds. Then repeat. The chest, not the abdomen, should move. **Be careful not to overinflate his lungs.**
STEP 4   **Check for independent breathing every few minutes.**

CPR Procedure

STEP 1   Place the cat on his side.
STEP 2   Slide your fingers under the cat's side at the fifth, sixth and seventh ribs (last few ribs before the abdomen).
STEP 3   Place thumb on top side of ribs.

272

STEP 4 Open the cat's mouth by inserting fingers at the mouth corners, and prepare to cover both his mouth and his nose with your mouth.

STEP 5 Squeeze chest (three squeezes in the time it takes you to say "one one-thousand"). Do a **total of fifteen squeezes** in the time it takes to count up to "five one-thousand." When you squeeze, you should feel a pulse in the groin.

STEP 6 Breathe **two short breaths** into his nose and mouth. The chest, not the abdomen, should move. **Be careful not to overinflate his lungs.**

STEP 7 Continue to repeat fifteen squeezes and two breaths. **Check for independent breathing and pulse every few minutes.**

STEP 8 Continue CPR until one of the following occurs:
- The cat begins breathing and his heart beats on its own.
- The Vet or another person relieves you.
- You become too exhausted to continue.

FIRST AID
(Shock, Poisoning, and Choking are described above)

Bites, Scratches and Wounds—Treatment for Cats

Symptoms	Treatment
PUNCTURE: A small hole (like a bite); deep, but not wide. You may not see these on the cat until the wound is infected—you'll feel a lump on or under the skin.	FOR SMALL WOUNDS: Clean the wound with hydrogen peroxide and watch for infection (warm, red or swollen). If infection develops, go to Vet. FOR DEEP WOUNDS: Stop bleeding by applying pressure to wound with dressing and fingers. Go to Vet immediately.
ABRASION: Scraping the skin	If abrasion is small, clean with hydrogen peroxide and watch for signs of infection.If the abrasion covers a large area, take the cat to the Vet.
LACERATION: A wide/deep, sometimes jagged cut	Apply pressure to wound with dressing and fingers to stop bleeding and go directly to Vet for sutures.

Cat Bite and Cat Scratch—Treatment for Humans
Note: If you are allergic to topical antibiotics, do not use them in treatment.

Problem	Treatment
CAT BITES: Report any cat bite to your physician, local animal shelter or health department. The animal may need to be	Wash the wound with soap and water. Pour hydrogen peroxide over the wound and rinse with water. Apply an antibiotic

quarantined. Read the information on bites in chapter 15.

CAT SCRATCHES

ointment and cover with a sterile dressing. Watch for signs of infection. Call your physician—a tetanus shot may be necessary.

Apply pressure, if necessary, to stop bleeding. Clean the wound with soap and water. Pour hydrogen peroxide over the wound and rinse with water. Apply an antibiotic ointment and a dressing if necessary. Watch for signs of infection. Call your physician—a tetanus shot may be necessary.

Bleeding

Symptoms	Treatment
Wounds is *not pulsing* blood and no bones are broken, slight wound	Apply pressure to wound with a clean bandage and your hand or fingers; hold till clotting develops (stops bleeding). Clean the area as directed for wounds above. If it is a wide wound or if bleeding doesn't stop after five minutes, get medical help.
Wound *pulsing* blood, major wound	Apply pressure only if no bones are broken, and go to Vet immediately. Do not use a tourniquet—hold cat so wound is higher than cat's heart.

Breathing Problems

Symptoms	Treatment
Rapid, irregular breathing patterns, panting, shallow breathing, noisy breathing	Call the Vet. If breathing stops during transport, use artificial respiration (directions above). Keep your hand on cat's chest—if chest moves, air is reaching the cat's lungs.

Burns

Symptoms	Treatment
More than singed fur or whiskers; flesh red or blackened	Do *not* put anything on the wound except clean, cool, damp pad or new burn dressings for people. Change as needed to cool the area. Take to the Vet immediately.

274

Fractures

Symptoms	Treatment
Limping, dragging a leg, leg at an odd angle, sudden large lump over bone	Splint before moving the cat; take to Vet. To splint leg or tail: • Roll up a thin magazine and form a V. • Crate the broken leg or tail in the V. • Tape the magazine to hold it together. For a break other than a leg or tail: • Gently roll or slide the cat onto a hard surface (cutting board, notebook, etc.). • Use a necktie or soft belt to secure.

Hyperthermia (Heat Exhaustion)

Cats left in a car even for a short time can easily overheat.

Symptoms	Treatment
Panting with a dry tongue; breathing heavily; body warm to the touch; drooling	Cool him off at once by spraying him with cool water, laying cool wet towels on him or putting him in a cool bath. Call your Vet. If cat is in shock or unconscious, take him to Vet immediately.

Hypothermia (Lowered Body Temperature)

A cat left outside in winter can become chilled to death.

Symptoms	Treatment
Cold to the touch; fur puffed out; shivering	Warm him by wrapping him in a towel, sweater or small blanket with a hot-water bottle or a heating pad set on low till shivering stops. Check with Vet, and offer a warm snack such as broth.
Weakness; pale-colored gums or tongue; unconscious	Wrap him in a towel, sweater or small blanket and take him to Vet immediately.

Something in Eye

Symptoms	Treatment
Pawing at eye, excessive tearing, squinting of one or both eyes, eye swollen or red	If object is easily seen and is **not** shaped to cause more damage, flush eye with warm water. Call Vet. If object cannot be seen or is shaped to cause more damage, do nothing to eye. Towel-wrap if needed to stop the cat from pawing his eye and rush cat to Vet.

Venomous Bites

By a snake, fire ants, wasps, bees, scorpions, etc.; repeated bites by ants, spiders (black widow and brown reclusive are most dangerous).

Symptoms	Treatment
Swelling at site of bites; drooling, strange behavior, pain, muscle cramps, paralysis	ID species (or capture in a jar for Vet to ID) and take cat to Vet immediately.